PRODUCING THEATRE

A Comprehensive Legal and Business Guide

by Donald C. Farber

DRAMA BOOK PUBLISHERS

New York

Library of Congress Cataloging in Publication Data

Farber, Donald C.
  Producing theatre.

  Includes bibliographical references and index.
  1. Theater — Production and direction — Law and
legislation — United States.   2. Theater — United States — Production
and direction.   I. Title.

KF4296.F37	343.73′078792	81-1025
ISBN 0-89676-051-0	347.30378792	AACR2

10 9 8 7 6 5 4 3 2   0 0   1   2 3 3 4 4 5 5 6 6 7 7 8 8 9 9

Manufactured in the United States of America

For my beautiful Annie,
who helped make it all happen

Greg Gordon assisted greatly with the research and writing of certain parts of this book and his assistance deserves particular credit and acknowledgment because it was most helpful and very special.

Table of Contents

Preface

THE SECOND BOOK I wrote, now out of print, was entitled "Producing on Broadway: A Comprehensive Guide." This book is an updating of "Producing on Broadway," but it is more than that; it is intended as a text covering the business of producing theatre anywhere in the United States — that is, on Broadway, in resident theatres, stock, or other productions.

The first book that I wrote, "From Option to Opening," published by Drama Book Specialists, attempted to explain in non-legal language all of the legal documents and relationships involved in the production of a play Off-Broadway. It was intended as a primer for those unfamiliar with theatrical producing, as many persons who produce Off-Broadway are, in fact, without any experience.

I still agree with most of the things that I wrote in the preface to the first edition of "Producing on Broadway," and, in fact, believe that the way I said it then was about as well as I am capable of saying it, so let me quote a portion of what I wrote:

> "Many lawyers are too word conscious. I may seem a traitor to some in my profession (although I would be a good deal more correct to label it "my business"), and am certain not to endear myself to all my fellow attorneys, but I must make the observation that people are more important than words. I go to all of the trouble to analyze, digest, edit, and compile a book consisting of words about words, and then I have the effrontery to ask you to read them and learn them — but they may not be so important as what it is they intend to accomplish. Words are only important to the extent that they are useful to

people, either functionally or artistically. It may be necessary to bend certain words and change certain concepts that are so carefully stated in a contract to accomplish a given result which is good for everyone. The words are not an end in themselves. One accomplishes nothing if he wins the battle of the words and the contract words are inviolate, if he has destroyed the client's show in doing this.

One must also bear in mind the distinction between "facts" (if there is such a thing, since facts change and are also subject to interpretation) and "opinions." It is, for example, a fact that a limited partner's liability is limited to the amount of his investment, providing that the limited partnership has been properly organized in accordance with the partnership laws of the state of New York. It is an opinion that a dramatic show without a star should not go out of town on a pre-Broadway tour.

There are a lot of statements in this book that are something in-between facts and opinions. These statements reflect ideas that are in reality a consensus but are so widely believed that they are, in fact, facts — although they are not easily provable as such.

In all events, the reader will not find facts and opinions labeled. If something is a fact, there is no problem. If the comment concerns something about which there may only be opinions, and if there are important and respectable but divergent opinions, I have tried to express them. If there are divergent opinions, I have expressed the opinion of what I believe to be the most highly regarded thinking in the business on the subject, tempered with what I consider to be a good measure of common sense. Certainly you will find different opinions. You may even uncover different facts. But, for the most part, the facts set forth herein are unvarying facts, and the opinions set forth are, in my opinion, the best opinions.''

Acknowledgments

MANY PEOPLE DESERVE THANKS for helping me prepare this book:

Special thanks to Judith Tuckman, my typist in the country, who did a professional job. Thanks also to my secretary, Phyllis Mandell, who helped to fill in when needed, to Ann Marie De Marco for helping by easing some of the office chores, and to Tom Burke for his cheerfully getting things there on time.

Warm thanks to my associate, William Apfel, for his assistance, and to my friends Leonard Soloway and Allan Francis, who checked out the theatre information.

Thanks to Daniel Brambilla for helping in the beginning of the writing and the rewrites. It turned out to be a much larger chore than he could possibly imagine, so although there is not a lot left of what he contributed, every bit helps and is appreciated.

Special warm thanks to Carl Schaeffer for his insight and understanding as well as his trust and confidence.

I am deeply appreciative of the most helpful and understanding editing of the manuscript by Kristen McLaughlin and the welcome assistance of Judith Rudnicki.

Last but not least, appreciation and thanks to my publisher, Ralph Pine, with this searching question — "For god's sake, Ralph, how could you do this to me again?"

Introduction

OF COURSE, there is no business like show business. That has to be the case, because the song says so. Many people accept this axiom without really fully accepting the fact that it is a "business." Show business is all kinds of things to all kinds of people. It represents excitement, glamor, and thrills for the uninitiated, at the same time representing backbreaking work, nervous anxiety, and emotional exhaustion for many on the inside looking out. The business is an overcrowded, highly competitive business for most of the people who are in it. It's a business of feast or famine, and even the stars — with all the glamour and the big money — will, with a few exceptions, never know the financial security that the person taking home a regular weekly paycheck enjoys.

The actor, when he's starting, must play for a marginal salary in stock or Off-Broadway so that his work may be seen. If he is lucky and makes it big, then he may work, but it may add up to a total of six or eight weeks a year. During his short time he may earn big money, which must be spread out so he can live the entire year. With the tax bite and with the star having to live like a star even when he's unemployed, there are often huge deficits by the end of the year for those who enjoy the privilege of having their name above the title.

During the last forty years the business has indeed grown. During the 1937–38 season, the total gross paid for tickets at the box office was approximately $11½ million. During the 1978–79 season, just forty-one years later, the total gross box office receipts were over $270 million. Of course, some of this may be accounted for by the inflation in this country;

we must not overlook the fact, however, that the business has grown. There is a demand for good theatre tickets. Theatre tickets, at the same time, cost more money.

The number of plays opening each year during this same period has substantially declined. For example, during the 1937–38 season there were a total of 111 new plays and revivals. During the 1978–79 season there were a total of 50 new plays and revivals. The cost of getting a play on has increased many times, and producers have become somewhat more selective.

In addition to growing, the business here is changing. There seems to be a larger importation of foreign productions. In fact, Actors' Equity has repeatedly made demands to restrict the number of foreign actors who are, at any one time, competing with American actors.

Contract agreements with unions expire and are renegotiated; budget requirements change just as theatregoers' preferences change. No one can be certain that anything he writes on this subject, or any subject, is immutable. At the same time, we should realize that certain basic concepts are less likely to change, and, if they do, the change will occur slowly.

Wherever a contract discussed in this book has a fixed terminable date, the date is noted. Changes which occur will, in most instances, be "non-basic" — the kind of facts and details that are easily ascertainable. It is of primary importance that the framework and the basic concept of the various contracts, as well as the relationships and obligations of the various contributing parties, be understood.

There are 41 Broadway theatres at the present time, 16½ of which are owned by the Shuberts. (Sometimes a producer will purchase a theatre so he doesn't have the problem of finding one when he wants to bring his show in.) During recent seasons there has been a critical shortage of Broadway theatres during the height of the season; that is, during September, October, November, and December. A critical shortage means that there are more shows waiting to get into theatres than there are theatres available. Perhaps this will be solved in the future with the building of new theatres and with the heightened sensitivity of producers to the kinds of plays that stand a chance of being successful.

If someone decides to go into "the business," he ought to know as much as he can about it. Contracts involved in producing a show are, in many instances, understood by too few people.

In a recent discussion with someone who should know, I was told nonchalantly that there are three or four attorneys who know and understand the Dramatists Guild contract. Now isn't that a shocker? Just think about it for a moment. The Dramatists Guild contract is used (and has been for many years) to option each and every play produced on Broadway by an American author (with only a few exceptions), and I am informed that maybe three or four attorneys in the business know and understand it. I would be much less disturbed if the person who said this had not been in a position to know exactly what he is talking about.

It's no secret that the Dramatists Guild contract is one of the most confusing, most ambiguous documents ever labeled a contract. Obviously it simply grew like so many other agreements which have been negotiated and renegotiated through the years. What happened, I presume, was that whenever a change was made, the parties were careful not to alter some other part of the contract that they had previously agreed upon. If they attempted to change the language, disagreement would develop, perhaps, about the language change. In spite of this, however, the contract — which includes a basic contract, a schedule of additional production terms, and an appendix — could be unified into one organized, cohesive document. Since the document is and has been (with few exceptions) used to option every play that has been written by an American and produced on Broadway, it should be understood whether one likes the format or not.

It is possible, of course, to produce a show without knowing anything about the agreements. One can, for instance, hire a competent attorney, manager, and accountant. These three people — who should know, or act like they know, the terms of most of the agreements — will deal with the various unions and parties. Ideally, however, the producer ought to know as much as he can about his relationship with the people he'll be working with. This relationship, being a contractual relationship, ought to be understood clearly in terms of the rights, duties, and obligations he has to the people he works with. No one should need to wave his contract under the other parties' noses, nor use it as a threat. But he should, however, understand it.

The Dramatists Guild contract, like the other agreements, is discussed with a view toward understanding each contract as a single cohesive unit and, at the same time, understanding it with respect to other contractual obligations that become legally binding when a producer produces a show.

In many instances there are disputes as to the meaning of certain contract provisions. It will serve no useful function to examine the detailed arguments supporting each point of view. For our purposes at this time it should suffice to know that there are discrepancies and disagreements in certain areas which someday may be resolved.

One should also bear in mind that what happens in reality is sometimes very far removed from the contract terms and provisions. In many instances a contract is entered into on the union form and the parties signing are little aware of most of the terms.

There are also instances where, through custom, certain ways of doing things have developed which are in direct contradiction to the specific contract terms setting forth how this should be done. In such a case, the parties (if they even know the contract terms) have simply not bothered to comply with the contract, because doing what they do is more suitable to accomplish the end. Little would be served by changing procedures to comply with a written document if the changed procedures did not serve some useful purpose.

If one were to study and learn the contents of this book, he would probably know more than any other single person usually knows about the contractual relationships involved in producing for the stage. As a practical matter, what usually happens is that some of the contracts discussed in this book are drafted after very careful consideration and negotiation between the attorney for the producer and the other party. However, in other instances there are contracts entered into by either the company manager or the house manager which the attorney for the producer never even sees. In fact, I would go so far as to say that there are many contracts the theatre makes with unions which affect the producer but which many people in the business, including attorneys, know nothing about or have never seen.

This book combines the contracts and agreements that would be within the scope of experience of the attorney for the producer, the house manager, and the company manager, as well as for the theatre.

It goes without saying, finally, that there is a vast amount of information that can never be learned from a book and will only be learned through the difficult but ever rewarding process of acquiring experience through *doing*.

PRODUCING THEATRE

A Comprehensive Legal and Business Guide

CHAPTER 1

Obtaining a Property

A N ORIGINAL WORK OF AUTHORSHIP, regardless of when it was created, is protected either by common law or by statutory copyright[1] unless the work has fallen into the public domain.[2] Copyright protection generally means that no one may use the work in any manner whatsoever without first securing the permission of the copyright owner or the person who acquired ownership of those rights through purchase, assignment, inheritance, or otherwise.[3] Failure to acquire permission can result in a lawsuit to collect the damages caused by the infringement, and can also give rise to an injunction to stop the unauthorized use. In order to avoid potential liability, and also to be fair to the owner of the work, a person interested in producing a copyrighted play in any manner — whether it be a Broadway production, an amateur production with free admission, or anything in between — should proceed first to acquire the performance rights. In so doing, the prospective producer must, among other things, determine if the rights are available and, if so, at what price and upon what conditions.

FINDING THE OWNER OF THE PROPERTY

In determining if the rights are available, the producer must find the person who has authority to deal with the property. If the author is alive, this can be done simply by contacting the author directly or by contacting his attorney, or other representative. The names, addresses, and phone numbers of these persons can be obtained from either the Dramatists Guild, if the author has had a play previously produced; the publisher of the play or music; the Writers Guild; or the Register of Copyrights in Washington, D.C.

If the play was previously produced in New York and was relatively successful, chances are good that one of the play licensing companies has the work in its catalogue (i.e., Music Theatre International, Samuel French, Inc., Tams Witmark Music Library, or the Rodgers and Hammerstein Library). In this instance a producer could contact the appropriate company rather than the author, his agent, or attorney.[4]

In all of the above cases the process of finding who owns or controls the rights is usually quite easy; however, when the author is either deceased, foreign, or deceased and foreign, complications can be encountered.

A deceased author's works are most often controlled by his estate through a literary executor who may be the author's spouse, child, or other relative. The literary executor could also be the author's attorney, agent, or bank if the works are held in trust. Tracking down the right person can be very time consuming, especially if the author has been dead for many years. The spouse may have died also, transferring the work to someone else; children may have married or remarried and taken different surnames; the trust may have terminated — the possibilities are too numerous to mention. If the deceased author's play was previously produced, however, there is the possibility that a licensing company will be handling the rights on behalf of the estate, thus simplifying the procedure.

A foreign author is, in most instances, represented by a foreign agent, and sometimes the agent has a U.S. representative. The problems of distance and language differences oftentimes present obstacles in determining the identity of the person who controls the rights. At the very least, trying to contact the proper person in a foreign country will usually require more time.

Needless to say, if an author is both foreign and deceased, it's likely that nothing short of perserverence and steadfastness of purpose will bring forth the identity of the owner of the work. And even then there can be little assurance that the person found is indeed the true owner of the desired rights. For this reason (as well as others which will be discussed later in Chapter 2), the producer's representative should always insist that the contract for the rights to the play include language to the effect that the person granting the rights: (a) warrants and represents that he is the owner of the copyright in the work; and (b) that he has full right and authority to grant the rights he is granting.

In addition to the problems sometimes encountered in finding the owner of the needed rights, the acquisition of performing rights in music and lyrics presents yet another obstacle. The person to contact in order to acquire these rights depends primarily on whether the producer needs grand or small performing rights, and the determination to be made as to which of these rights is needed in a given situation depends on a number of intertwining factors.

Grand rights are those needed to perform the music in a dramatic fashion while only small performing rights are required for non-dramatic performances. The determination of what is dramatic and what is non-dramatic seems to be the essence of the problem, and in attempting a definition it becomes apparent that although the extremes are clear, the dividing line is not. If there exists a story connecting the songs together, the performance is considered a musical play and dramatic, thus requiring grand rights. If there is no story but just improvised patter connecting the songs, the performance may be more like a non-dramatic night club act requiring only small rights. But the kind of dialogue between songs is not the only basis on which to decide if a storyline exists. Sets, costumes, and props could, with the music and lyrics, create a dramatic sequence conveying a story, especially if one or all of those elements are similar to the sets, costumes, and props used in a play from which the songs were originally performed. Thus, although television, radio, night club, and concert performances of songs usually require only small performing rights, if a story is conveyed through any of the elements of dialogue, sets, costumes, and props, grand rights may be required. In certain instances grand rights are necessary if all the songs from a musical play are used in concert in the same sequence in which they were originally performed, even if none of the above elements are present. There are no definite rules that apply in order to determine whether a story is being told or not. However, if a producer has any question of which rights to acquire, it's always safer to get the grand rights, if possible, to avoid any lawsuits or injunctions for copyright infringement.

If the producer receives assurances from the apparent owner of the rights that the owner controls those rights which the producer needs, without specifying whether those rights are grand or small, the producer needing grand rights may be lulled into a false sense of security. The producer may be made to believe either that the owner has the grand rights, when in fact he controls just the small rights, or that the grand rights are not needed for the production, when in fact they are. In such an instance, the producer should try to have the person or company granting the rights give him a warranty and indemnity on any losses he may sustain due to their granting the small rights in the event the grand rights are in fact required. This will rarely be granted, but in the event it is, the indemnity should not be limited to the amount of money paid by the producer to the grantor of the rights for the use of the music. The amounts paid may be so small as to be of little value to the producer in the event of a lawsuit for infringement.

Small performing rights are usually licensed by either one of three major companies: ASCAP, BMI, or SESAC. Payment of either a designated fee per song or a blanket payment covering all the songs in the company's catalogue will authorize the use of the music. Although grand rights are safer to have, they are usually more expensive and sometimes more difficult to acquire than small performing rights.

The composer and lyricist of the songs will usually hold the grand rights to their compositions, but there are times when the music publishing company will be the owner. Songs written for the movies is one example of such ownership. These songs are usually considered works for hire (i.e., the film companies paid the composers and lyricists or employees to write the songs), and under the copyright law the employer enjoys complete ownership in the works. Since many of the major film companies have publishing companies as subsidiaries, a producer wishing to acquire the grand rights to such songs would have to contact either the film company or the music publishers rather than the composers and lyricists.

Another example of complete ownership of a song by a publishing company is the situation where a young unknown writer will sign an exclusive songwriter's contract with a publishing company which gives the writer an advance payment against future royalties. In exchange, the company owns all of the writer's musical output during the duration of the contract.[5]

In any event, whomever the owner may be, the cost for the grand rights for the music and lyrics will vary anywhere between $100 per song per performance week to a percentage of the gross weekly box office receipts, as discussed later in this book.

It should be noted that this procedure of separately acquiring the grand performing rights to songs is only necessary when a producer intends to present on stage, and in a dramatic fashion, songs that were never part of a play, that were part of a play but did not merge with the play when presented, or that did merge with the play but have been released by permission.[6] The rights in the book, music, and lyrics to a musical play — either old or new — are acquired simultaneously.

DETERMINING HOW AND WHERE TO PRESENT THE PROPERTY

Before obtaining the property — in fact, even before determining who the owner of the rights is — the producer should have a clear idea of how and where he intends to produce the play (i.e., Broadway, Off-Broadway, stock, first- or second-class tour, regional or amateur theatre). This will be one of the factors determining whether he will acquire an exclusive option to produce the play, which he hopes would include the right to earn certain additional and subsidiary rights, or merely a non-exclusive license to present the play for a specified number of performances. In most cases, stock, second-class tours, and all amateur theatres acquire only a simple license. Broadway, Off-Broadway, and pre-Broadway tours, first-class tours, and some regional theatres will usually get options with the amount of additional and subsidiary rights varying greatly (this will be discussed in more detail in the next chapter).

The reason for granting an option rather than a license is based in part on the potential contribution the production will make to the play. If a producer intends to mount a first-class production to open on Broadway, the play will receive a great deal of exposure both by the number of people attending and the press coverage. This increases the future subsidiary market for the play in the stock, touring, and amateur circuit; and, in addition, can be the catalyst for the making of a movie, television series or mini series, and cast album. If the play is produced Off-Broadway, a future market is also created, although perhaps to a somewhat lesser degree since the play's exposure may be less intense.

The contribution made by the production would not be possible without the large contribution of money made by investors to produce the play in a first-class manner. Since investors generally want to see their investment returned, they have learned to expect that the production company producing the play will participate in future profits derived from sales of the play to subsidiary markets. The investors' reason for this is simple: if they and the producer took an unknown property and made it into a successful play, which in turn caused it to make even more money by subsidiary uses, they should share in the author's receipts from those other sources. This advantage is achieved by the producer entering into an option agreement with the author, who will not be unwilling to give up a share of his future earnings from the play since he is aware that his play would have little future without a successful first-class production.

Generally, the more remote the production becomes from a first-class presentation, the less the author will be inclined to share in future earnings since the chance of that production being the cause of future earnings becomes proportionately remote. There are, of course, exceptions to this general rule for other than first-class productions performed in major theatres in major cities in the United States; however, Broadway and other first-class productions still reign supreme.

It should be added here that a simple license is almost always granted to a producer provided he agrees to pay the license fee. A license, however, may not be available if an agreement exists granting the exclusive production rights to another. This usually occurs when a producer holds the exclusive option to present the play, or when a play has been produced while under an option agreement, whereby the producer acquires additional exclusive rights to continue to produce the play. There are occasions when a producer who holds these exclusive rights will release them to another for a stock or amateur presentation, provided that such a production will not be within a competitive radius of one of his productions of the play.

In contrast to the often ready availability of a license, an option may sometimes be impossible to acquire even if the property is available and even if the producer is willing to pay an exorbitant price. The reason for this is that an author is sometimes more interested in having his work produced, directed, and acted by certain persons at certain times. If those persons are not interested or available at the right time, neither is the author or his play. Practically speaking, this situation will often be found with the estate of a famous deceased author where the trustees or executors of the estate sometimes become overzealous in protecting the integrity of his works.

METHODS OF ACQUIRING RIGHTS TO A PROPERTY

A person wishing to produce a play can acquire the rights in one of the following methods.

Produce a Play in the Public Domain

As mentioned earlier, all original works of authorship are protected either by common law or statutory copyright unless the work has fallen into the public domain. A work in the public domain is available to be used in any manner imaginable without the need to acquire or pay for rights. In order to understand how a work gets into the public domain, a basic understanding of the copyright law (both old and new) is necessary.

Under the old copyright law, once a play was written it automatically enjoyed the protection of a common law copyright. If anyone misappropriates the work, the author can sue the wrongdoer in a court of law. This common law copyright can exist forever, provided the author does not "publish" his creation by distributing it to the general public.[7] If such publication[8] occurs, in order to have statutory copyright protection the author must comply with the provisions of the copyright law, which provides that a "copyright notice" be prominently displayed on the work — i.e., © (or copyright) 1977 John Doe. Failure to affix this notice upon publication will usually cause the work to fall into the public domain. There are some rare exceptions to this rule which are written into the copyright law. For example, an inadvertent failure to affix the notice may not be fatal in certain instances.

Once the work was published with the copyright notice affixed, the common law copyright terminated and the work was then protected by statutory copyright under the old federal copyright law.[9] Although the common law copyright was perpetual, the statutory right under the old law granted protection for only a certain number of years. Prior to January 1, 1978,[10] the copyright term was twenty-eight years with the opportunity of renewing the protection for an additional period of twenty-eight years, thereby bringing the total to fifty-six years. Since under the old law the federal copyright became activated when the work was published with a notice of copyright, the term of fifty-six years is measured from the date of publication. After the period of fifty-six years the work falls into the public domain.[11] Furthermore, if the copyright was not renewed before the first twenty-eight-year term expired, the work can similarly become part of the public domain.

The new copyright law — effective January 1, 1978, for works created on or after that date — changed the term for the duration of copyright to the life of the author plus fifty years with no renewal term. The term begins from the date the work was created (if on or after January 1, 1978) and is not therefore measured from the publication date as under the old law. Furthermore, there is no longer any common law copyright since the new federal law preempted the area by providing statutory copyright protection upon creation of the work. Consequently, works created on or after January 1, 1978, no longer have a perpetual common law copyright until first publication. As under the old law, failure to publish with a copyright notice affixed will invalidate the copyright except under certain specific circumstances.

Although it may appear that determining if a work is in the public domain is simply a matter of adding fifty-six to the date of publication for a work created prior to 1978, such is not the case. The new copyright law provides many exceptions to the general rules mentioned above, and only a careful reading by a person familiar with the law will give an accurate answer. One such example of where the general rules do not apply (and where a producer intending to present a play in the public domain should proceed with caution) is with works whose renewal term (second twenty-eight years) was in existence in 1962, when the Congress began to write the new law. Since Congress quickly realized it was going to take a considerable amount of time to revise the old law — and that it would be unfair to penalize authors whose copyrights would expire by the time the new law became effective, thus depriving them of the benefits of its provisions — the Congress enacted legislation beginning in 1962 which extended the copyright of those works for a period of two years. Similar enactments (extending the copyright for one- or two-year periods) were made eight times more during the course of the revisions extending those copyrights up until the date of effectiveness of the new law, which again extended all copyrights then in their renewal term to seventy-five years from the date the original copyright was secured. The effect of all these extensions is that works copyrighted anytime after September 18, 1906, whose copyright was duly renewed, now enjoy copyright protection for seventy-five years or, at least, through 1981. Therefore, a less than fully informed person attempting to determine whether such work first published in late 1906 was in the public domain would add fifty-six to 1906, come up with 1962 as the last year of copyright protection, and incorrectly conclude that the work would be in the public domain and thus free to use.

The copyright office, for a fee of $5 per hour, will make a copyright search to determine if and when a work in question was copyrighted and if and when the renewal registration was filed. The office will not, however, render a legal opinion as to whether a work has fallen into the public domain.

Although great care must be taken in determining if a work is actually in the public domain, a producer can save a great deal of money by producing such a play. There are no royalties to be paid, and no negotiations for an option. One of the drawbacks is that there is also no exclusivity. Anyone else can produce the same play in the theatre next door, and the producer will find himself in competition with the play he is producing. The chances of this happening, however, are somewhat remote, since the other producer would find himself similarly situated. Another drawback is that the producer and his investors will receive no income from the distribution of the subsidiary rights since the work no longer enjoys the protection of a copyright; neither the author (if he is still alive) nor his estate have any rights to distribute. The work is free to be used by anyone without charge.

Commission an Adaptation of a Public Domain Work

The work in the public domain which attracts a producer's interest need not be restricted to a play. A novel, short story, or epic poem, for example, can be adapted into a stage play. Although the underlying work (i.e., the novel) may be free to use, the person commissioned to do the adaptation would usually hold the copyright on the dramatized version. In a rare instance, a producer may "hire" an adaptor as an employee. In such a case, the producer would be the owner of the copyright, since it would be considered a "work for hire." The normal procedure, however, is for the producer and author (as well as composer and lyricist, if it's to be a musical adaptation) to enter into a Dramatists Guild Minimum Basic Production Contract if the producer intends to mount a first-class production. If it is to be other than first class (such as an Off-Broadway presentation), an option agreement drawn by the producer's attorney will be used. [12]

Even if the producer's intention is to present the play as a second-class production in a remote location, he will still, in most instances, acquire some form of option rather than merely a license. This is so because the producer is offering to pay the author to write the adaptation, and if the producer does not get what he wants in return regarding a future interest in the play, he will simply not commission that author. Of course, the protection normally afforded to a producer by entering into an option (wherein he receives the exclusive rights to present the play) does not strictly apply in this case. Although the producer will have the exclusive right to produce the adaptation, the underlying work is in the public domain, and anyone else can come along and present a different adaptation — thus creating the competitive situation mentioned before. But, once again, the chances of this happening are somewhat remote. A problem which can more readily arise, however, whenever anyone uses a public domain work, is that if the production is successful, other producers around the country (or even the world) can produce a similar show and cut into the producer's potential stock, amateur, and other subsidiary markets by flooding them before he gets there. Furthermore, if a movie company thinks that adapting the work is a good idea for a film, it may not bother to negotiate a film deal for the producers' adaptation if it can do its own for a fraction of the cost. It is important to note in this context that although the idea for the adaptation may have been uniquely and originally that of the producer, an idea is not copyrightable. Therefore, others can use the same idea, provided they do not copy the producer's newly created version. In some circumstances they can even use the same title, since titles — like ideas — do not enjoy copyright protection. [13]

Commission the Translation of a Public Domain Work

If the work in the public domain is a foreign-written play and there is no need for a dramatic adaptation, commissioning a translation would be appropriate. [14] What was said in the preceding section concerning adapting a public domain work is equally applicable here. In this area a producer may find it easier to hire a translator as an employee and retain complete copyright ownership himself. This is, of course, a matter of negotiation and depends to a large extent on the reputation of the translator. Although a translation can be done by a person with little knowledge of the theatre, the final product may be awkward and unplayable, and the producer may own the copyright of a relatively useless translation. Paying more for a well written and constructed translation by a talented translator will increase the chances of producing a good play.

Acquire the Rights to the Adaptation or Translation
of a Public Domain Work

The previous two sections dealt with a producer hiring or commissioning an author, composer, lyricist, or translator. However, if a producer finds a previous adaptation or translation which he feels has chances for success, he can produce that version without commissioning a new version. The fact that the underlying work may be in the public domain does not mean that the adaptation or translation is also free to use. As stated before, any new versions are themselves protected by a copyright — unless, that is, they have also fallen into the public domain.

The same problems of competition attendant to producing other public domain works apply here.

If the producer intends to present the play as a first class production, he would ordinarily negotiate and enter into a Dramatists Guild contract with the translator or adaptor. For other than first-class productions there is no standard option agreement which is generally used. The producer's attorney will usually draft his own contract.

Acquire the Rights to an Original Copyrighted Work

In contrast to public domain works, which are free to use without permission, are original works of authorship which enjoy full copyright protection. These works could be completely new and unproduced or could be old standards which have been on the boards many times. In either case, if the producer has in mind a Broadway or other first-class production he will probably enter into a Dramatists Guild contract.[15] If other than first class, the option to be signed will vary as previously indicated. These options usually provide that the producer has the exclusive right to present the play, thereby eliminating the possibility of a competing production. Bear in mind that an idea cannot be copyrighted, therefore another author could write a different play based on the same idea.[16]

Depending on the reputation of the author, a producer may not be able to option the rights to produce a play unless he plans on putting the play on Broadway, off-Broadway, or in a major theatre in a major city in the United States. Since the author wants the production of his play to be the best possible if the producer is going to share in his future royalties, he will usually grant only a simple license to smaller theatre companies and producers.[17]

Acquire the Rights to an Adaptation or Translation of an Original Copyrighted Work

Just as a work in the public domain may be adapted or translated, so may an original copyrighted work. A producer desiring to present such a play would enter into the appropriate option agreement with the author of the translation or adaptation. Part of the option agreement should provide not only that the new version of the work is original with the author, but also that the author has full right and authority to grant the rights. This would include a warranty that the author had acquired the rights from the owner of the basic work to do the adaptation or translation, and a clause holding the producer harmless in the event the author breaches the warranty. In the event the producer is sued because he produced an unauthorized version of the basic work, he could in turn sue the author for breach of contract and recover any losses he sustained as a result of the author's misrepresentation.

Acquire the Rights to Adapt or Translate an Original Copyrighted Work

Unlike a work in the public domain, a producer cannot legally commission an author to adapt or translate a copyrighted work and produce it without first obtaining the rights from the owner of the basic work. Provided the rights are available, the basic works such as novels, short stories, poems, plays, motion pictures, radio and television shows, and even comic strips can be translated, adapted, dramatized, or made into musicals. Usually the owner of the basic work will enter into an option agreement which will provide that the producer, upon exercise of the option, will own the rights in the basic work to adapt it for the stage in accordance with the terms of the literary purchase agreement annexed to and signed simultaneously with the option.[18] It is important that the agreement with the author of the basic work provides that the producer has the exclusive right to do the adaptation he desires and that the owner will not, during the term of the agreement, grant similar rights to anyone else. If he can no longer grant those rights to others, he will want to make sure he gets the best possible production in the best possible location.[19] For this reason, the owner of the basic work will not usually grant adaptation or translation rights to a producer who does not intend eventually to have a New York or other first-class production.

Commission an Original Work to be Copyrighted

A producer who has a unique idea can commission a playwright (preferably one with a reputation) to transform that idea into a play.

The terms of the contracts entered into between the producer and author will vary depending on the type of production, as previously stated. The contract will almost invariably be an option with additional rights rather than merely a license, since the producer is taking some risk in producing an unknown property and will want to provide investors with an added incentive to part with their money.

A possible area of interest in the commissioning of new plays is that of dramatizing the lives of famous people or certain interesting or unusual events in the news concerning people known or unknown. A producer desiring to commission the writing of such a play should first acquire good legal counsel, since such a production could give rise to a lawsuit under the right of privacy laws which virtually every state now has either by statute or court decision. The privacy statute in New York is found in the Civil Rights Law, Sections 50 and 51. Section 50 states "A person, firm or corporation that uses for advertising purposes or for purposes of trade, the name, portrait or picture of any living person without having first obtained the written consent of such person, or if a minor of his or her parent or guardian, is guilty of a misdemeanor." Section 51 states that the person so wronged can sue for an injunction and for money damages. The question of what is "for trade" is vague and has often come into conflict with the First Amendment guarantees of freedom of speech.

The statute has been further defined and refined by numerous court cases. The results of each case depend on the particular facts. Suffice it to say that if a producer intends to produce a play about a living person, he would be well advised to consult a knowledgeable lawyer.

Write or Adapt a Play to Produce

Since we are enumerating the ways to acquire a play to produce, we must not overlook the fact that the producer could, of course, write or adapt a play, or compose music and lyrics, or do any or all of these things. If a producer does any or all of these things, it would, perhaps, be wise for him to find someone else to produce. If no one else wants to produce the work, one might observe that the producer is less than unbiased toward the writer's work, and the producer's objectivity and business judgment should be carefully considered. Perhaps there are people who can write well, compose well, direct well, and then also produce well. There just aren't many. Most people would do well to handle any one of these jobs with a degree of professionalism.

CHAPTER 2

The Option For Other Than A First-Class Production

A FTER THE PRODUCER has determined that he wishes to acquire the rights to a property, who controls the rights and where, and how he intends to produce the play, he must then negotiate the terms of the agreement to acquire the rights. If the producer is acquiring a license with no additional or subsidiary rights, the negotiation process and the terms will be relatively one sided in favor of the author. The amounts due the author for a license are usually fixed at a percentage of the gross box office receipts or a flat fee, and the only variable is how much of an advance against royalties the producer need pay.

If, on the other hand, the producer is acquiring what is referred to as an "option," he should know what terms an option agreement can contain. This chapter will explain the most common terms found in option agreements, their purpose, and how they vary, depending on the bargaining power of the parties. After the reader has acquired a basic understanding of an option, the Dramatists Guild Minimum Basic Production Contract (which is a form of option most always used for first-class performances[1]) will be discussed in detail in the following chapter.

OUTLINE OF CONTRACTUAL PROVISIONS

1. Warranties of author and producer as to ownership and originality of the property

17

2. Author's grant of rights
3. Non-competition clause
4. Payments to author
5. Producer's subsidiary rights
6. House seat allocation
7. Billing credits
8. Producer's additional rights to tour
9. Producer's additional rights to produce or move the play to Broadway
10. Producer's additional rights to produce the play in England
11. Producer's additional rights to produce other first-class productions
12. Approval of director, actors, and designers
13. Duration of right to produce the play
14. Right to assign option
15. Arbitration clause
16. Script changes
17. Legal clauses

A sample option agreement containing the basic language of these terms appears at the end of the book. You will be able to refer to the contractual language easily, since the numbers to the left of the terms cited above correspond to the same paragraph numbers in the contract.

Warranties of Author and Producer as to Ownership and Originality of Property

In Chapter 1 we discussed the necessity of the producer acquiring the rights to do the play to avoid a lawsuit. The language in this paragraph should serve to guarantee that he is, in fact, making a valid acquisition after he has found the person whom he believes to be the owner of the property. The clause sets forth that the author or owner warrants and represents that the work: (a) is original and does not violate anyone's copyright (i.e., the author did not copy from another author); (b) does not violate any other rights of any person (this would include such areas as the right of privacy, defamation of character, libel, slander, and unfair competition); (c) is unencumbered by any claim made by someone against the author which adversely affects the play or the copyright (someone may be claiming a prior grant of the same rights being conveyed; this would be a claim that adversely affects the play. Producers want to option potential hits, not lawsuits); (d) is solely owned by the author, or owner, and that he has the right and power to enter into this agreement and to deal with the rights granted in the option.[2]

The author or owner also agrees to "indemnify" (pay) the producer for any losses the producer may suffer due to a "material" (substantial) breach of any of the above warranties. What is material may be a question for the court or an arbitrator to determine. If the court or an arbitrator finds the breach is material, the author must pay the producer's legal fees in addition to other damages, such as lost profits and any payments owing under contractual obligations which the producer undertook (i.e., fees for actors, designers, theatre, etc.) and which he cannot fulfill due to the inability to open or continue the play. The author also agrees to hold the producer "harmless" from any claims, demands, lawsuits, etc. This means that if the producer is sued by a third party, such as a real or a bogus owner of the play, the author must assume the responsibility so that the producer is not harmed by the claim.

If these provisions seem harsh and unfair to the author, one should realize that a producer spends great amounts of time and money to produce a play, and his investors would like to be assured that the already risky business of investing in plays is not made more hazardous by producing a play which infringes on someone else's rights, not to mention the fact that the author is, in reality, the one person who ought to know whether he stole the material or whether it is original — and he should be willing to guarantee such facts.[3] The paragraph will also provide that the producer will similarly indemnify the author with respect to any material which the producer, director, stage manager, etc., puts into the play, for which the author suffers damages.

Although the author warrants that the play is original and owned by him, this warranty does not extend to the title of the play, since — as previously mentioned — a title cannot be copyrighted. Because the use of a title similar to one which has established a secondary meaning can be considered unfair competition, a producer may suggest that the author change the title to avoid trouble. If the author refuses, the producer will want to add a clause to the above provisions whereby the author warrants that the title will not infringe on anyone's rights.

Author's Grant of Rights

The producer purchases from the author or owner the right to produce the play within a specified period of time in a specified place. This is, in fact, the option, and if he does so produce, the rest of the agreement becomes effective. If the producer does not present the play within the option period, the agreement terminates and all rights revert to the author.

The amount the producer pays for the option will vary greatly depending on numerous factors — including, among other things, the fame of the author and the amount of competition to produce the play. It is not unusual for a six-month option for an Off-Broadway production to cost $500, and the agreement may contain a provision for an automatic extension for an additional six months upon payment of $500 more, prior to the expiration of the first six-month term. It is possible for the option to cost up to $1,000 for six months. No matter what the option costs, the payments are most usually considered as advances against the royalty payments due to the author once the play opens.

Producers should try to negotiate the option terms so that they pay a smaller amount for the initial six-month period and a larger amount for the six-month extension. After the first six months, the producer should be in a better position to know if he will get the play financed and the cast he wants. If the show is close to coming together, the larger second payment can be money well spent and, in most cases, will be an advance against the royalties due the author when the show opens. [4] If, however, the producer finds that the show cannot be produced, his exposure will be limited to the smaller initial option payment.

A producer will always try to keep the option payment as small as possible, because if the play does not open, the option money belongs to the author and need not be returned to the producer. The option payment purchases the exclusive right to produce the work for a given period of time, during which time the author cannot sell the rights to another producer.

The producer will acquire the rights to produce the play in a definite location — i.e., New York City (on or off Broadway, or a middle theatre), a specific theatre such as the Kennedy Center in Washington, D.C.), or a specific kind of theatre (such as a stock or resident theatre.) The author will want this specified so he knows what kind of production it will be. Since the author is also under certain circumstances and conditions granting additional and subsidiary rights, he will want to make certain that the play will be presented in a manner that will create a future market. In order to help get a good production, the author may also grant the producer the right to present the play as a tour prior to its presentation at the designated location.

Bear in mind that the author may grant more than one extension and that the extensions may be more or less than six months. An original one-year option with a six-month extension is probably most common for New York productions, whether on or off Broadway. An author will rarely grant a producer an option and extensions that will add up to more than two years. If the producer cannot get the play on in two years he probably cannot get it on at all, so the author will want to give it to another producer who can.

Non-Competition Clause

Although paragraph two states that the producer is acquiring the sole and exclusive rights to present the play in a certain location or a specific theatre or kind of theatre, it does not specify whether the author can grant the production rights in the play to another producer in another location. Paragraph three further provides that the rights granted to the producer are the sole and exclusive rights to produce the play throughout the United States and Canada.

The author usually agrees that he will not grant anyone the rights to do a movie version of the play which would be released either during the option period, the run of the play, or any period in which the producer may have any rights to produce the play in the United States, Canada, or the British Isles. A movie released during these periods would possibly directly compete with the play and could cause the play to lose business.[5] This clause protects the producer from such competition; however, it will permit the author to dispose of the movie rights provided the producer grants his prior written approval, which will not be unreasonably withheld.[6]

The author may agree that he will not grant anyone the rights to perform the play in any media (except movies) in the United States, Canada, or the British Isles during the period the producer retains any rights or options to produce the play anywhere in the United States or the British Isles.[7]

Payments to the Author

In addition to the option payments received by the author, the producer also agrees to pay the author a percentage of the gross weekly box office receipts received from the sale of tickets. As mentioned earlier, the option payments are usually advances against these royalties and are therefore deducted from the first royalties earned by the author.[8]

The royalty to the author is usually a minimum of 5 percent of the gross weekly box office receipts, although this figure can and does vary. Some regional theatres have paid as little as 4 percent and some even get by with a flat fee of $100 or $125 per performance.

If the play is by a famous author, or if it is a play which more than one producer wants to option, the royalty may go above 6 percent of the gross weekly box office receipts but usually not over 10 percent. As will be seen in the next chapter concerning the Dramatists Guild contract, the royalties for a first-class dramatic play are on a sliding scale.

If the producer is presenting a musical, a 6 percent royalty is not unusual. It is usually divided 2 percent to the bookwriter, 2 percent to the lyricist, and 2 percent to the composer. Of course, if one of the collaborators is more famous than the other, or if his contribution is greater, that person may receive more than half of the gross weekly box office receipts.

In an effort to achieve a balance, the producer will sometimes offer the authors a smaller percentage of the gross until the production budget has been recouped, and a higher percentage thereafter. If, for example, the authors are demanding 7 percent and the producer wants to pay 6 percent, the resulting compromise could be 6 percent until the production budget is recouped, and 7 percent — or maybe even 7½ percent — thereafter. Once the play has returned the initial investment, the producer should be more comfortable giving the authors an extra 1 or 2 percent of the gross. Until recoupment, the extra 1 percent could mean the difference between staying alive during a difficult period or folding.[9]

Another compromise is for the producer to give the author some percentage of the producer's profits. Since profits are relatively rare in producing plays, an author will usually opt for more concrete remuneration.

If the producer[10] is presenting a musical adaptation of a copyrighted basic work, in addition to paying a percentage of gross box office receipts to the authors of the adaptation, he will most usually have to pay the owner of the basic work 1, 1½, or 2 percent of the gross weekly box office receipts. The payment for the right to adapt a basic work will include an option payment, which will usually range between $1,000 and $10,000 for two one-year options (and can be more or less). In the contract for the acquisition of the adaptation rights, the owner of such basic work will, in return for this sum, grant the producer (or whomever acquires the rights) a fixed period of time in which to complete the adaptation (usually one year) and an additional fixed period of time in which to produce the play (again, usually one year). The up-front option payment (or some part thereof) is generally considered as an advance against the 1, 1½, or 2 percent royalty earned by the owner when the play opens.

In addition, the owner of the basic work will want, and will be entitled to, an interest in the play's subsidiary rights. Usually the owner of the basic work will receive that proportionate part of the author's share of receipts received from all subsidiary uses of the play[11] which his royalty bears to the total aggregate royalties payable to all of the creators of the new work, the adaptors (bookwriter, composer, lyricist), including in this total the payment to the owner of the basic work. The owner of the basic work should want a limit placed on the aggregate royalties for the purpose of this computation. The limit may be 10 or 12 or 13 percent so that the producer is not able to dilute the interest of the owner of the basic work. The adaptors may be more than the bookwriter, composer, and lyricist. For example, the producer might hire a talented director and choreographer whose work is so unique that their contributions qualify them as creators.[12] The director and choreographer would, as part of their contract with the producer, receive a percentage of the gross as an "author's" royalty, and would want to share in the subsidiary income as well. As the total aggregate royalty increases to the creative personnel, the percentage of subsidiaries payable to the owner of the basic work decreases. Therefore, the limit of 10 or 12 or 13 percent will at least guarantee a limit on the dilution of the share of the owner of the basic work.

For example, the proportionate share of subsidiaries of the owner of the basic work would be computed as follows: If the owner of the basic work were paid a royalty of 1 percent and all the creative personnel (bookwriter, composer, and lyricist) jointly receive 6 percent, then the owner of the basic work would share in receipts from subsidiary income by receiving one-seventh of the share of such receipts, since 7 percent is the total aggregate royalties. If there is a 10 percent limitation written into the contract and the owner of the basic work receives a royalty of 1 percent, then he cannot receive less than one-tenth of such subsidiary receipts even if the total aggregate royalties payable to the adaptors and owner of the basic work exceeds 10 percent of the gross weekly box office receipts.

The term "gross weekly box office receipts" has been frequently referred to. The contract defines it as all receipts at the box office from the sale of tickets, less: theatre party commissions, discount and cut-rate sales, all admission taxes presently or to be levied, Ticketron charges or the cost of any other automated ticket distributor, those sums equivalent to the former 5 percent New York amusement tax (the net proceeds of which are now set aside in pension and welfare funds of the theatrical unions and ultimately paid to said funds), any subscription fees, and actors' fund benefits.

The contract provides that the royalties for each week must be paid to the author usually by the Wednesday following that week's performances. The producer must enclose with the payment a signed copy of the box office statement. The author has the right to examine the books of the producer at any time during regular business hours upon giving the producer reasonable notice. To avoid unnecessary harassment, the producer will attempt to limit such inspections to not more than semi-annually.

It should be noted that the contract contains a clause which provides that the author will waive his weekly royalty payment. This waiver clause is intended to assist the play to stay alive at critical times. In an effort to help keep the show alive, the author may agree to waive his royalty, but will want to waive only so much of it, if paid, as would cause the play to operate at a loss. An author may agree with such a waiver only if the producer agrees that he waives his producer's fee, and all other royalty recipients, similarly, waive. [13]

Producer's Subsidiary Rights

As previously mentioned, the producer is acquiring only the rights to present the play with live actors on the stage. The producer's production will make a contribution to the value of the play for use in other media if it runs for a certain length of time.

In consideration of the contribution the producer makes to the play, the author agrees to share with the producer a percentage of the net receipts received by the author from the future exploitation of his work in other media.

A Broadway production probably contributes most to the value of a play in other media. [14]

The receipts from subsidiary rights in which the producer shares [15] are usually from the following sources: (a) worldwide — motion pictures rights; (b) the continental United States and Canada — any of the following rights: radio and television; touring, stock, Broadway, Off-Broadway, amateur, and foreign language performances; condensed tabloid and concert-tour versions; commercial uses; original cast album, tapes, cassettes, records, and video cassettes.

Although the producer shares in the receipts from all the above uses, he does not control the disposition of the rights. The author is the owner and controls the rights. The producer is a third party beneficiary and shares in what the author receives.

In the case of the original cast album for a musical production, the producer as well as the bookwriter, composer, and lyricist will negotiate and enter into the agreement. The fact that the producer is part of this agreement is not because of any interest in subsidiary rights, but rather because the original cast album will be made using the original cast — i.e., members of the show who are employed and furnished by the producer.

Even though the author controls the future uses of the property, he must deal in good faith in disposing of those rights. The author may not make a deal in which he sacrifices one of the properties he has written in which the producer shares so that he might make a better deal on another of his properties in which no one shares. For instance, say an author has a play that a movie producer is anxious to make into a film and for which the author has been offered $100,000. In the event a producer produced the play and acquired an interest in subsidiary rights, the author should not be able to offer the movie producer the right to do the film for $75,000 on the condition that the movie producer will at the same time purchase another of the author's works for $150,000.

In other than a first-class production, later discussed, the number of performances the play has to run in order for the producer to share in the proceeds from the subsidiary rights may be computed in the following manner: 10 percent if the play has run for at least twenty-one consecutive paid performances; 20 percent for forty-two performances; 30 percent for fifty-six; and 40 percent for sixty-five consecutive paid performances. It is not usual for a producer to receive more than 40 percent.[16] The percentage is calculated on the author's net receipts earned from the disposition of subsidiary rights (less the agent's commission) if the contract for the disposition of such rights is entered into during a fixed period (usually seven or ten years after the opening or closing of the original production), even though the receipts may be received after the fixed period expires. All the performances must be consecutive (without a lapse between performances) and must be for paid admission attended by the public.

Preview performances are paid public performances, but since they are prior to the critics reviews, their contribution to the value of the property may be less. If the play officially opens, up to seven paid preview performances may be counted by the producer in making this computation.

As noted above, the producer's participation in the author's receipts from subsidiaries for a limited number of years after the last performance of the play in New York City (or after the first performance). The producer will continue to participate in all receipts earned from any disposition of subsidiary rights for as long as those receipts are earned by the author, provided that the contract for the disposition was entered into within the agreed upon number of years after the last or first performance. It is usually between seven and eighteen years, the extremes being three years or for the duration of the copyright in the play (fifty-six years under the old copyright

law or the life of the author plus fifty years as under the new law). As a
practical matter, the period is usually set on either side of ten years. An
example of this is as follows: the option agreement states that the producer
would share in the author's net receipts from any subsidiaries disposed of
before the expiration of ten years from the date of the last public performance in New York City. The play opened on January 1, 1970, and ran
consecutively until June 15, 1976. The author sold movie rights in July 1980
for $10,000. The producer would receive (assuming he earned 40 percent)
$4,000. Although more than ten years transpired from the time the play
opened, if the period is measured from the close of the play, then only four
years and one month would have elapsed. If the author did not receive
another payment from the movie company until July 1990, the producer
would still get 40 percent of the new payment. Although the payment in
1990 comes more than ten years after 1976, the movie contract was entered
into within the ten-year limitation period. It is for this reason that the
contract contains the parenthetical phrase that the producer shall receive the
percentage of net receipts *(regardless of when paid)*. The date of the
contract, not the payment, is usually the controlling factor. The receipts of
any contract entered into after the specified period (i.e., June 16, 1986, in
the above example) will not have to be shared with the producer; however,
all receipts from contracts entered into prior to that date continue to be
shared.

The negotiations for subsidiary rights can be very important. If the play
is a flop, the fight over subsidiaries may have been in vain.[17] However,
since few people — including producers — can predict with accuracy which
play will be successful and which will flop, every producer enters into
negotiations with the thought in mind that the play will be a hit. The
producer, the author, and, most importantly, the investors know the value of
subsidiary rights. If a producer does not get a fair deal on the subsidiaries
from the author, the author could have a hollow victory. Investors may not
invest, and without their money neither the producer nor the author have a
show.[18]

The previous breakdown of percentages per number of performances
(10 percent for twenty-one, 20 percent for forty-two, 30 percent for fifty-
six, and 40 percent for sixty-five) is one of the common arrangements for an
Off-Broadway production.[19] Under the Dramatists Guild Contract a producer of a first-class production, which includes Broadway, will get 40
percent after twenty-one consecutive performances in New York; or sixty-
four performances in or out of New York within eighty days of the first
performance; or one performance if the parties to the agreement have
selected a certain option in the agreement, as will be later discussed in

detail. Elsewhere the numbers may vary. A New York City production can negotiate a better subsidiary rights deal than a Kansas production. The outcome of any such negotiations depends on various factors, probably the most important of which includes the theatre, its location and size, the prestige of the producer or producing company, the total cost of the production, the eagerness of the producer, the stature of the author, the availability of financing, and the sophistication of the investors.

An author will usually not object to granting an interest in the subsidiary rights if it is for an important enough production. If an Off-Broadway show is having a pre-New York tour, it may make sense to count part of the pre-New York performances toward subsidiaries. The parties, for example, may agree to count up to twenty-five out-of-town performances. Thus, if sixty-five performances in New York City would result in the producer getting a 40 percent interest, if the play ran twenty-five or more performances in Boston or elsewhere, only forty additional New York performances would be needed to get that 40 percent.

In selecting a property to produce, the producer may find that the play was previously produced and that another producer has acquired and continues to retain an interest in the author's subsidiaries. Since the author does not want to give away another 40 percent of his interest, and since the new producer will have difficulty in financing the play without giving his investors an interest in subsidiary rights, a compromise must be reached.

One method of resolving this problem is to convince the producer of the first production that he ought to assign some part of his subsidiary rights interest to the new producer if the new production runs for a required number of performances. The original producer may not be unwilling to do this in view of the fact that a successful new production could increase the value of the subsidiary rights for all concerned. In such a situation, the author may also part with some of his subsidiary interest as well in order to assist the new production. If the original producer — who had earned a 40 percent interest in subsidiaries — gives up one-half (a 20 percent interest), and the author — who has the other 60 percent — gives up a 10 percent interest, the new producer would have a potential 30 percent interest in the author's receipts from the disposition of subsidiary rights. The original producer would retain 20 percent and the author would still have 50 percent.

House Seat Allocation

One of the areas of an option agreement which generates less controversy is that of house seat allocation (house seats are usually the best and most expensive seats in the theatre). The producer will usually offer the author a pair of house seats for all performances and ten pair for the night of the official opening. The reason for the absence of controversy is that house seats are not free, but they are valuable and everyone gets some. The tickets are held at the box office only until 6:00 p.m. of the day before each evening performance and 12:00 noon of the day before each matinee. If the author or his designee do not pay for and pick up the tickets by those times, the tickets become available for sale to the general public.

The attorney general of the state of New York has set forth rules and regulations concerning the use of house seats, and the author must agree to keep accurate records in accordance with the law.

Billing Credits

One area of sharp negotiations is that of billing credits. Everyone agrees that the author should receive credit, but where it should appear and how big it should be is open to negotiation. The author usually gets credit in all advertisements (except ABC and teaser ads),[20] programs, billboards, and houseboards wherever the name of the play appears. Sometimes the author will want to place a condition on the provision that he need not receive credit in ABC, shallow double, and teaser ads; that condition being that his name need not appear provided no other name appears.

Depending on the bargaining power of the author, the size of his name will vary anywhere from one-third to 100 percent of the size of the title. If the author is famous, the producer will not raise much of an argument on the size of the author's name, since this will be what sells tickets.

Authors will usually want their name to be the biggest name with only the title of the play being bigger. The producer may want to hire a director or star of prominence who, as part of their contract, will insist that their name be the largest. An author will often have to accept a clause which provides that no names will be larger than his except those of a star or director of prominence.[21]

In negotiating billing, in addition to the size of type used for the author's name, the style, boldness of type, and coloring of the type is established in relation to other names. Placement is also important. Authors usually insist that their name appear on a separate line beneath the title of the play.

When there are multiple authors, as in a musical, the names are usually listed as bookwriter, composer, and lyricist in that order.

Producer's Additional Rights

If the play is produced in accordance with the terms of the option agreement, and if certain conditions are met — such as the play running twenty-one performances, or opening before a paid audience, or running for any number of performances which may be arbitrarily decided upon — then certain additional rights accrue to the producer.

The rights to tour the play, to produce the play in England, and to produce subsequent productions in different parts of the country are usually options which the producer acquires. These options must be exercised within a certain period of time after the opening or closing of the original production. It is not unusual that the rights must be exercised within six months after the first production of the play before a paying audience. In each instance, to exercise the option the producer must give notice and send an option payment to the author.

The agreement will usually provide that the option to produce the play for a tour of the U.S., or in England, or for other productions must be exercised by sending the author notice and a payment of $500 or $750 or $1,000 for each of the rights to open the play in any of these areas, within one year after the giving of the notice. Since it requires more time to set up a tour, it is wise to provide that the tour must be commenced within fifteen or eighteen months instead of a year. For each city in which the producer desires to produce the play other than a tour, he must make a payment of $500 or $750. The agreement will provide that the royalties in each instance will be in an amount the same as the royalties provided in the original option agreement.

The agreement will probably provide that the producer may move the play to Broadway at any time during the run of the play, or within six months (or one year) after the close of the original production of the play, by entering into a Dramatists Guild Minimum Basic Production Contract on the terms and conditions set forth.

Approval of Directors, Actors, and Designers

It is usual for the author to have approval of the director, actors, and designers, or some of them. The producer's representative will try to qualify the approvals to provide that they will not be unreasonably withheld by the author. Without such a provision, the author may be as arbitrary as he or she wishes with respect to the approvals. The provision that approvals will not be unreasonably withheld creates a litigatable or arbitratable issue which can be resolved by someone other than the author. A producer could then go ahead and hire the director even without approval, and at a later date a court or arbitrator would determine whether the author was being unreasonable in withholding the approval. Without such a provision, the author could arbitrarily withhold approval of anyone for whatever whimsical reason he or she wanted.

Duration of Right to Produce the Play

The agreement will provide that the producer can produce the play during the continuous run of the play. The continuous run will usually be defined to mean that the run continues so long as there are no more than two or three or four weeks between paid performances before a live audience. There are, of course, other ways of defining continuous run, but one should make certain that the agreement is clear as to the continuing right of the producer to produce the play and when those rights cease and terminate.

Right to Assign Option

The producer must have the right to assign the option, since, in all probability, he is going to assign the production rights to a limited partnership, which will be formed to produce the play. The author, on the other hand, has consented to this producer producing the play and will not want him to make a complete assignment to someone else and walk away from the production. The relationship between an author and producer is a very personal relationship, and although in many instances the successful author and his producer are not madly in love, it does make life simpler if they have mutual respect for one another and a working relationship. It is not unusual to provide that the producer may assign the contract to a partnership or a corporation in which he is one of the principals, without any other approvals, but if the producer wishes to make an assignment to an entity in which he is not one of the principals, then the author must approve of such assignment.

Arbitration Clause

If there is a dispute with respect to the contract, either party may ask a court of law to resolve the dispute. There is a better way of resolving disputes, however, which I feel is particularly applicable to theatre differences. It may be provided in the agreement that the dispute will be resolved by arbitration. The advantage of arbitration is that (1) the parties can select an arbitrator who is knowledgeable in theatre; and (2) most often a quicker decision may be reached. It is usual to provide that the arbitration will be in accordance with the rules and regulations of the American Arbitration Association.[22]

Agreements of this kind will sometimes provide that disputes may be settled by a party specifically designated by the parties to the agreement. For example, if there is a dispute of an artistic nature, the author and producer may consent that the director will cast the deciding vote. It there is a business dispute, the parties may agree that the dispute may be settled by either the attorney for the production or the general manager for the show.

Script Changes

Almost always the option agreement will provide that there will be no script changes without the approval of the author. Although rarely granted, it is usual to ask the author not to withhold such approval unreasonably with respect to the script. It is most usual to give the author sole and complete control even to the extent that he may be unreasonable.[23]

Legal Clauses

There are a few boiler-plate legal clauses usually added to the end of an option to produce a play. It may be provided that the agreement will be interpreted under the laws of the state of New York (or any other state where the agreement is being drafted), that this agreement is the entire agreement between the parties and anything previously said or written is invalid, that the parties are not to be considered joint venturers or partners, and such similar provisions.

CHAPTER 3

Movie Deals

INVESTORS EXPECT TO SHARE IN SALE OF MOVIE RIGHTS

M OTION PICTURE RIGHTS deserve special attention. As was pointed out, usually the investors in a show share in the proceeds
from the sale of subsidiary rights if the play runs for a certain length of time.
One of the most lucrative possible sources of income for a production, its
investors and its adaptors is a share in the sale of the motion picture rights.
A distinction must be made between (1) the rights to deal with the motion
picture rights in the play; and (2) the rights to base the play in whole or in
part on the movie.

If a play is adapted from a work that has already been made into a
movie, then the movie rights have already been disposed of and, unless the
rights have reverted to the owner of the basic work (which is not likely in
most instances), some kind of deal ought to be made with the company
owning the movie rights.

FILM COMPANY MAY ALSO OWN BASIC RIGHTS IN WORK

A play and a movie may be based on the same basic work (a novel, a
record, etc.), or a producer or adaptor may want to base a play on a movie

33

(which, in this instance, would make the movie the basic work). The movie may have been an original, or it may have been based on another basic work that the moving picture company acquired all rights to, including the dramatic rights. In either event, appropriate arrangements should be made. The only basic difference in these two instances is that if the play is to be based on a movie, then the motion picture company will expect a larger payment. The reason for this is that in addition to permitting the adaptor to deal with the play to make a movie sale based on the play, they are also granting the rights to do the play based on the movie. If the movie is the basic work, the motion picture company is in a much stronger bargaining position than if it only owned the film rights and the film was based on another work. Why would anyone want the rights to base a movie on a play based on a movie? The answer is simple. The play, although based on the movie, might become a totally different property. If the play is a success there is surely a market — especially if the play is a musical adaptation of a dramatic work.

One should always be prepared to bargain for the motion picture rights, so that if the play is a success it may then be made into another movie.

DRAMATIC RIGHTS

If the motion picture company owns the dramatic rights, that part of the negotiations is the same as negotiating with anyone else for the dramatic rights, which has already been discussed in detail.

FILM RIGHTS — OPTION OF FIRST REFUSAL

For the most part, aside from the dramatic rights, one may expect that the company owning the film rights will want an option of first refusal to make a movie based on the play for one-third less than any other bona fide offer. There may also be a fixed amount set forth in the agreement for which they may purchase the movie rights — such as $150,000 plus an amount equal to 2, 5, or 10 percent of the first year's gross box office receipts for the play, but in no event more than another fixed amount, which might be $1 million. These, of course, are hypothetical figures and could vary greatly in either direction.

SHARE OF SALE TO OTHER FILM COMPANY

In addition, if the motion picture company chooses not to make the film and the rights are sold to someone else, they will expect one-third of the proceeds of the film sale.

The motion picture company will expect a certain percentage of the box office receipts from the play — an amount such as 2 or 3 perceny is not unusual. They might also insist upon a payment, at the time that the agreement is entered into, as an advance against the box office receipts, or merely as a fee. This amount may vary between $1,000 and $5,000, but very often is not even demanded, agreed to, or paid.

FILM COMPANY MAY WANT CAST ALBUM AND PUBLISHING

An owner of the motion picture rights may try to get the rights to publish the music and to make the original cast album if the play is a musical. Many of the major film studios have associated companies which do publishing and recording. It is not advisable for a producer or an adaptor to permit them to have these rights unless it is unavoidable. The producer may have to rely on an investment from a record or publishing company in exchange for the rights to the album, and if these rights have been tied up and are not available, he may lose this investment source. It is better to give the motion picture owners an option of first refusal on these rights, so that at the very least they will have to match any other bona fide offers.

Sometimes the motion picture owner will agree to cease distribution of the original movie, and sometimes not. In most instances, they will cooperate in every way, including making copies of the print available for viewing, for if a deal has been made at this point, they will in fact have a vested interest in the outcome of the play.

The negotiations would be similar whether the play will be a musical or a drama, except with a drama there would be no discussion of music publishing. A dramatic cast album is a possibility, but of much less importance, so that it is less a subject of sharp bargaining. The dollar amounts and percentages might vary, but not substantially. But, more important, bear in mind that most adaptations are for musicals rather than for dramas.

CHAPTER 4

Option for a First-Class Production — The Dramatists Guild Contracts

THE OPTION TO PRODUCE a Broadway show is almost always a Dramatists Guild Minimum Basic Production Contract, sometimes referred to as the "Dram Guild Contract."[1] There are separate contracts for a dramatic production and for a dramatic musical production. There are also Dramatists Guild contracts for a review, for stock tryouts, and for a collaboration. If the author is not a member of the Guild and you wish to option his play for a Broadway production, then he will most usually become a member of the Guild.

The Dramatists Guild Minimum Basic Production Contract is used for the optioning of a completed play, and is also most usually used as the agreement between the producer and adaptors (bookwriter, composer, and lyricist) when the producer has acquired rights to do an adaptation of a basic work. A producer acquiring such rights in a basic work will acquire the rights for the sole purpose of conveying them to the adaptors. Unless broad rights are acquired, the producer will have problems getting top notch adaptors. A hot bookwriter, composer, and lyricist would be willing to do an adaptation only if they would be in a position to make a film sale of their successful stage adaptation of the basic work. The producer conveys the rights to do an adaptation in this same Dramatists Guild Minimum Basic Production Contract, which, in turn, grants the producer the option to the production rights in the play effective when the play is completed.

For many years there was an agreement that producers signed with the Guild which contained the same provisions now contained in the agreement entered into by a producer with a specific author. In 1961 that agreement lapsed, and now only the individual contract with each author for each show is signed.

Although the League of New York Theatre Owners and Producers does not contract with the Guild as it does with other unions and associations, it negotiates the terms of the contract. This leaves the parties — that is, the producer and the author — in a position to voluntarily use the contract. If the League contracted, there would be a binding obligation on its members (virtually all producers and Broadway theatres) to use the contract. Even if a producer were not a League member he could not get into a theatre under such circumstances. Although voluntary now, the Guild contract is almost always used. [2]

Guild Membership

In order to become a member of the Guild, one must first become an associate member after approval by the membership committee and payment of a $20 annual fee. After a first-class performance, the associate member — again with approval — becomes an active member and the fee is $35 annually. Active members may vote. In addition to the $35 annual fee, the Guild retains 2 percent of the author's royalty on a dramatic show if the royalty payable to all authors on that particular show is $3,000 per week or less, and 3 percent of the royalty if the author's total royalties exceed $3,000 that week. On a musical the Guild retains 2 percent of the royalties payable to the bookwriter, composer, and lyricist if the weekly royalties payable to all the authors (which would mean all bookwriters, composers, lyricists, and authors of underlying properties' receipts combined) is $4,000 or under, and 3 percent if the total payable to all authors is over $4,000 that week. In addition, whether the property is dramatic or musical, the Guild is paid 2 percent of an author's receipts from the motion picture sale.

Terms Sometimes Above Minimum

The Dramatists Guild contract — which is, as previously stated, a minimum basic contract — contains the minimum terms that must be given to an author. There is nothing to prevent the author's agent, attorney, or other representative from demanding more than the minimum terms, nor is there anything to prevent the producer from paying more. Some contracts are essentially upon the minimum basic terms. If the author is a well-known personality, he may demand and receive a higher percentage of the gross box office receipts than the minimum for his royalty payments.

On a musical, if the author, composer, and lyricist have never had a show produced before, the contract may be on the minimum royalty terms of 6 percent. With veterans, it is not unusual to pay a 7 or 8 percent royalty until production costs are recouped, and then an extra 1 percent. Sometimes, however, the royalty on a musical is either a straight 7 or 8 percent.

There will be other areas where there may be a variance from the Minimum Basic Production Contract terms, and in each instance I will try to call these to your attention as we go along.

Guild Approval

After it is signed by the producer and the author, the Minimum Basic Production Contract is forwarded to the Dramatists Guild for its approval. If there have been changes which reduce the author's rights or income below the minimums, then the Dramatists Guild may not countersign the agreement and it will not be valid. There are certain established rules which the Dramatists Guild will follow. There are, however, some occasions when they will vary in certain ways from the minimum terms to effect a contract, but there are limits to the extent of the variations permitted.

Contract Parts

The Dramatists Guild Minimum Basic Production Contract actually consists of three parts. There is the basic contract, which is signed at the end by the parties to the contract. Appended to the contract is what is known as the "Schedule of Additional Production Terms." Also appended to the contract is "Appendix A to the Schedule of Additional Production Terms," which consists of instructions to the film negotiator.

The contract in its section on definitions defines "contract" as the Minimum Basic Production Contract plus the Schedule of Additional Production Terms. It is questionable whether or not the instructions are actually a part of the contract and binding upon the parties. Since they are instructions to the film negotiator, they are nevertheless important terms which, whether binding upon the parties or not, certainly affect the parties to the agreement.

In addition to the three basic parts of the contract, there is one paragraph, Paragraph TENTH, which is a blank paragraph filled in at the time the

Contract is pre-paged and contains provisions which are specifically applicable to that particular contract. Paragraph TENTH contains variances from the printed form as well as additional provisions in the contract.

Some Confusion in Contract

One of the reasons that the Dramatists Guild contract is very often difficult to read and is not easily understandable is that the Minimum Basic Production Contract will often make reference to certain items which are discussed in greater detail in the Schedule of Additional Production Terms. There are constant cross references from one paragraph to another or from one paragraph in the contract to a paragraph in the Additional Production Terms, with further reference back to a provision of the contract. In analyzing the contract, it will be noted which part contains the term under discussion; however, although a term may be found in more than one part of the contract or schedule, it will be discussed as if it were all written into the contract in one place.

Contract is a License to Produce a Play

The Dramatists Guild Minimum Basic Production Contract is an option for the producer to produce a play on the speaking stage in the United States and Canada. If the producer does produce the play in accordance with the terms of the contract, the producer shares in other proceeds of the play and acquires certain other benefits.

DRAMATIC PRODUCTION CONTRACT

Option Cost

There are alternative ways of paying for the option. One contract provision provides that the producer pay a minimum of $500 upon the signing of the contract for the first three months, a monthly payment of $100 for each of the next three months, and $200 each month for the next six months. These payments constitute a non-returnable advance against royalties. A producer may alternatively pay the sum of $200 each month for twelve consecutive months, which would also constitute a non-returnable advance against royalties. Not all option payments are advances against all royalty payments; there are certain royalty payments, which will be discussed later, for which option payments are not considered an advance.

There is no usual way of arranging the option payments, but perhaps the most common method is for an annual payment of between $2,000 and $2,500. This may be paid in various ways during the year, such as one-half on signing and the other one-half after six months, or one-quarter every three months. Of course, a neophyte for a first play may get the minimum, payable as above provided, in the contract. Which method of payment is used for the option, as well as for royalties, is agreed to by the parties or their representatives during the contract negotiations.

Length of Option

The standard Minimum Basic Production Contract will run for a period of one year, which means that the play must have a first-class performance before a paid audience on or before one year from the date of the contract, or one year from the date of delivery of the completed play. The producer, of course, will want to make provision to extend the option to produce the play after the one-year period. If the year runs out and the play has not been produced, he will have invested a great deal of time, energy, and effort in what will prove fruitless unless he can get an extension and get the play on. It is not unusual to have a special provision in Paragraph TENTH which provides that for an additional payment of a certain amount of money, which may be an additional $200 per month, the option may be extended for an additional six months. The Dramatists Guild is reluctant to permit a producer to extend an option except under certain circumstances. The Guild takes the position that the $200 per month is not as important to the author as a production of the play, and to tie the play up, if there is little chance of it being produced, is not in the best interest of the author. For this reason, the contract must provide that, in order to extend the option beyond a year, there must have been certain circumstances which prevented the producer from getting the play on during the one year period. The clause may provide that extension of the option is conditioned upon the producers having entered into a contract with a star to appear in the show, or with a director to direct the show during the six-month period that the option is extended, and the star or director are unavailable to appear until the period covered by the six-month extension. Theatre unavailability until the extended six-month period is also a valid reason for extension. Such additional option payments are normally considered advances against the royalties in the same manner that the original option payments are deemed advances against royalties.

The author's representative will try to include a provision in the agreement in Paragraph TENTH which provides that if the play is not in rehearsal by a certain date, all rights will revert to the author. The basis for this is that if the option is for one year, and if the play has not gone into rehearsal at least four weeks before the expiration of the one year, it would be impossible for the play to open within the one year. If there is not an option extension, and it appears that it will be impossible for the producer to get the play on in time, the author would want the rights to revert so that he may sell the option to another potential producer.

In the event that the play has not been completed at the time the contract is entered into, the one year runs from the date the completed play is submitted to the producer. A completed dramatic play for the purposes of the agreement means a minimum of 110 pages single spaced.

Actually, pursuant to the contract, the producer is not obligated to pay any money until the date of delivery of the manuscript; however, payment is almost always made at the time the contract is signed, but the option time does not start to run until delivery is made.

Minimum Basic Royalty Payments

It should be noted that the minimum royalty payments to the author (which are provided in the largest percentage of contracts) are 5 percent of the first $5,000 of gross weekly box office receipts, plus 7½ percent of the next $2,000 of gross weekly box office receipts, plus 10 percent of the gross weekly box office receipts over $7,000. Bear in mind that these are the minimum terms, and under certain circumstances some authors may demand and receive a straight 10 percent royalty, more or less, but rarely more.[3]

Variances from Minimum Basic Royalty Payments

The contract provides for certain deviations from the minimum royalty payments of 5 percent, 7½ percent, and 10 percent. These are the following, each of which will be discussed in detail:

1. Reduced royalty to author based on reduced royalty to other artistic personnel.
2. Limitation of royalty during the first four weeks out-of-town.
3. Alternative royalty payment for the first three weeks commencing with the official New York opening performance.

4. Alternative royalty payment commencing with the fourth week following the official New York opening.
5. Limitation on royalty payments for road companies after the New York run. [4]

Reduced Royalty for all Artistic Personnel

If the producer pays $200 each month for the option, then the producer may elect a certain provision of the contract which may become effective and permits reduced royalty payments to the author if the other artistic personnel in the production accept similar reductions. This provision of the contract was a result of long negotiations which took place between the Dramatists Guild and the League of New York Theatres in 1961; the provision is complicated, somewhat difficult to comprehend, and seldom used, but nevertheless part of the Minimum Basic Production Contract. [5]

In effect, it provides that if the producer makes similar arrangements with the director and actors, and with respect to the fees of the producer himself, then the author will accept compensation for not in excess of seventeen consecutive weeks (including all out-of-town performances prior to the New York opening, New York preview performances, New York performances, or performances after the New York run), commencing with the first paid performance of the play or until the "production expenses" are recouped (as production expenses are defined in the contract), at the rate of one-half of the compensation otherwise provided, or 5 percent of the gross weekly box office receipts, whichever is greater. If the producer is entering into a contract upon the minimum terms, then the one-half would mean 2½ percent of the first $5,000 gross weekly box office receipts plus 3¾ percent of the next $2,000 gross weekly box office receipts plus 5 percent of the gross weekly box office receipts over $7,000, so that in such event the alternative of 5 percent of the gross weekly box office receipts would be greater and would be the amount that would be paid. After payment of this compensation for seventeen weeks or after the production expenses have been recouped, then the payments provided in the contract are made, so that if the contract is based on the minimum terms — 5 percent, 7½ percent, and 10 percent would be paid. In the event that there are no out-of-town performances, then the seventeen consecutive weeks commence with the first New York performance.

In determining whether production expenses have been recouped or not, one must take into account all income to the producer derived directly or indirectly from the production of the play, including not only income from the first-class performances, but also from other activities such as the sale of souvenir gifts, payments from music publishers, and any share of net receipts to which the producer may become entitled due to the disposition of any subsidiary rights in the play during any such week, even though later received.

When it is said that comparable arrangements must be made with the director, with the actors, and with respect to producer's fees, it means that during the period the author accepts a reduced payment, the director must be paid an amount equal to one-half of the percentage of weekly box office receipts which he will receive during the New York run. However, he will not be required to be reduced below 1 percent of the gross weekly box office receipts. During this period each actor must also receive one-half of the guaranteed salary and/or one-half of the percentage of weekly box office receipts which he will receive during the New York run. However, no actor during said period shall be required to be reduced below $1250 per week. No arrangement need be made with any actor who receives less than this amount and who does not receive a percentage of the box office receipts. During this period any management fee or percentage of gross weekly box office receipts payable to the producer will be one-half the amount of the management fee and/or percentage of weekly box office receipts that exceed ½ of 1 percent of the gross weekly box office receipts. The producer will not pay or make any charge for office expenses in excess of $300 per week during the period that the author's payments are reduced. The contract also provides that the director's, actors', and producer's fees need not be reduced proportionately more than the author's fees are reduced during this period.

The contract provides that the producer will furnish the author and the Dramatists Guild with copies of all contracts with the director and actors, all contracts which concern the production or management fees, and all other documents and financial statements or reports which are issued by the producer to the investors, and that these materials must be furnished within ten days after their execution and no later than two weeks prior to rehearsal. There is further provision that the Guild or the author may examine the producer's books.

It must be understood that although the producer may, at the time he enters into the contract, if the author agrees, select this alternative to take advantage of a reduced payment to the author for seventeen weeks, or until recoupment, whichever is sooner, he is under no obligation to do this. If, after beginning production, the producer decides that these arrangements cannot be completed or are impractical or undesirable, then the contract is effective but that particular provision is inoperative, and the royalties would be paid in accordance with the contract terms applicable as if this alternative had not been selected.

Limitation of Royalty During First Four Weeks Out-Of-Town

As was noted, the most usual royalty arrangement is that the author be paid 5 percent of the first $5,000 of the gross weekly box office receipts, plus 7½ percent of the next $2,000 of such receipts, plus 10 percent of all such receipts in excess of $7,000. The contract also provides that such payments shall not exceed $750 in any of the first four weeks of the out-of-town performances prior to the New York opening. This restriction to $750 during that period is one of the provisions of the Minimum Basic Production Contract that the persons representing authors sometimes try to have deleted. Sometimes it is and sometimes it isn't. It also should be noted that this $750 limitation is not applicable if the previously discussed limitation of a reduced royalty for all artistic personnel is selected and becomes applicable.

Alternative Payments For First Three Weeks in New York

In the event that the producer has not elected to pay the reduced amount to the actors, director, and consequently to the author, there is another alternative method of paying royalties which is provided for in the agreement. However, the author's representative often will not permit the producer to elect this alternative. It provides that for the first three weeks, beginning with the official New York opening, the sum of $3,000 shall be paid at least one week prior to the first rehearsal, and held by the Guild in escrow for the benefit of the author. Immediately after the official New York opening, the Guild turns this money over to the author. If the producer elects this alternative, and does not pay the $3,000 as provided in the agreement at least one week prior to the first rehearsal, then royalty payments will be at the 5 percent, 7½ percent, and 10 percent rate. However, the author has the option of terminating the agreement if he so desires upon written notice to the producer within three days of the default in payment of the $3,000.

If the play is abandoned, and does not officially open in New York, the $3,000 is returned to the producer. Although, as was noted, option payments are usually considered advances against royalties, this royalty payment is an exception, for if the producer pays the sum of $3,000 for the first three weeks, this royalty is in addition to the option payments. The option payments are not deemed advances against this royalty payment of $3,000. The opportunity to make the payment of $3,000 for the first three consecutive weeks is very important to the producer for one reason. As discussed later, the producer acquires certain very valuable rights if the play runs for a certain length of time. If the $3,000 payment is made, the play need only officially open in New York City for these rights to belong to him.

Alternative Royalty from Fourth Week in New York

The contract also provides an alternative payment for each week commencing with the fourth week after the New York opening. However, this alternative cannot be selected if the producer has elected to pay the author the reduced payments during the seventeen weeks or until recoupment, as previously discussed. The alternative is a payment of $250 per week plus 25 percent of the weekly operating profits (as defined in the contract) until the week in which the production expenses (as defined in the contract) have been recouped. After the production expenses have been recouped, the payments resume at the regular 5 percent, 7½ percent, and 10 percent rate. One should bear in mind that if this alternative is selected, the payments of $250 per week and the 25 percent cannot be credited against the advance which was paid for the option, but are payments in addition to the advance. After recoupment, however, if the advance has not been fully credited against royalties earned, any further royalties payable to the author are credited against so much of the advance payments still uncredited.

Road Company Limitation

It is not unusual for the author's representative to try to include in Paragraph TENTH a provision that the compensation for road company tours after the New York run shall be 5 percent of the first $5,000 of gross weekly box office receipts, plus 7½ percent of the next $2,000, plus 10 percent of the receipts over $7,000 without the limitation that is provided in the contract, to the effect that, if the payments would result in there being no operation profits for a particular week, the author would receive only such compensation for that week so as not to result in an operating loss — in no event, however, less than $250.

Author's Warranties

Guarantees of Originality

In consideration of the payments to the author, the author guarantees that he is the author of the play and has the right to enter into the agreement, and that he will perform such services as may be reasonably necessary in making revisions. Since the warranties (a warranty is a guarantee) in the contract are only to the effect that the author is the author and has the right to enter into the agreement, Paragraph TENTH may sometimes provide that to the best of the author's knowledge the play is wholly original with him and that use of the script will not conflict with or infringe upon the rights of any other person or corporation.[6]

No Warranty of Title

In the case of the title, there is usually no warranty or representation by the author of ownership, as one may not own a title in the same sense that one may own other works that one creates and enters on a page. A title cannot be protected by copyright. Therefore, in Paragraph TENTH it may be provided that the author gives a representation that he has not himself done anything which affects his right to use the title of the play, and that as far as he knows he has the right to use the title.

It is possible for a title, after continued usage, to become identified with a particular show; in such a case, the title may thereafter have a protectable value which cannot be used by others. This is not the usual case with a play title if the play is being optioned for the first time. In the event that there is a change in the title, it is not unusual to provide in Paragraph TENTH that the title change will become the property of the author. Of course, no change may be made in the title, just as no change may be made in any other part of the play, without the author's prior approval.[7]

Grant of Production Rights

The author grants the producer the exclusive right to produce the play in the United States and Canada and agrees that he will assist in selection of the cast and will consult and advise the producer, director, dance director, conductor, and scenic and costume designers in all of the problems arising out of the production. He further agrees that he will attend rehearsals of the play as well as out-of-town performances prior to the New York opening.

However, he may be excused from attending out-of-town upon a showing of reasonable cause.

Author's Billing and Credits

The producer agrees to announce the name of the author as the sole author of the play on all programs and in all advertising matter in which the name of the producer appears.

Paragraph TENTH will usually elaborate on the author's billing, listing the places where the author will receive credits. Sometimes the size of type used for the author's name will be designated, such as at least one-quarter, one-half, or three-quarters the size of the type used for the title of the play. There may be a provision that the author's name is larger than any other name or larger than any other name except the star and a director of prominence. One must be especially careful, as it is imperative that most stars' names be larger — and the names of some important directors as well. The author may defeat his purpose by insisting that his name be larger if, in so doing, the producer cannot hire the star or director who would be right for the play. The billing credits usually provide that the author need not receive credit in so-called "ABC" and "teaser" ads as well as shallow double ads, provided the producer's name does not appear. The extent of the contract provisions on billing credits varies. Some well-known authors do not find it necessary to insist upon any specific billing credits, knowing that they will receive prominent billing because their names sell tickets.

Paragraph TENTH may also sometimes contain a provision that if there is a motion picture, or a live or taped television program or series based upon the play, the author must use his best efforts to have credit given to the play producer, to the effect that the play was originally produced on Broadway by this producer.

Author's Approval

In the contract the producer acknowledges that the play is the artistic creation of the author and agrees that the author will have cast and director approval and, where appropriate, conductor and dance director approval.

After opening, any cast change or replacement of director, conductor, or dance director will also be subject to the author's approval, which approval the author may grant to another person who may act on his behalf.

If the author is outside the United States, he gives up his approvals unless he has designated someone else who is in the United States to act for him.

In all cases, where the approval or consent of the author is required, an unresolved disagreement among several authors of the play is resolved by a majority of the authors, unless a different method of decision is provided for in the production contract. If there is a tie vote and the authors cannot resolve the disagreement, the Schedule of Additional Production Terms provides that the president of the Guild, upon the request of the producer or the authors, or either of them, may appoint a single arbitrator to pass upon the unresolved disagreement.

Changes in the Script

After delivery of the completed script, no addition, omission, or alteration may be made without the consent of both the author and the producer. The author owns any changes in the play. If the producer feels that the author is unreasonable in refusing to make changes or additions, he may complain to the Guild, which will appoint a representative or representatives, and if they deem it advisable they will use their best efforts to prevail upon the author to make the suggested changes. One must bear in mind, however, that the Guild does not have the power to compel an author to agree to changes in his script.

The author's right with respect to play changes and approvals of cast and director shall similarly apply to any British production. [8]

Rights Acquisition Time

The producer, by successfully producing the play in a first-class production, makes a contribution to the value of the play for other uses. Therefore, the contract — together with the Schedule of Additional Production Terms — provides that if the play runs for a certain length of time, the producer will acquire certain rights which could prove to be very valuable.

These additional rights accrue if the play is presented for one of the following: (1) twenty-one consecutive performances in New York; or (2) sixty-four consecutive performances in or out of New York (however, traveling time out of New York does not break the continuity of consecutive performances so long as sixty-four of the performances are given within eighty days of the first performance); or (3) one performance in New York if the producer has made the payment of $3,000 provided in the contract for the royalty covering the first three consecutive weeks from the New York opening. Any one of these will be referred to as the "rights acquisition time."

If the part of the contract is selected and becomes operative which permits the reduced payments to the author if the other artistic personnel take similar cuts, then each preview performance in New York within ten days of the official opening in New York (even though not consecutive) will be considered a consecutive performance in New York for the purpose of determining whether the play has been presented for the period of "twenty-one consecutive performances in New York," provided that the author is paid the compensation as set forth in the contract and provided that the gross box office receipts of each performance are at least 65 percent of the capacity of the theatre (computed at the announced New York prices).

Additional Production Benefits

This measurement of the time necessary for the acquisition of additional rights is important in that if the production runs for the length of time as stated above, the producer: (1) acquires an interest in the subsidiary rights as set forth in the contract; (2) acquires the right to do an English production in accordance with the contract terms; (3) may reopen the show after it closes; (4) becomes entitled to special concessions which may, under certain circumstances, reduce the compensation to the author; and (5) acquires a bargaining position with respect to the motion picture rights. (Each of these rights will be discussed later in detail.) Of course, the contract provides that all of the producer's rights in the play terminate unless the play does run for this number of performances, which was referred to as the "rights acquisition time."

Interest in Subsidiary Rights

As we have noted, the contract states that if the producer successfully produces a play, the production makes a contribution to the value of the uses of the play in other media. Therefore, if the play has been produced for the rights acquisition time, namely for twenty-one consecutive performances in New York, or for sixty-four consecutive performances outside of New York, if the producer made the payment previously discussed in the amount of $3,000 for the first three weeks' royalties after the New York opening, the producer acquires a percentage interest in the net receipts received by the author from the sale or disposition of the property for other media. Bear in mind that the author alone owns and controls the play with respect to all other uses, and that any sale, lease, license, or other disposition will be by the author. The subsidiary rights or additional rights discussed here are the rights to share in the proceeds and not the rights to control the play.[10] The author does agree, however, that he will not permit, without the producer's prior consent, any outright sale (as distinguished from a lease, license, or other disposition) for motion pictures throughout the world or within the United States and Canada, for radio, television, second-class touring performances, foreign language performances, condensed and tabloid versions, so-called concert touring versions, commercial uses, play albums of records, stock performances, amateur performances, Off-Broadway performances, and musical comedy, operetta, or grand opera based upon the play. In no event will there be an outright sale of any of such rights prior to the first-class production of the play, except that an outright sale of motion picture rights prior to such first-class production of the play may be permitted if made in accordance with certain terms set forth in the Schedule of Additional Production Terms, the terms of which will later be discussed in detail.

Basic Rights Covered

The rights in which the producer may acquire a financial interest are the motion picture rights throughout the world and within the United States and Canada, radio, television, second-class touring performances, foreign language performances, condensed and tabloid versions, so-called concert tour versions, commercial uses, and play albums of records.

Percentage Interest

The producer will receive 40 percent of the author's net receipts, if any, if the above set forth basic rights are disposed of within ten years after the last performance pursuant to the contract; 35 percent if disposed of within the next two years; 30 percent if within the next two years; 25 percent if within the next two years; and 20 percent within the next two years. Stock performance and amateur performances within the United States are also included, provided that the producer has not elected the clause, and paid the director, actors, and the author a smaller amount for the first seventeen weeks or until the production has recouped its production expenses.

If that part of the contract is selected and becomes operative which

provides that the author may be paid a reduced royalty during the first
seventeen weeks or until recoupment, then in lieu of the percentage above
stated for stock and amateur performances, the producer would receive 40
percent of the net receipts, if the stock performances and amateur performances (Off-Broadway performances are also included here) within the
United States and Canada are disposed of within five years after the last
performance under the contract.

With respect to a first-class performance of a musical comedy, operetta,
or grand opera based on a straight dramatic play, the producer will receive
40 percent of the net proceeds received by the author for any performances
given within eighteen years after the first-class run of the play has ended.

The producer will receive the percentage of the receipts as above set
forth for the disposition of the motion picture rights; however, it should be
kept in mind that if the original contract for the motion picture rights grants
motion picture sequel rights upon payment of additional compensation,
and if such additional compensation is paid, the play producer will receive
one-half of the respective percentage for the sequels, as above set forth for
the motion picture rights.

Interest in British Subsidiary Rights

If the play has been produced by the producer in the British Isles in
accordance with the terms of the contract, then the producer acquires the
same financial interest in the net profits received by the author for the
subsidiary uses when exploited in the British Isles, exclusive of motion
picture rights.

Interest outside United States, Canada, and England

The contract also provides that the author has the exclusive rights to
negotiate and contract for all performances or for other purposes outside the
continental United States, Canada, or the British Isles. However, the author
agrees to pay the producer 40 percent of the net proceeds that he receives
from any such contracts so executed within seven years after the New York
opening.

The contract nowhere specifically provides that the producer's interest
in the author's share from productions outside the United States, Canada,
or the British Isles is dependent upon the play running for any particular
length of time; however, it is most usual for Paragraph TENTH of the
agreement to contain a provision to the effect that this interest is only

acquired when the producer acquires his interest in the subsidiary rights — that is, when the play runs for the rights acquisition time.

Restrictions on Other Grants by Author

The contract, in the Schedule of Additional Production Terms, provides for certain restrictions on the author's granting of other rights in the play. The reason for this is obvious, as the producer of a first-class production — having invested a good deal of time, money, effort, and energy in the play — does not want to compete with television, film, or other productions. Therefore, the contract provides that the author will not permit the release of stock presentations, amateur presentations, musical comedy, opera, or grand opera based upon the play, as well as foreign language performances in the United States, radio, television, second-class touring rights, condensed and tabloid versions, concert tour versions, and Off-Broadway performances at any time until after the end of the first-class run; provided, however, that selected songs from a musical production may be released for radio at any time. Commercial uses and mechanical reproduction of the music will not be permitted until after the initial first-class performance of the play, and publication of the music may be simultaneously with, or at any time after, the initial first-class performance.

The Schedule of Additional Production Terms provides that the author retains sole and complete title to all rights and uses except as otherwise specifically provided in the contract and also reserves all rights and uses which may hereafter come into existence. However, the rights reserved by the author will not be exercised by the author only as specifically provided in the contract. There is a provision that all contracts for the publication of music and lyrics of a play shall provide that the copyright be in the name of the composer and lyricist.

English Production

The Minimum Basic Production Contract further provides that if the producer has produced the play for the rights acquisition time, the producer acquires the exclusive right to produce the play in the United Kingdom of Great Britain and in Ireland (referred to in the contract as the "British Isles") upon the same terms and conditions applicable to a New York production. Within six months after the date of the New York opening, the producer may — without payment of any advance royalty payment — send the author written notice that he intends to produce the play in the British Isles within said six month period. If the producer wishes to extend the option to present the play to open within an additional six month period, he may do so upon payment to the author of $500 before the expiration of the initial six-month period. He may further extend the option for a second six-month period upon payment of an additional $500 prior to the expiration of the first extension of six months. These payments, if made, are considered non-returnable advances against the British royalty payments.

English Royalty Payments

The producer agrees to make royalty payments to the Guild for the account of the author as follows: 5 percent of the first 750 pounds of gross weekly box office receipts, plus 7½ percent of the next 500 pounds of gross weekly box office receipts, plus 10 percent of the excess over 1250 pounds of gross weekly box office receipts.

The London theatre scene is somewhat unique, and it is almost imperative that an American producer associate himself with an English producer to present a play on the West End of London. The Dramatists Guild Minimum Basic Production Contract provides that the producer may associate himself with an English producer or may produce the play under a lease to a British producer — subject, however, to the author's written consent.

Paragraph TENTH will sometimes include a provision that if the play is produced in Great Britain by the producer in association with a British manager or on lease to a British manager, and if the producer receives an advance against royalties or profits, or a workable sum in lieu of royalties, then 50 percent of the amount received by the producer must be paid to the author as an advance against the author's royalties for the British production. If this advance is larger than the advance provided for in the contract provision covering a British production, then this payment shall be deemed inclusive of the original payment.

Alternative Interest in English Production

If the producer does not produce the play in the British Isles within the period provided for in the Dramatists Guild contract, then such rights revert to the author. However, the producer will still receive 25 percent of the net proceeds received by the author as a result of any contract for the production of the play in the British Isles made within five years after the New

York opening, which includes any proceeds received by the author from subsidiary rights. Although the contract is not explicit on this subject, it is assumed that before the producer will receive this 25 percent of the net proceeds, the first-class production must have run for the rights acquisition time — that is, for at least the twenty-one performances, the sixty-four performances, or one performance with the $3,000 payment.[11]

Right to Reopen Play

The contract in the Schedule of Additional Production Terms makes provision for the producer to reopen the play, but this right is only acquired if the play has run for the rights acquisition time.

This right to reopen is provided because the producer may find it necessary to close the play for vacations, to permit the star to appear in another medium, or for any number of reasons. If the play is closed at a time when it is still doing business, and there is some reasonable probability that business would continue for some length of time, it should not be necessary for the producer to start all over to again produce a play which he has already successfully produced. If the play has run the rights acquisition time, then the producer may, within 4½ months after the close of the initial first-class run of the play, notify the author in writing that he wishes to reopen the first-class production of the play in the United States and/or Canada. He must, simultaneously with sending the notice, pay the author the sum of $100 plus $100 each month thereafter until the first performance of the renewed run takes place. The production must take place not later than 6 months after the date of mailing the notice to the author; however, if the 6-month period expires between May 1 and September 14, the producer may reopen the play not later than September 15 of that same year.[12]

If the producer does reopen the play and the rerun is for a period of at least twenty-one consecutive first-class performances in New York, or sixty-four first-class performances outside of New York, or partly in New York and partly outside New York within a period of eighty days, then the producer shall continue to be entitled to further reopenings, in each instance in accordance with the procedure above set forth. This means that the producer may continue to open, close, reopen, close, reopen, and so on, indefinitely, so long as each first-class production runs for a least twenty-one consecutive performances in New York or sixty-four performances within a period of eighty days either in or out of New York.

There are other provisions in the contract for reopening the play which one should be aware of. If the play is first produced outside of New York in accordance with the terms of the agreement, for at least three consecutive performances, and the producer closes the play within one month after the third performance, the producer may reopen the play provided he reopens it no later than three months after the closing and gives the author written notice of his intention to do so within thirty days after the closing. No further payment is required for the producer to reopen during the first month after the closing, but the producer must pay $200 per month to reopen during each of the next two successive months. This reopening, like the other reopenings discussed above, may result in the producer acquiring the rights to further reopen the play if the play, when reopened, runs for the twenty-one consecutive first-class performances in New York or sixty-four first-class performances in or out of New York within the period of eighty days after reopening.

Right to Reopen English Production

The Schedule of Additional Production Terms contains a similar provision for reopening a British production. If the British production has acquired exclusive first-class production rights by running: (1) for twenty-one consecutive performances in London if first produced in London; or (2) for a total of sixty-four consecutive performances, within eighty days after the first performance, partly in London and partly outside of London; or (3) if it is first produced outside of London and runs for at least sixty-four performances outside of London within eighty days after the first performance, then the producer may, within three months after the close of the initial first-class British run of the play, notify the author in writing that he intends to reopen the first-class production of the play in the British Isles. Simultaneously with the sending of the notice of intention, the producer must pay $100 to the author plus $100 for each month thereafter until the first performance of the renewed run takes place. The production must take place within three months after mailing of the notice; however, if the three-month period expires between October 1 and October 14, the producer may reopen the play no later than October 15 of that same year.

If the producer reopens the play under the provisions above referred to, and thereafter has a run of twenty-one consecutive first-class performances in London or sixty-four consecutive first-class performances outside of London within a period of eighty days, then he will continue to be entitled to further reopenings, in accordance with the procedure set forth above, until the first-class run in the British Isles ceases.

Special Concessions

The contract in the Schedule of Additional Production Terms provides for certain special concessions which may be acquired by the producer. If the play has run the length of time we have referred to as the rights acquisition time, then, after eight weeks of out-of-town performances, it is possible for the producer, with the written consent of the author and the Guild, to reduce the royalties below the 5 percent, 7½ percent, and 10 percent which is provided in the contract for out-of-town performances.

If the play has run the rights acquisition time, a similar reduction may be agreed upon for the period commencing with the fourth week after the New York opening. You may recall that the contract provides for a royalty payment during this time of either $250 per week plus 25 percent of the weekly operating profits until production expenses are recouped and then 5 percent, 7½ percent, and 10 percent or, in the alternative, a minimum of 5 percent, 7½ percent, and 10 percent. If the producer has elected the former payment in the amount of $250 plus 25 percent of the profits until recoupment, then the reduction may not be granted during the period of recoupment.

One reduction for not in excess of two weeks duration may be made without the consent of the Guild, provided that the author and producer enter into an agreement in writing which is filed with the Guild within a week after the reduction is agreed upon. No reduction is permissible during the period of reduced compensation for the author if the contract clause is in effect which provides for reduced compensation to the author if the director, cast, and producer take similar cuts.

Other Concessions

There is a clause which provides that under certain circumstances certain concessions, other than financial, may be made. Any such concessions must be made in such a way that there is no discrimination, so that concessions granted to one producer or author will be made to others under similar circumstances. The Guild does not bind itself to follow prior decisions, and reserves the right to adopt new or different policies from time to time. The Guild does, however, agree that when Guild approval is required it will not be unreasonably withheld, although the Guild may not be held liable in any matter involving the exercise of discretion.

Sale of Motion Picture Rights

If the play runs for the rights acquisition time, as previously mentioned, the producer acquires an interest in the share of the author's net receipts from the disposition of certain subsidiary rights. Included among these is the motion picture rights. It is possible that conflicts might arise between a play and a movie of the same property.

A substantial portion of the Schedule of Additional Production Terms as well as the entire Appendix A to the schedule is devoted to the procedure in connection with a film sale — and for good reasons, because the sale of motion picture rights to a play can mean substantial income for both the author and the production which shares the receipts. Because a production is sometimes financed by movie money, the producer under such circumstances might find himself having an interest in the seller on the one hand and being the purchaser on the other hand. An author, however, might be tempted to make a movie deal that sells the property for less than it is worth, in exchange for an extravagant overpayment to the author for writing or assisting with the screenplay. This, of course, would be unfair to the producer who shares in the proceeds of the sale of the film rights but shares nothing of the revenue from the author's services to the film company, independent of the script.

It is important that a movie sale be consummated upon terms that are to the best interest of all of the parties. The contract sets forth, in detail, terms which provide for the appointment, duties, and procedure of a film negotiator to represent the author in the disposal of world-wide motion picture rights, in the hope that this objective might be gained.

Prior Disposition of Motion Picture Rights

If the author sells or leases the motion picture rights in a property prior to making a contract for its production as a play in the United States, then the schedule provides that no contract may be made for the play production until one year after the sale or lease of the motion picture rights.

In the event that the motion picture rights are disposed of after a contract for the production of the play has been entered into but prior to the production of the play, then the motion picture contract must be signed before the beginning of rehearsals of the play. Any such contract must be made on the basis of a minimum guaranteed payment, or an advance plus, or on account of, percentage payments based on the picture receipts or the box office receipts of the play, or both, and is subject to the approval of the Guild and the producer.

Play Revival

If the play is produced for the first time and the producer is entitled to share in the motion picture proceeds but no motion picture rights have been sold, then before the author grants any other producer the right to revive the first-class run, or before he himself revives it, the author must offer the producer who first produced the play the right to revive the play upon the same terms and conditions that the author is willing to accept from another producer, or, if the author wishes to revive the play himself, upon the same terms as the original production. The offer must be made in writing to the producer by registered mail. If the producer does not accept the offer, in writing, within ten days after mailing of the notice by the author, the producer will be deemed to have rejected the offer and the author may produce the play himself or grant the rights to another producer within ninety days thereafter on terms at least as favorable to the author as those offered to the original producer who rejected them.

If the motion picture rights have not been disposed of within five years after the close of the first-class run, and the producer has not exercised the option to revive the play, then if there is thereafter a revival of the play by a new producer or by the author, the percentage of the author's profits to which the original producer would be entitled is one-half of the share otherwise provided in the contract.[13] If the revival or new version runs for the rights acquisition time, then the producer who produces the revival or new version shall receive the other one-half of the percentages specified as the producer's share from the author's receipts from the sale of movie rights.

There is an unresolved question as to whether or not the original producer and the revival producer share the profits with the computation of the ten, twelve, fourteen, sixteen, or eighteen years computed from the termination of the revival or new version, or whether the original producer's participation is computed from the termination of the original production and the revival producer's participation is computed from the termination of the revival or new version. This question may or may not be resolved in the near future.

In the event that the revival or production of a new version does not run for the rights acquisition time, the original producer would have full participation in the share of the author's receipts from the disposition of the motion picture rights in the same manner as if there had not been a revival or new version.

The Film Negotiator—Duties

The film negotiator acts as the representative of the author in connection with the disposition of the motion picture rights in a play, and has the right to offer such rights to motion picture producers and to carry on negotiations for the sale or other disposition. The negotiator has the right to consummate a sale or lease after consultation with the producer (reporting details of all offers or proposed contracts) and approval of the author, and to receive and distribute the monies received for the sale or lease. All contracts for the sale of the movie rights must also be countersigned by the Guild.

Temporary Replacement, Alternate, or New Negotiator

The Schedule of Additional Production Terms makes provisions for the replacement of a negotiator and also for the appointment of a temporary negotiator if the negotiator dies, resigns, or is unable to perform his duties. There is also provision for the appointment of an alternate negotiator (if the negotiator is temporarily ill or away) and for the selection of a new negotiator, if required. If the negotiator, in a sale, has a conflict of interest due to his relationship with the producer, the motion picture company or the author, or upon the request of the author or producer, the General Advisory Committee of the Guild may replace him with a substitute negotiator.

No Author Conflict of Interest Permitted

The author agrees to cooperate with the negotiator, to promptly submit all offers to the negotiator, and to make a full disclosure of all offers. He further agrees that unless the producer consents, he will not insist on any commitment or agreement with a motion picture producer for the author's personal services either as author, actor, director, or in any other capacity, as a condition of the disposition of the motion picture rights to such motion picture producer.

Aggrieved Producer's Rights

If the producer deems himself aggrieved by the disposition of the motion picture rights, the producer's sole recourse is against the author — and then only for fraud or wilful misconduct. The author's refusal to grant motion picture rights to make a sequel is no basis for the producer's being aggrieved. The Schedule of Additional Production Terms specifically states that the producer has no recourse against a purchaser or lessee of the motion picture rights or against the negotiator, the Guild, or other producers who voted for the selection of the negotiator.

Procedure Followed by Negotiator Varies

Appendix A (instructions to the negotiator) sets forth specific procedures to be followed by the negotiator in effecting a sale or lease of a play for a motion picture production. The sales are divided into two kinds: (1) plays produced by producers independently of motion picture backing; and (2) plays which are financed either in whole or in part by motion picture producers. The plays financed either in whole or in part by motion picture producers include three kinds:

1. Those in which the producer has disclosed — in writing to the author upon signing of the Dramatists Guild contract — the fact that the producer is, or desires to be, motion picture financed;
2. Those in which the producer does not make such a disclosure upon signing the production contract but makes it before the date of the play's first rehearsal;
3. Those in which the producer has made no such disclosure at any time but at the time of the negotiations for the play's sale for motion pictures is not able to satisfy the negotiator of his complete independence of motion picture financing.

The procedure is different in each instance.

The instructions to the negotiator suggest the negotiator should request that every producer make a voluntary disclosure of any relationship which he may have which conflicts with the basic relationship of the producer and the author being jointly interested in the proceeds of motion picture monies.

Play Produced by Backers Independently of Motion Picture Backing

Producer, Author, and Negotiator Joint Effort

The negotiator is instructed to offer the producer a full opportunity to satisfy the negotiator that the producer is certain that no substantial part of the play's backing is furnished directly or indirectly by any motion picture producer. If the producer does satisfy the negotiator that no substantial part of the financing was derived from the motion picture industry, then it is recognized that the producer's interest in securing the highest price and the best conditions of sale is identical with that of the author and that it is to the author's advantage to have the producer's advice and experience throughout the negotiations for the screen rights to the play.

If the producer does not satisfy the negotiator that no substantial part of the financing of the play is motion picture money, then the negotiator may use his best judgment as to the producer's participation, bearing in mind that the negotiator is not responsible or liable for the exercise of his discretion.

Thus, in addition to acquiring an interest in the proceeds from the sale of the movie, if the show has run the rights acquisition time, and if the producer is to participate, Appendix A instructs the negotiator to call a conference to which the producer is invited to help fix the price at which the play will be offered for sale. [14]

If the negotiator, the author, or the producer deem it advisable to either raise or lower the price, the negotiator is instructed to again call a conference to establish a new price. The price must not be changed in either direction without affording the author and producer an opportunity to confer. Any offer received by the negotiator must be immediately communicated to the author or his agent and to the producer.

Procedure if Author's Terms are Unacceptable to Producer

It is, of course, most desirable that the sale price of the movie rights be mutually satisfactory to both the author and the producer. If the author decides to accept a definite offer which is unsatisfactory to the producer, and if the producer is not associated with or employed by a motion picture producer and has not been partly or completely financed by a motion picture producer or an officer of a motion picture company, then the negotiator must advise the producer by telegram of the price, method of payment, and release date. Unless the producer, within twenty-four hours (exclusive of Saturdays, Sundays, and holidays) of the giving of the notice, advises the negotiator by telegram that the offer is rejected and the reason therefore, the negotiator may accept the offer. If the producer does reject the offer he must — within five days from the receipt of the notice — submit to the negotiator a definite offer from a party of financial standing for a price in excess of the price acceptable to the author and on other terms at least as favorable to the author as those contained in the offer which the author is willing to accept. If the producer brings in such an offer within this time, this offer is accepted. If the producer fails to bring in such an offer within the time, then the original offer acceptable to the author is accepted. In the event that there is a disagreement between the author and the producer as to (1) the financial capability of the producer's offer; or (2) the price; or (3) the terms being better than the original offer, then the negotiator may, in his sole discretion, decide the issue or may request the American Arbitration Association to appoint two persons who, together with the negotiator, will make the determination. If the negotiator's relationship with one of the parties might be such that he would be unfairly influenced, then — if requested by either the author or the producer, or upon the negotiator's own initiative — he may ask the American Arbitration Association to appoint three persons to decide the issue. The determination, whether by the negotiator, or by the arbitrators with or without the negotiator, is binding upon the parties.

If the determination is with the assistance of arbitrators, then the arbitration must take place on two days' notice and the author and producer equally share the cost of the arbitration. The negotiator is instructed that he has the right to make the decision himself except in such situations where the determination is a close one.

If, during the negotiations or after the sale, the negotiator or the author doubts the producer's statement that he does not have financial backing from a motion picture producer, then the author or the Guild may demand an arbitration to determine whether or not the producer has misrepresented.

Plays Financed by Motion Picture Producers in Whole or in Part

As enumerated above, there are three classifications with respect to plays financed by motion picture producers.

1. Procedure Where Producer Discloses Motion Picture Backing at Contract Signing

The instructions to the negotiator set forth the fact that it is desirable that the producer disclose in writing, prior to entering into the production contract, if his production is, or if he desires it to be, motion picture backed. If such disclosure is made, it is assumed that the author, in entering into a production contract for the play, is satisfied with such financing, and that the motion picture backer should enjoy certain advantages.

If the producer has produced the play and it has run the rights acquisition time, then the negotiator, as the author's representative, determines when the play will be offered for sale or lease, and after consultation with the producer and author arranges for the author to fix a holding price. If the negotiator suspects any collusion between the motion picture producer and the author, then the negotiator is instructed to report such suspicions to the council of the Guild as a violation of the Minimum Basic Production Contract.

Offer to Motion Picture Backer

After the price is fixed, the negotiator first offers the rights at this price to the motion picture backer who has invested in the play, with the stipulation that he will have forty-eight hours to accept or reject the offer. If the motion picture backer does not accept the offer within forty-eight hours, the play may be offered on the open market with the rejected price as a minimum and no further opportunity will be given to, or bids received from, the motion picture backer to meet or better any other bids in excess of the price rejected by him. If the play is not sold in the open market at the price fixed, or better, the negotiator and the author may reduce the holding price; however, if they do so, they must follow the procedure just outlined. They first must offer it to the motion picture backer before placing it on the open market. It may be thereafter successively offered at a reduced price, if found necessary, following the same procedure each time.

Proof of Motion Picture Backer's Interest

After any rejection by the motion picture backer, the author and negotiator may demand that the motion picture backer submit an offer as evidence of his interest in the property. In the event that the motion picture backer does not submit an offer within one week of the negotiator's request, then the play shall be considered free and clear of any obligation to the motion picture backer and may be offered in the open market without the further necessity of first offering it to the motion picture backer or giving the backer the opportunity to bid or better any price.

If the motion picture backer wishes to express interest, he must do so by submitting a specific offer either as a fixed sum or as a fixed sum plus a percentage of receipts, together with a summary of the other terms of the proposed contract. The author would then have one week in which to accept or reject the offer. If the author rejects the offer he may still use it as a minimum holding price at which to offer the property on the open market, but no bid will be considered from the motion picture backer in excess of this holding price. If no offers are received in excess of this holding price, the author may offer the play on the open market at a sum at or below the price set by the motion picture backer which was rejected by the author. In such a case, however, the motion picture backer will be free to file offers with the film negotiator in competition with any other motion picture company, but no bid from the backer in excess of such minimum holding price will be considered in such competition. But if the author receives a bid from any other motion picture company at the same price as that offered by the motion picture backer, the backer's bid (if kept open) will receive preference provided that the other terms offered by the backer are as favorable as those offered by the other motion picture company.

In all cases of such a motion picture-financed-play production, the negotiator is instructed to keep the author fully informed of all facts relating to the sale or lease, including offers received, steps in negotiation, etc., but not to reveal any of these facts to other than the author and the Guild. The negotiator should caution the author against disclosing any such information to the motion picture-backed producer.

2. Procedure Where Producer Discloses Backing After Signing But Prior to First Day of Rehearsal

If the producer has made no written disclosure of motion picture financing upon signing the production contract, but has made it prior to the date of the first rehearsal of the play, then the author may instruct the negotiator to: (1) follow the procedure, as set forth above, for a producer who has given written notice upon signing the original production contract; or (2) follow the procedure, as hereinafter set forth, applicable to a producer who has made no disclosure at any time but cannot satisfy the negotiator of his independence of motion picture backing.

3. Procedure Where Producer Makes No Disclosure But Cannot Satisfy Negotiator of Independence of Motion Picture Backing

Where the producer has not at any time in writing disclosed to the author that the play has motion picture financing, or cannot at the time of the negotiations for the sale or lease of the motion picture rights satisfy the negotiator of his independence of motion picture financing, or the producer has received motion picture backing at some time after the date of the first rehearsal and prior to the offering for the sale or lease, whether such backing is disclosed or not, then the negotiator is instructed to use his utmost efforts to secure a competitive open market for the picture rights to the play without any of the advantages to the motion picture backer previously discussed. The author, is, under such circumstances, doubly cautioned by the negotiator to not disclose to the producer any offers.

Compensation of Negotiator

The Guild retains 1¼ percent of all monies received from the disposition of motion picture rights.

Producer's Defaults

In the event that the producer is in default in making any payment to the author, the Guild may file a memorandum with the negotiator, who will thereupon withhold that amount from the producer's share of the film sale. Unless the producer demands arbitration within ten days after the negotiator mails notice to him of the withholding of the funds, the negotiator pays the amount due to the Guild on behalf of the author.

If the producer has furnished a bond which the Guild has drawn upon because of the producer's default, the Guild may likewise give the negotiator notice of this fact, and the negotiator will withhold the amount necessary to replenish the bond from the producer's share of the film sale. Similarly, if the producer, within ten days after the mailing of the notice, notifies the negotiator in writing that he disputes the claim, an arbitration follows. If the producer does not dispute the claim, the negotiator will pay the amount to the Guild necessary to replenish the bond.

Debts by Author

On the other hand, if the author is indebted to the Guild or to the producer, the Guild may file a memorandum to that effect with the negotiator, and the negotiator will withhold the amount from the author's share of the profits of the movie sale and pay the same either for the Guild or on behalf of the producer.

Motion Picture Release Date Conflicts

The schedule specifically provides that the release date of the motion picture must not interfere with either the New York or the road run of the play. The author, after fixing the film release date, notifies the producer of this date by mail or telegram. If the producer objects to the release date, he must notify the negotiator within three days after the notice is sent or given to him — Saturdays, Sundays, and legal holidays excepted. The producer should also state the reason that he objects to the release date, and the negotiator will then give due consideration to the producer's objections and fix a release date which is binding and conclusive on the parties.

Producer's Participation in Sequels

As previously mentioned in our discussion of subsidiary rights, if the motion picture producer in the original contract for the motion picture rights is granted the right to make sequels upon payment of additional compensation, then when the additional compensation is paid, the producer is entitled to receive one-half of the percentage amount otherwise provided in the contract for payment to the producer as his share of the motion picture rights. That is, if additional compensation is paid for a sequel sold during the first ten years after the last performance pursuant to this contract, the producer would be entitled to one-half of 40 percent or 20 percent. If the additional compensation is paid for the sequel sold during the next two years — that is, within twelve years after the last performance — then the producer is entitled to one-half of 35 percent or 17½ percent. If the receipt is for a sale within the next two years, the producer would receive one-half of 30 percent or 15 percent, and if within the next two years, one-half of 25 percent or 12½ percent, and if within the next two years, one-half of 20 percent or 10 percent.

House Seats

Paragraph TENTH usually has a provision that the author, or authors if there be more than one, shall each be entitled to purchase a certain number of house seats. House seats are not free seats, but seats which are held for the author and others involved in the production, to be purchased by them usually on or before 6:00 p.m. of the night before each evening performance, and on or before 2:30 p.m. or 3:00 p.m. of the day before each matinee performance. It is not unusual to provide that for each performance each author will be entitled to purchase either one or two pairs of adjoining house seats in the first eight or ten rows of the center section of the orchestra, nor is it unusual to provide that each author will be entitled to either six, eight, or ten additional pairs of house seats for opening night of the show.[15]

Stage Manager's Script

Paragraph TENTH almost always provides that prior to the close of the play or prior to one month after the New York opening, whichever is earlier, the producer will furnish the author a legible copy of the "stage manager's script" in the usual form which includes lighting, costume, and property plots and all other details and information to be found in a stage manager's script. This is an extremely valuable property, especially if the play is a success, since all of the diverse elements that go into making up the play and contributing to its success are contained in the stage manager's script and in no other one place.

Author's Reservation of Rights in Foreign Grant

If the author disposes of any foreign uses including uses in the British Isles, he must, in his contract, reserve for his own use all motion picture and television rights in such foreign territory, and the contract that he enters into for such a production must provide that the exercise of such reserved rights — that is, the motion picture and television rights — by any other person in the foreign territory shall not be deemed competitive with any rights so disposed of.

Author's Agent

The contract authorizes the author to employ an agent and to pay the agent up to 10 percent of the amount of the author's receipts from any sale or lease of the property, except that the agent may be paid up to 20 percent from a disposition for amateur performances.

Author's Agent May Take Share From Producer

If the producer consents to the agent representing him with respect to other uses of the play, then the agent's commission of 10 percent may be taken from both the author's share and the producer's share. It is, of course, to the producer's interest not to permit the agent to represent him with respect to the motion picture sale. This is not always easy, since the producer is dealing with the agent in acquiring the play production rights. If the agent becomes insistent (and rest assured he will), the outcome will depend upon the relative bargaining strength of the parties.[16] There is also something to be said for the concept that the producer ought to pay for the services of an agent also, if the agent's work accrues to the producer's benefit as well.[17] The authority to employ and use an agent is set forth in the Schedule of Additional Production Terms; however, Paragraph TENTH of the contract almost always additionally states who the agent is and the fact that payments must be made to the agent who may retain his 10 percent, or 20 percent in case of amateur performances, from the amounts that the author is entitled to. The amount of space required to set forth the agent's duties and responsibilities depends upon the particular agent and varies widely.

Author and Producer May Not Use Same Attorney or Agent, and Other Conflicts

The contract provides in the schedule that the author must not appoint a producer, or any corporation in which the producer has an interest, or any employee of the producer, or the attorney for the producer as his agent or as his representative.[18] No author's agent may act as agent and producer of the same play.

Payments

All payments for the disposition of the motion picture and other subsidiary rights may be made to the author's agent but only if the author's agent is a member in good standing of the Society of Authors' Representatives or of the Dramatists Play Service. Otherwise, the monies are paid to the Guild, which pays the money directly to the author, agent, and producer as their respective interests appear.

Neither the author nor the producer may make any claim for commissions in connection with any disposition of the play for any purpose, nor will the producer be reimbursed for any expenses or disbursements unless the author, prior to the expenditure, agrees in writing to the payment of such disbursements and the agreement has been countersigned by the Guild. For this reason, producers should be careful in making any expenditures on behalf of an author.

Arbitration

Arbitration Obligation

Any claim, dispute, or controversy arising between the producer and the author in connection with the contract or its breach must be submitted to arbitration as set forth in the Schedule of Additional Production Terms, with the exception previously noted that if any part of the author's payments are withheld by the producer, since they are deemed to be trust funds, the author may at his option pursue any remedy at law or in equity without first going to arbitration.[19] The Guild receives notice of the arbitration and has the right to be a party to the arbitration.

Arbitration Procedure

Judgment upon any arbitration award may be entered in the highest court of the forum, state or federal, having jurisdiction, which means simply that the results of the arbitration may be made the ruling of a court and entered as an order of the court.

The Complaint

The schedule states that a complainant must file with the American Arbitration Association five copies of a written complaint setting forth the claim, dispute, difficulty, misunderstanding, charge, or controversy to be arbitrated and the relief which the complainant requests. One copy of the complaint is mailed by the American Arbitration Association to the party complained against and one copy is mailed to the Guild.

The Answer

The party to whom the complaint is addressed has eight days from the mailing to him in which to file five copies of a written answer with the Association. The Association mails one copy to the person who filed the complaint and one copy to the Guild. If the person to whom the complaint is mailed is more than five hundred miles from New York, he shall have three additional days to file his answer. If no answer is filed within the period, it will be considered that he denies everything that the complainant is complaining of.

Guild Participation

The Guild has authority pursuant to the contract to file a complaint and demand arbitration with or without the author's consent, and in such event the author becomes a party to the arbitration and cannot discontinue the arbitration without the consent of the Guild. If an award is rendered in an arbitration against the author where the producer is the complainant, the Guild may discipline the author in the manner it deems advisable, and this proposition is specifically set forth in the schedule.

Selection of Arbitrators

Within ten days of the mailing of the complaint, the author, or the Guild if it has initiated the arbitration, appoints one arbitrator from the author's slate and the producer appoints one arbitrator from the producer's slate. If either party fails to appoint an arbitrator within the ten days, then such appointment is made for the author by the Guild and for the producer by the American Arbitration Association. Within five days after the appointment of the two arbitrators, the third arbitrator is selected from among the persons on the public slate by the two arbitrators who were chosen.

Power of Arbitrators

Arbitrators are empowered to award damages against any party in a controversy upon such terms as they deem fair and reasonable, to require specific performance of a contract, or to grant any other remedy or relief whether by injuction or otherwise which they deem equitable. Simply stated, an injuction is an order to someone to do something or to cease from doing something. Arbitrators may render a partial award before making a final award and will determine in their award who pays the cost of the arbitration.

Immediate Arbitration

There is provision for an immediate arbitration under certain circumstances set forth in the schedule, in which case the entire arbitration proceeding is speeded up and decision is quickly rendered.[20] The necessity for speedy arbitration in the case of a theatrical production, under certain circumstances, is understandable. The conditions under which a speedy arbitration may be held are: (1) if the complainant alleges a violation by the author in not attending rehearsals of the play, or out-of-town performances without having been excused for reasonable cause; (2) if the producer fails to get the author's approval for cast, director, and other approvals where appropriate, or for changes or replacements; (3) if the producer fails to announce the author's name as provided in the agreement; and (4) if the producer makes any alterations, additions, or omissions in the script without the author's prior approval.

In an immediate arbitration the hearing is held within three days after the filing of the complaint. The copy of the complaint must be delivered or telegraphed to the party complained against, and he must file the five copies of the answer within twenty-four hours after receipt of the complaint. The complainant must set forth in the complaint the name of the arbitrator selected by him, and the other party similarly sets forth in the answer the name of his selection. Within twenty-four hours after receipt of the answer by the American Arbitration Association, the third arbitrator is chosen by the two already selected.

Definitions

Author

The contract defines author as each dramatist, collaborator, or adaptor of the play and each composer, lyricist, novelist, or author of any other literary or musical material used in the play but not including a person whose service is only that of a literal translator.

Commercial Uses

Commercial uses are defined as toys, games, figures, dolls, novelties, or any physical property representing a character in the play or using the name of a character or the title of the play or otherwise connected with the play or its title, provided that the author has consented to such use.

End of First-Class Run

End of the first-class run is defined as the time when the producer loses his rights to reopen the play or has in writing declared that he will not reopen it.

New York and Off-Broadway

New York is defined as the theatrical district of the Borough of Manhattan in the city of New York, and Off-Broadway performances are defined as performances in theatres located in the city of New York which are classified pursuant to the terms of the Minimum Basic Contract of Actors' Equity as "Off-Broadway." The Actors' Equity Minimum Basic Contract defines Off-Broadway as the Borough of Manhattan outside the area bounded by Fifth and Ninth Avenues, from 34th Street to 56th Street, and by Fifth Avenue to the Hudson River from 56th Street to 72nd Street. An Off-Broadway theatre, in addition to being outside that area, is not more than 299 seats.[21]

Production Expenses—Weekly Operating Profits

In a previous discussion it was pointed out that it is possible for the producer to elect a certain part of the contract which provides that for the first seventeen weeks the author, providing others have taken similar cuts, will receive a reduced royalty payment until the production expenses have been recouped, or for a maximum of seventeen weeks. There is also a provision previously discussed which provides that during the week commencing with the fourth consecutive full calendar week, the producer may elect, if the author consents to it, to pay a royalty of $250 per week plus 25 percent of the weekly operating profits during each week up to and including the end of the week in which the production expenses have been recouped. For these reasons, "production expenses" and "weekly operating profits" should be and are defined in the contract.

Production expenses are defined as fees of designers and directors; cost of sets, curtains, drapes, and costumes; cost of props, furnishings, and electrical equipment; premiums for bonds and insurance; unrecouped advances to authors; rehearsal charges; transportation charges; reasonable legal and auditing expenses; advance publicity and other expenses actually incurred in connection with the production and presentation preliminary to the opening of the play in New York, including any compensation to the producer or to any person rendering the services of a producer other than a charge for office expenses not to exceed $250 per week commencing two weeks before the opening of rehearsals and continuing until the New York opening. No items charged as "production expenses" shall be charged against operating profits, or vice versa.

Weekly operating profits are defined as the difference between the producer's share of the box office receipts (after meeting any theatre minimum guaranty) and the total weekly expenses determined as follows: $250 (in the Dramatico–Musical Minimum Basic Production Contract this amount is $500) for author's compensation; salaries of the cast, business manager, press agent, orchestra, and miscellaneous stage help; compensation payable to the directors; transportation charges; office charge not to exceed $250 (in the Dramatico–Musical Production Contract this amount is $450); advertising; rentals; miscellaneous supplies; and all other reasonable expenses of whatever kind actually incurred in connection with the weekly operation of the play as distinguished from production costs, but not including any compensation to the producer or a person rendering the services of a producer, nor any monies paid by way of percentage of the receipts or otherwise for the making of any loan or the posting of any bond.

Gross Weekly Box Office Receipts

Whereas production expenses and weekly operating profits are defined in the body of the contract, the Schedule of Additional Production Terms states that "gross weekly box office receipts" means receipts from all sources including sums over and above the box office prices of tickets received by the producer or by anyone in his employ from speculators, ticket agencies, ticket brokers, or other persons, and other additional sums received from the production of the play. If the play is performed by more than one company, the percentage compensation accruing from each company is computed and paid separately.

Paragraph TENTH should provide that although gross weekly box office receipts are computed as set forth in the Schedule of Additional Production Terms, in making the computation there should be deducted from the receipts any federal admission taxes or similar taxes imposed on admissions, any commissions paid in connection with theatre parties or benefits, and those sums equivalent to the former 5 percent New York City amusement tax, the net proceeds of which are now set aside for pension and welfare funds of the theatrical unions and ultimately will be paid to said funds. If the clause concerning the former 5 percent tax appears, there must be a sentence added stating that if the League of New York Theatres and the Dramatists Guild later agree on another definition of "gross weekly box office receipts," it will be applicable.

Defense of Law Suits

Since a play is a joint effort, and there are many contributions to the play after what is originally put down on paper by the author, there are certain specific provisions in the schedule with respect to who is responsible for the play in the event that there is a libel action or an action for infringement or interference with the rights of any other person. In the event of such an action, the producer and author jointly conduct the defense of the action and equally share the expenses, unless the infringement, libel, or other interference is found to have been caused by either the producer or author alone, in which case no part of the expense would be paid by the one not responsible. If the producer furnishes the author with an idea or material and the author writes the play based on this, then if an action is brought on the grounds of plagiarism, the producer must defend the action at this own expense and pay any and all damages that may be assessed as a result of the plagiarism, as well as any judgment against the author. The author, of course, is not responsible for any material in the play which is not written by him. If a suit is brought against either the author or the producer, the party sued must promptly inform the other one of the lawsuit.

Assignments of Contract

The contract provides that it will be binding upon and inure to the benefit of the parties and their respective successors in interest, but that any assignments (an assignment is a transfer of the rights and obligations) of the contract, with the exceptions hereinafter noted, will be effective only when approved in writing by the author, and countersigned by the Guild. The Schedule of Additional Production Terms contains a more specific provision to the effect that no assignment is effective without first obtaining the consent of the author in writing and the counter signature of the Guild, except that an assignment may be made to a corporation in which the producer has the controlling interest, or in which he is the directing head, or to a partnership in which the producer is one of the general partners. [22] Any assignee must assume all of the obligations of the contract, and the producer who originally signed the contract also remains personally liable for the fulfillment of the contract in the same manner as though no such assignment has been made. A copy of the assignment must be filed with the Guild.

Adaptation

The Dramatists Guild, as well as protecting the rights of an author of an original work, also protects the rights of an adaptor. There is a provision in the Schedule of Additional Production Terms that if an English language adaptation is made from a foreign language play or from another literary property, the adaptor must receive at least one-third of the minimum compensation payable to the author.

Repertory

If a play is produced in repertory, the percentage compensation is computed on the basis of eight performances constituting a week. The times for payment or mailing must be agreed upon in the production contract; however, in no event can it be later than four days after the end of every calendar month in which the play is performed, regardless of the number of performances during that month.

Producer Cannot Offset Claims Against Author

The Schedule of Additional Production Terms contains a provision that the producer may not deduct from the compensation owed to the author any amounts which the producer claims to be due to him from the author (unless covered by a written agreement between them); however, a deduction may be made if it is less than $100 and the author has signed a memorandum which acknowledges his indebtedness.

Author's Expenses Out-of-Town and Transportation

The contract in the Schedule of Additional Producation Terms provides that the producer must pay reasonable hotel and traveling expenses for the author on trips outside New York City (or to New York City if the author is a non-resident of New York City) to attend rehearsals, attend out-of-town performances prior to the opening, attend the New York opening, and at any other time when the presence of the author is required by the producer. It is most usual for Paragraph TENTH to set forth more precisely the amount payable for expenses on a daily basis. This additional provision will provide that the author must receive payment for economy jet transportation and will sometimes, but rarely, provide that the author will receive first-class air transportation. For each day that the author is in New York, away from his home, or outside New York if New York be his home, a per diem payment of $75 is most usual, or something between $60 and $75. It will be provided that such living expenses are paid to the author if he comes to New York from out-of-town only until opening night.

If there is a British production, then it is most usual for the contract to provide that the producer will also furnish the author with round-trip transportation from his home to London, plus the equivalent amount of pounds sterling per day during the rehearsal tryouts and up until the opening of the first-class production in England. It should be borne in mind that if the author is a resident of the New York City metropolitan area, the per diem payment is paid to the author out-of-town during the out-of-town tryouts or at other times if the producer requests the author's presence for rewrites, for consultation, or for any other reason.

Author's Money Held by Producer in Trust

The contract provides that all sums due the author which are in the hands of the producer are deemed to be trust funds. The significance of this is that legally there is a very strict duty owed by one who holds trust funds. As noted previously, if there is a breach of trust and the funds are not paid to the author, the contract provides that in lieu of the arbitration procedure the author may pursue his remedies at law or in equity.

To Whom Checks Payable and to Whom Sent

The contract provides that all checks must be sent to the Guild. The checks in payment of the option, or to extend the British Isles option, and the check in payment of the $3,000 for the first three weeks' royalties if this is applicable, are made payable to the Guild, and all of the other checks are made payable to the order of the author, or the author's agent if the author so instructs the producer in writing, and if the agent is a member in good standing of the Society of Authors' Representatives, or of the Dramatists Play Service.

Producer Furnishes Statements

The producer agrees to forward to the Guild, within seven days after the end of each calendar week, the amounts that are due as compensation together with the daily box office statements of each performance during the week, signed by the treasurer or treasurers of the theatre and countersigned by the producer or his representative. Box office statements and payments for plays presented more than five hundred miles from New York City may be furnished and paid within fourteen days after the end of each week, and if the play is presented in the British Isles, within twenty-one days. If the payment depends upon operating profits or losses, then the weekly operating statements must also be furnished to the Guild.

It is most usual that paragraph TENTH will provide that copies of box office and any other statements sent to the Dramatists Guild pursuant to the contract will also be furnished to the author's agent.

Address of Notices

The schedule provides that the producer will supply the Guild, in writing, with his address. Notices are sent to the address furnished, and a notice sent by registered mail is deemed due notice to the producer. All notices to the author must be sent to him by registered mail to the address stated in the production contract, and a copy must be sent to the Guild.

Guild Countersignature Corporate Producer

The contract must be countersigned by the Dramatists Guild before it is effective. Any change or modification of the contract must be in writing and also countersigned by the Guild. In the event that the producer is a corporation, then an individual who is in control of the corporation who owns a majority of the stock, or will be named as the producer, must personally guarantee the contract. One can understand the necessity for this if one realizes that a corporation need not be responsible in the same way that an individual is. If a corporation runs out of assets, it can simply go out of business. An individual would be more responsible, hence the Guild insists that an individual be personally obligated to the terms of the contract, in addition to the corporation.

Author Approves Co-Producer

The contract provides that the producer may not use the name of any person, firm, or corporation as participating in the production of the play without the author's consent in writing.

Closing

When the producer decides to close the play, he must immediately give written notice of this fact to the author.

Termination of Contract by Author

If the producer does not make any payments when due, or fails to fulfill any of the other terms of the contract, the author may send notice by registered mail or by telegraph requesting that the producer correct such failure or breach within three days after the mailing or telegraphing. If the breach is not corrected within three days, the contract ceases, and all rights revert to the author. Sundays and legal holidays are not included in computing the three-day period. If the producer has his office or place of business more than one hundred miles from where the notice is sent, the notice must be by telegraph.

Automatic Termination

All rights revert to the author automatically if the producer: (1) fails to produce the play during the option period or the period as extended; or (2) the play fails to run the number of performances which we have referred to as the "rights acquisition time"; or (3) if the producer does not make any option payment within ten days after it is due; or (4) the producer files a petition of bankruptcy or is adjudicated a bankrupt, or makes an assignment for the benefit of creditors or takes advantage of any insolvency act, liquidates his business, or a receiver is appointed for his property; or (5) if a corporate producer, with Guild consent, is involved in a merger, consolidation, or reorganization; or (6) if the corporate existence of the producer is terminated. In the event of a termination of the contract, the producer must immediately return all manuscripts, scores, parts, and any other literary or musical material to the author except for one copy of the manuscript which he may retain but not use or sell.

Contract Interpretation

If any part of the contract is in conflict with any law of any state, the validity of any other portions or provisions are not affected.

DRAMATICO–MUSICAL MINIMUM BASIC PRODUCTION CONTRACT

Payment for Option

There are a few differences between the dramatic contract and the Dramatico–Musical Production Contract. Although the dollar amount of the option minimums are the same, if the producer elects the reduced royalty payments based on reduced royalty to other artistic personnel, and pays $200 per month for the option, it must be a payment of $200 each to the bookwriter, composer, and lyricist. If the reduced royalty for artistic personnel is not selected; then the $200 each month is shared by the bookwriter, composer, and lyricist. If a minimum payment of $500 for the first three months is made, the $500 is likewise shared by the bookwriter, composer, and lyricist. What percentage each receives will have been decided based on the relative bargaining power of the parties.[23]

Completed Book

A completed musical work is a book of at least 80 pages, single spaced (it will be remembered that a completed dramatic work is at least 110 pages single spaced), plus a score consisting of music and lyrics for at least twelve songs.

Minimum Royalty Payments

The minimum weekly royalty payment payable to the author (bookwriter, composer, and lyricist) is in the amount of 6 percent of the gross weekly box office receipts.

Variances From Basic Minimum Royalty

Reduced Royalty for All Artistic Personnel

The provisions in the contract which provide that the author may be paid reduced payments if the director, actors, and the fee of the producer are accordingly reduced in the musical contract also provides that the fees of the choreographer must be similarly reduced.

Comparable arrangements with the actors means that during the period each actor will receive one-half of the guaranteed salary and/or one-half of the percentage of weekly box office receipts which he will receive during the New York run; however, no actor during this period will be required to be reduced below $2,000 per week (in the dramatic contract it was $1,250 per week).

Comparable arrangements with the choreographer means that the choreographer must receive as compensation during the period one-half of the percentage of weekly box office receipts which he would receive during the New York run; however, the choreographer's compensation during this period need not be reduced below one-half of 1 percent of the gross weekly box office receipts.

The cash office charge may not be in excess of $350 per week during this period that the author's payments are reduced, as distinguished from $300 per week in the dramatic contract.

The payments to the author under such circumstances is one-half of the payments otherwise provided for, or 4 percent of the gross weekly box office receipts, whichever is greater.

Minimum Royalty and Limitation of First Four Weeks Out-of-Town

For the first four weeks' out-of-town performances before the New York opening, the payments need not exceed $1,500 per week. The dramatic contract as noted limits this to $750 per week. As with the dramatic contract, this limitation does not apply if the reduced royalty for all artistic personnel is selected and becomes applicable.

Alternative Royalty Payment for First Three Weeks in New York

The alternative royalty payment for the first three weeks beginning with the official New York opening, which is in the amount of $3,000 in the dramatic contract, is in the amount of $6,000 in the musical contract. Similarly, the other advantages accrue to the producer if the $6,000 payment is made in that the play need only run for one performance in New York as the "rights acquisition time" for the producer to acquire the additional rights previously referred to.

If the $6,000 is not paid, then the minimum royalty payment provided in the musical contract during this first three consecutive weeks, beginning with the New York opening, is in the amount of 6 percent of the gross weekly box office receipts.

Royalty after Fourth Week

Unlike the dramatic contract, the musical contract does not offer alternative payments for the royalty payments commencing with the fourth consecutive full calendar week after the New York opening, but sets forth instead a minimum royalty for a musical of 6 percent of the gross weekly box office receipts.

Road Company Limitation

For each week of road performances after the New York run, the minimum royalty payment also is 6 percent of the gross weekly box office receipts. If, however, such payment would result in there being no operating profits for a particular week, then the author is paid only such compensation as will not result in an operating loss, except that in no week will the author receive less than $500. You will remember that in the dramatic contract this limitation is for not less than $250 for each week.

Royalties in British Isles

If a musical is done in the British Isles, the royalty payment is also a minimum of 6 percent of the gross weekly box office receipts.

Author's Approval and Billing

The reference in the musical contract to author's approvals also include approval of the conductor and dance director. The producer must announce the names of the composer and lyricist as well as the bookwriter in the billing. There is a provision that where consent of the author is required, composers, lyricists, and bookwriters vote as separate units with one vote to each unit.

There is also a provision in the musical contract which does not appear in the dramatic contract to the effect that in any case where the play has run for at least three weeks in New York City and the producer, because of an emergency, requests the author's approval to make changes or replacements, if the producer is unable to obtain any composers', lyricists', or bookwriters' response to such requests, then seventy-two hours after having sent telegrams to the individuals and to the Guild, the non-responsive parties' right to vote is forfeited and the vote of the others controls.

The dramatic contract provides that if the play runs the length of time referred to as the "rights acquisition time," the producer will receive 40 percent of the author's net proceeds from performances of a first-class stage musical, comedy opera, or grand opera based on the play within eighteen years after the first-class run of the play has ended. Of course, no such provision is contained in the musical contract.

In the definition of weekly operating profits the weekly expenses are stated to be $500 for author's minimum compensation (rather than $250 as appears in the dramatic contract) and the office charge is not to exceed $450 (rather than $250 as stated in the dramatic contract).

Interest in Subsidiary Rights

In the listing of the subsidiaries in which the producer will share a percentage of the profits, if the play runs the "rights acquisition time" the musical contract includes "grand opera," but omits "play albums."[24]

Division of Receipts

Paragraph TENTH of the musical contract will customarily contain most of the provisions contained in a dramatic contract and, in addition, should include a very detailed statement setting forth how the bookwriter, composer, and lyricist (as well as the substitute bookwriter, if any, substitute composer, if any, and substitute lyricist, if any) share in the royalties and also specifically how they share in the subsidiaries. It is sometimes provided that the bookwriter, composer, and lyricist share equally, so that if a royalty of 6 percent of the gross weekly box office receipts were paid, each would receive 2 percent. It is sometimes provided that the bookwriter receives one-half and the composer and lyricist receive the other one-half, which would mean that the bookwriter would receive 3 percent and the composer and lyricist would share 3 percent. The sharing of the interest in the subsidiary rights is usually related to how the parties share royalties on the Broadway show. It is, however, most usual to provide that the composer and lyricist own and control the music and lyrics to the extent that they are usable separate and apart from the play as an entity.

Cast Album

The interest that the author, composer, and lyricist respectively share in the original cast album is always subject to sharp negotiation and the difference of opinion is accentuated by the argument that the recording is usually mostly music and lyrics. The bookwriter's answer is that if it weren't for the book, there would not be an original cast album. It is not unusual that they share equally — that is, one-third of 60 percent to each, with the producer receiving 40 percent.

Musical Schedule Terms

Revue Numbers

All of the provisions of the Schedule of Additional Production Terms are applicable to a musical contract. However, there are some specific provisions of the schedule which are applicable only to a musical.

There is a provision that any sketch or number from a revue, or any musical numbers in a musical play which have not been used on opening night in New York, or within three weeks thereafter, or are omitted for any three consecutive weeks, may be withdrawn by the author and used by the author for any purpose free of any claim by the producer subject only to a participating interest in additional uses which the producer may have previously acquired. If a sketch or song is omitted from a condensed or tabloid version of the play, the author whose work is omitted will nevertheless share in the proceeds from such version, provided that his contribution has been included in at least one-half of the prior presentations in New York. In such case, the authors would share in the profits of such a condensed or tabloid version in the same proportion that they shared in the original production.

Producer Furnishes Score of Music

The producer agrees to furnish all orchestral scores, conductor's scores, orchestra parts, or vocal parts at his own expense which thereafter belong jointly to the lyricist and composer. Such scores and parts may be used by the lyricist and composer at any time after the close of the first-class run of the play.

Producer May Get Reimbursed Up to 50 Percent for Score

There is provision in the schedule for the producer to reimburse himself for an amount up to 50 percent of his expenditure for the orchestral score, conductor's score, orchestra parts, and vocal parts. The producer may deduct from the compensation of the composer and lyricist (but not from the payment for the option, not from the $6,000 for the first three weeks beginning with the New York opening, if this is provided for in the contract, and not from the royalties for the road performances after the New York run) up to $100 each week as payment toward the 50 percent of the cost. The producer must pay the monies so deducted to the Guild until the producer has presented evidence to the Guild of such expenditures for which the Guild will then return the amount up to 50 percent to the producer. The deduction, unless otherwise agreed upon, is borne by the composer and lyricist according to their respective percentages of compensation. The provision that the score and parts will belong to and may be used by the lyricist and composer after the close of the play is not conditioned upon the deductions provided for having been completed. The composer and lyricist may — at their option, at any time — pay the producer an amount equal to 50 percent of the amount which he spent for the score and parts, or the balance which may then be unpaid.

Composer and Lyricist Control Publishing

The composer and lyricist alone have the right to contract for the publication of the music and lyrics without prejudice to the right of the producer to arrange for separate payment to him by the publisher. The composer and lyricist alone may permit reproduction of the music and lyrics by phonograph records, tapes, or other devices. [25]

Musical Score Available to Guild

The producer must, upon the request of the composer and lyricist, or the Guild, make the orchestral score available to the Guild as soon as possible after the opening for the purpose of making a copy. Upon the close of the run of each company, the producer agrees to deliver the complete orchestral score, conductor's score, orchestra parts, vocal parts, and prompt book to the composer and lyricist. The producer may retain a copy of these items but not for use or sale.

Song for Movie Use

The schedule provides that a separate song or sketch from a revue may be disposed of for motion picture purposes only after eighteen months from the close of the first-class run, except that if the producer — within five days after notice to him — objects to such disposal, then the approval of the general advisory committee of the Guild must first be obtained. The author's share of the profits is shared only by the authors of the song or sketch so disposed of unless there is specific agreement to the contrary.

No Publishing Until First Performance

As has been stated above, the schedule provides that the author will not — without the producer's consent in writing — release publication of the music nor will he permit publication of the music or mechanical reproduction of the music until after the initial first-class performance of the play. We have also already noted that all contracts for the publication of the music and lyrics of any play shall provide that the copyrights be in the names of the composer and lyricist.

Waivers on a Musical

Although the Guild opposes such action if it learns of it, on most musicals, the bookwriter, composer, and lyricist enter into a letter agreement with the producer wherein they waive or defer collection of a certain percentage of their royalties under certain circumstances. They sometimes waive the royalties, but usually agree to take less during certain weeks and recoup the deferred amounts at some later date if the show makes money. A typical letter agreement of this kind might provide that if the show grosses below $125,000 during a week, then the bookwriter, composer, and lyricist would collect 75 percent of the royalty otherwise provided for; if it grosses $120,000, they would receive 50 percent of the royalty otherwise provided for; if it grosses less than $115,000, they would only receive 25 percent of the royalty otherwise provided for; and if it grosses less than $110,000, they would defer collection of the royalty completely during that week. Bear in mind that these figures are arbitrary and subject to negotiation, and could be in amounts higher or lower than above stated, depending upon the weekly operating expenses.

OTHER DRAMATISTS GUILD CONTRACTS

There are three other less commonly used Dramatists Guild Contracts:

Revue Production Contract

The Revue Production Contract — with the supplemental provisions recommended by the Dramatists Guild for incorporation in the Revue Production Contract — is used for a musical revue. At the present time, musical revues are out of vogue on Broadway. When and if the form is used, it is necessary to complete a form with a good number of blanks which have to be filled in. The supplemental provisions set forth certain recommendations of the Guild which may or may not be incorporated into the Revue Contract. All in all, the form may prove helpful in suggesting areas that should be covered in a contract.

Collaboration Contract

The Dramatists Guild "Collaboration Contract" is a form that is suggested for use by persons collaborating on the writing of a play.

The necessity for its use is very often avoided by incorporating all of the terms of the collaboration into the Minimum Basic Production Contract entered into with the producer. If the parties are collaborating on a property to be written which has not as yet been sold to a producer, they may wish to use this form.

Stock Try Out Production Contract

The Dramatists Guild, Inc., also has a Stock Try Out Production Contract. If this contract is used, it is prepared together with a Dramatists Guild Minimum Basic Production Contract, which is annexed to the Stock Try Out Production Contract. If the play is produced in stock, the producer has an option for not more than thirty days from the opening performance to enter into the Minimum Basic Production Contract upon the terms set forth in the annexed contract as prepared.[26]

CHAPTER 5

The Producing Company

PARTNERSHIP OR CORPORATION

Why a Limited Partnership?

Tax Benefits

FOR THE MOST PART, limited partnerships are used as the producing entity rather than a corporation, a joint venture, or a general partnership. Although there are various complicated schemes for using corporations to accomplish certain specific purposes, by and large the tax advantages of a partnership — namely that the profits are only taxed once, and in the event of a loss, the loss can be offset against ordinary income — are advantages that most investors look for, expect, and sometimes even insist upon. With a corporation, the profits are first taxed as income to the corporation and then, when paid out to the investors as dividends, are again taxed to the investors. Since the investors have purchased common stock in the corporation, any loss is a capital loss, which can first be offset against capital gains, and the balance, if any, may then be offset against up to $1,000 of ordinary income. Most theatre investors have more need of a loss which can be offset against ordinary income than they have for a capital loss.

It is also possible to arrange for the investors to make loans to a corporation in which the producer is the sole stockholder. Up until 1942, when the Internal Revenue Code was changed, this was a common procedure. This was abandoned for the reason that a non-business bad debt, unless by a corporation regularly engaged in the lending business, is considered a capital loss rather than an ordinary loss.

Limited Liability

A general partnership is seldom used as the producing entity, because it does not give the investors the protection of limited liability, which is the essential feature of a limited partnership. A limited partner's liability is limited to the amount of his investment.[1]

A joint venture is a fancy name for a kind of general partnership. The investors under such circumstances would be considered general partners with all of the liability of a general partner. There have been some producing companies (one rather well known) which have used joint venture agreements where the investors were led to believe that they enjoyed limited liability. Although he may not have to expend his own funds above the original investment, a joint venturer does not, as a matter of fact, enjoy limited liability and is exposed to the same liability as any other general partner in a general partnership.

Corporation May Be a General or Limited Partner

The laws of the state of New York were changed effective September 1, 1963, to provide that a corporation may be a general partner or limited partner. This, of course, means that it should be possible to combine the advantages of a corporation and the advantages of a partnership by having the producer or producers first organize a corporation which becomes the general partner of the limited partnership. In this way the investors, being limited partners, would have all of the tax benefits of a partnership; at the same time, the producer as well as the investors would enjoy the advantage of limited liability, since the producer, as a stockholder, would not be exposed to general liability. If the corporation has large assets and is substantial, there may be good reason why one ought to do this.[2] If, however, a corporation is organized solely for the purpose of becoming a general partner of a limited partnership, and the corporation has no assets to speak of, then the Internal Revenue Service would consider the producing company to be a corporation for income tax purposes.

Of course, there is nothing to prevent an affluent producer from convincing one of his less affluent co-producers to be the general partner of the limited partnership together with a corporation belonging to the affluent member. So long as there is an individual who is one of the general partners, there is no problem with any number of corporate general partners. The Internal Revenue requirements would be complied with if there is this single partner, and the partnership would be taxed as a partnership rather than a corporation, no matter how rich or how insolvent the individual partner is.[3]

Characteristics of Corporation for Tax Purposes

In order for the partnership to be taxed as a partnership and not as a corporation, it must have certain basic characteristics. There are four characteristics of a corporation which distinguish it from other entities: continuity of life, centralization of management, free transferability of interests, and limited liability.

1. It is for this reason that the Limited Partnership Agreement will generally provide that the partnership will end upon the death or insanity of a general partner or of one or more corporate officers. Such a provision is adequate to avoid continuity of life.
2. The agreement will almost always state that the management of the affairs of the partnership shall not be centralized in one or more persons acting in a representative capacity. In fact, the Internal Revenue regulations actually provide that a limited partnership organized under the laws of the state of New York does not have centralized management unless substantially all of the interests in the partnership are owned by the limited partners.
3. Under a limited partnership, if properly drawn, a partner may assign the right to receive a share of capital and/or net profits, but ought not grant the right to become a member of the partnership in his place. It is usually desirable to limit an assignment of a limited partner's interest by requiring the consent of the general partner. This limits free transferability.
4. The limited partners in a limited partnership have limited liability, and if the general partner is an agent acting on behalf of the limited partners, for tax purposes the partnership is deemed to have limited liability.

It is not easy to set forth fixed rules always applicable in determining whether the entity will be considered a partnership or corporation for tax purposes. Each of the characteristics of a corporation has relative importance, and in making a determination all of the factors are taken into consideration. There is no doubt but that if all four characteristics of a corporation are present, it will be considered a corporation for tax purposes. If less than all four of the characteristics are present, it may or may not be considered a corporation, depending upon a number of factors which it is impossible to set forth here in detail. Suffice it to say that one must be aware of the problem so that the partnership does not inadvertently end up being treated as a corporation for tax purposes.

Limited Partnership Agreement

There is no standard theatrical Limited Partnership Agreement. There is a very old and dated printed form which some attorneys use and adapt for each particular show. The printed form omits some provisions which should be included, and the job of properly adapting it can be extensive. For this reason most attorneys who do this kind of work use their own form, which will contain some of the provisions that are found in the printed form.

Basic Provisions

There are certain basics which all or most all Limited Partnership Agreements used in theatre production have in common. It is usually these few important elements which the producer knows and discusses with the investor. Many investors who have invested in theatre before are aware of these basic provisions. For example, almost all theatrical Limited Partnership Agreements provide that the first net receipts of the partnership are used to repay the investors their original investment, and after the investors have recouped their investment, all net profits are shared equally with the producer. The producer receives 50 percent and the investors share 50 percent proportionately, in accordance with the amount of their respective investments. Most Limited Partnership Agreements provide that the investors will share in all of the profits of the producing company, including profits from subsidiaries. There are, however, instances where the producer will share only the box office receipts with the investors, just as there are rare instances where the producer will give the investors 60 percent of the profits, rather than 50 percent.[1]

The Limited Partnership Agreement is usually signed by the investor at the time the investment in the production is made. After all of the limited partners have invested and the production is completely financed, the attorney for the production will prepare a conformed copy of the agreement (a conformed copy is a duplicate of the original with the signatures of each partner indicated) and will forward a copy to each of the investors.

Usual Provisions

The discussion which follows will cover most of the terms, items, and provisions found in most Limited Partnership Agreements. Some things will be mentioned, however, which might not appear in all agreements.

One should bear in mind that each general partner assumes all of the obligations and liabilites of the producing company. Between them the general partners might have an arrangement for sharing the liabilities, but each is responsible for all of the obligations to creditors.

If additional funds are needed after the limited partners' money is used up, it must come from the general partner. In exchange for the obligations of the partnership, the general partner has the right to make all of the decisions for the partnership. He is — and should be — responsible, since he is making the decisions.

The Limited Partnership Agreement will state that it is being made between the producer and those persons who sign the agreement as limited partners. It will set forth the main address of the partnership, as well as the name and address of the attorney for the partnership.

Definitions

Most Limited Partnership Agreements contain certain definitions.

"The Play"

Since "The Play" is referred to throughout the agreement, it is not unusual in the beginning to define "The Play" as the specific play or plays that the partnership will be producing.

"Contributions of Limited Partners"

The term "contributions of limited partners" is generally defined in the agreements as the amounts which the limited partners contribute to the partnership.

"Aggregate Limited Contributions"

The term "aggregate limited contributions" means all of the contributions of all of the limited partners required to be made by them.

"Sinking Fund"

After a show opens, even if it is making money, the production company should not disperse all of the profits to the partners because of the nature of the theatre business. It is not unusual to have a period of very successful business followed by several weeks or more of difficult times. If all of the profits have been paid to the partners, then there would be nothing in the partnership to get over the rough times. Accordingly, most agreements provide that a "sinking fund" may be established and retained by the partnership. The amount of the sinking fund is defined in the agreement and will usually be between $50,000 and $100,000, the amount depending upon the show's total weekly expenses.

"Estimated Production Requirements"

The amount of money the producer intends to raise for the production is known as the "estimated production requirements." The "estimated production requirements" should be defined as the amount of cash which, together with any bonds or guarantees furnished, totals the specific dollar amount the producer will attempt to raise. As we shall later see, it may be possible for the production to commence with something less than the estimated production requirements, since it might be possible to produce the show for a small amount. However, under all circumstances the agreement should state the minimum specific dollar amount which must be raised for a production before the investors' money can be used. Investors want to know that when an investment is made, it will be used only if enough money is raised to produce the show.[5] The estimated production requirements of a dramatic show will range between $250,000 and $350,000, and for a musical between $1,000,000 and $1,500,000.

Gross Receipts, Expenses, Production Expenses, Running Expenses, Other Expenses, and Net Profits

In order to define "net profits," it is necessary to also define "gross receipts" and the various kinds of expenses: "expenses," "other expenses," "running expenses," and "production expenses." "Net profits" is defined as the excess of "gross receipts" over all "production expenses," "running expenses," and "other expenses," as these terms are defined in the Limited Partnership Agreement.

The term "gross receipts" means all sums derived by the partnership from any source whatsoever from the exploitation of all rights in the play, including all proceeds derived by the partnership from the liquidation of the physical production of the play at the conclusion of its run, and from return of bonds and other recoverable items included in "production expenses."

The term "production expenses" is defined to include the fees of the director and designers; the cost of sets, curtains, drapes, costumes, properties, furnishings, electrical equipment, premiums for bonds and insurance, and cash deposits with Actors' Equity Association or other similar organizations by which — according to custom or usual theatrical practice — such deposits may be required to be made; advances to authors; rehearsal charges and expenses; transportation charges; cash office charges; reasonable legal and auditing expenses; advance publicity; theatre costs and expenses; and all other expenses and losses of whatever kind (other than expenditures specifically precluded by the contract) actually incurred in connection with the production of the play preliminary to the official opening. The agreement may further state that the general partner has incurred or paid, and prior to the inception of the partnership, will incur or pay, certain production expenses as set forth in the contract, and that amount, and no more, shall be included in the production expenses of the partnership, and (but only if the aggregate limited contributions in full shall have been paid in) the general partner shall be reimbursed for the expenses paid by him.

"Running expenses" is deemed to mean all expenses, charges and disbursements actually incurred as running expenses of the play including, without limitation, royalties and/or other compensation to or for authors, business and general managers, director, orchestra, cast, stage help, transportation, cash office charge, reasonable legal and auditing expenses, theatre operating expenses, and all other expenses and losses of whatever kind actually incurred in connection with the operation of the play and taxes of whatsoever kind and nature other than taxes on the income of the respective limited and general partner. The running expenses shall include payments made in the form of percentages of gross receipts as well as participations in profits to or for any of the persons, services, or rights referred to in the contract.

"Other expenses" is defined as all expenses of whatsoever kind or nature other than those referred to in the two preceding paragraphs hereof actually and reasonably incurred in connection with the operation of the business of the partnership, including but without limiting the foregoing, commissions paid to agents, monies paid or payable in connection with claims for plagiarism, libel, negligence, etc.

The term "expenses" shall be deemed to include contingent expenses and liabilities, as well as unmatured expenses and liabilities, and until the final determination thereof, the general partner shall have the absolute right to fix, as the amount thereof, such sums as the producer in producer's sole discretion deems advisable.

"Author"

"Author" is defined as the author, adaptor, and/or owner of the play and includes the singular or plural, as the case may be. A person may inherit or otherwise acquire the rights to produce the play, and would be the owner, although not the author of the play. An owner may sell the production rights to the producer.

Miscellaneous

There is usually a provision which states that the phrase "general partners" shall be construed to mean the plural, if more than one person signs the agreement as general partner, and all pronouns shall be deemed to refer to the masculine, feminine, neuter, singular, or plural as the identity of the person or persons, firm or firms, corporation or corporations may require.

Representations and Warranties by the General Partner for a First-Class Production

The general partner warrants and represents (which, simply stated, means that he guarantees) that he has acquired the first-class production rights in the play by contract under the terms of a Minimum Basic Production Contract of the Dramatists Guild. If the terms vary from the Minimum Basic Production terms, then the agreement must set forth the variance. Usually the agreement states that the limitations, restrictions, conditions, and contingencies of the partner's right to produce the play is as set forth in the Minimum Basic Production Contract, and that a copy of the contract is on file at the office of the attorneys for the partnership and is available for inspection by the limited partners.

For Other Than a First-Class Production

The general partner will warrant and represent that he has acquired the rights to produce the play upon the terms and conditions set forth in the option agreement. The terms will, of course, vary depending upon the type of production, whether Off-Broadway, in a residence theatre, or in stock.

Warranties of Sufficiency

The general partner further warrants and represents that, in his opinion, the total cost of opening a first-class production of the play including all bonds, cash deposits, production expenses, and the cost of an out-of-town trial run, if anticipated, will not exceed the amount which is set forth as the estimated production requirements.

Formation of Limited Partnership

The agreement will state that the parties do form a limited partnership pursuant to the Partnership Law of the state of New York, for the purpose of managing and producing the play and for the purpose of exploiting all rights held by the partnership in the play. The rights which the production company owns are the rights which were originally obtained by the general partner when he entered into the option agreement. The option agreement is assigned (an assignment is a transfer of rights and obligations) to the partnership after the partnership is formed by the general partner who acquired the rights.

Term of Partnership

The agreement will usually provide that the partnership will commence on the day when the Certificate of Limited Partnership is filed in the office of the county clerk and will terminate upon the death, insanity, or retirement of any individual general partner or upon the dissolution of a corporate general partner. The Certificate of Limited Partnership is a document which must be filed in the county clerk's office in the county in which the partnership is organized. The agreement usually provides that the general partner will file such a certificate and will immediately thereafter publish the Notice of the Limited Partnership, which means publishing a copy of the certificate or a digest of the certificate once a week for six weeks in two publications in the county.[6] The partnership may also be terminated when all rights of the partnership in the play have terminated. Upon termination, the general partner must immediately liquidate the affairs of the partnership.

Death of Limited Partner

If a limited partner dies, his executors or administrators — or, if he becomes insane, his committee or other representative — will have the same rights the limited partner would have under the agreement until the termination of the partnership. The share of such limited partner in the assets of the partnership is subject to all of the terms, provisions, and conditions of the agreement as if the limited partner had not died or become insane.

General Partner May Add General Partners

The agreement provides that the person who executes the agreement as general partner is the general partner of the partnership. However, the general partner may nevertheless enter into agreements with other persons to undertake the obligations and the privileges of general partners. The limited partners consent to the general partner entering into such an agreement, providing that the general partner is not relieved of any of his obligations under the agreement.

Rights in Play Assigned to Partnership

The general partner agrees to assign to the partnership all of the rights held by him or any rights acquired by him in the play.

General Partner's Expenditures

The general partner is generally reimbursed for all legitimate expenditures made prior to the formation of the general partnership. The general partner may be reimbursed for the full cost of the option agreement, attorneys' fees, accountants' fees, script duplication costs, and similar expenses. The agreement may state an exact dollar amount which the general partner has expended to date, or it may simply state that he is to be reimbursed for those expenditures he may reasonably spend or incur, including but not limited to advances to the author.

Use of Funds Invested

Each limited partner in the agreement agrees to contribute a specific amount, which is set forth in the agreement, to the capital of the partnership, which money may be used by the partnership for the payment of production, running, and other expenses.

Investment of Bond or Theatre Guarantee

In lieu of a cash contribution, a limited partner may make his investment in the partnership by furnishing a bond to Actors' Equity Association, or one of the other associations, or by furnishing the theatre guarantee. The agreement provides that such an investment is the same as a cash investment by the limited partner. If the play closes before the limited partner's contributions have been repaid to them in full, and before the partnership has paid any of the obligations covered by the bond deposit, then each limited partner who furnished a bond must pay the partnership the full principal amount which was originally pledged by him as a bond or guarantee, less any amounts which he may already have been called upon to pay. There is an advantage to furnishing a bond or guarantee, since an association will accept an investment in a savings bank account if it is given together with an assignment to the association to be held as security. Under such circumstances, a party putting up bond money does not lose the bank interest, whereas all other investors in the producing company would receive no interest on their investment. This provision of the agreement is not intended, to substantially discriminate in favor of such bond-furnishing investors, but it does. In the event that the play closes and the other limited partners have lost part or all of their investment, a proportionate share will be taken from the bond-furnishing limited partners to the extent that the bond is not used and is returned to them.

There is also a provision in most agreements that the general partner may arrange for the deposit of bonds or other deposits based on an agreement which provides that the first net profits received shall be paid to the association or theatre holding the bond for the purpose of releasing the bond to the investor who put up the bond. This would mean, in effect, that such an investor would have a distinct advantage over the other investors in that his funds are first returned to him. It is most usual for the contract provision to provide that such an arrangement may not reduce the percentage of net profits payable to the other limited partners. This means that the general partner will have to compensate those persons who furnish bonds by giving them a share of the producer's profits. If a producer is having difficulty raising the last money needed for the show, and he is very close to being financed, he may under such circumstances make such an arrangement for the furnishing of the bond. Most general partners do not want to prefer one limited partner over another, but if it means getting the last $50,000 necessary for the production to go on, and it might not otherwise go on, then the general partner might be more inclined to make such an arrangement.

Use of Funds—Smaller Capitalization Finally

The general partner agrees that he will not use the funds given to him by the limited partners until a specified amount of money — whatever the producer states is sufficient to produce the show — has been raised.

Bear in mind that the producer will, of course, try to raise the estimated production requirements. However, the estimated production requirements, although a more desirable amount, may be an amount in excess of the amount which is actually needed to produce the show. The producer may, for example, try to raise $300,000, which will be set forth in the partnership agreement as the estimated production requirements, but may, however, be able to get the production on for $250,000 with a somewhat smaller reserve. The partnership agreement will provide that the partnership may use the invested funds when between $250,000 and $300,000 has been raised and that under no circumstances may any of the limited partner's investment be used without prior written approval from such limited partner, until at least $250,000 has been raised. If the amount necessary to produce the show is not raised, the general partner agrees to return all of the funds collected to the respective limited partners.

If the play is finally capitalized for less than the estimated production requirements, then instead of returning money to the investors, each limited partner will end up with a larger percentage of the show for his investment. For example, if a limited partner invests $3,400 for a 1 percent interest in the profits of a $170,000 show, and if the producer later decides to capitalize the show for $155,000, then the $3,400 investment would purchase 1.09 percent of the net profits of the production, and the investor would receive this share. An investor is investing a fixed dollar amount, and he may get more than 1 percent for his $3,400 investment in such case, but he may not get less than 1 percent for such an amount.

Overcall

The partnership agreement may provide that each limited partner must, upon demand of the general partner, make an additional contribution of 10 percent, 15 percent, or 20 percent of his original contribution. The agreement will usually also provide that if the limited partner fails to make the contribution when demanded, the general partner may bring an action against the limited partner, and he will be responsible for such unpaid additional contribution, plus all disbursements, costs, and expenses (including reasonable counsel fees), of bringing and maintaining the action to collect this amount.

Investment Held in Special Bank Account

It is most usual for each limited partner to make the investment at the time that he signs the Limited Partnership Agreement, but this may not, in fact, happen. If the agreement is signed and the contribution is not made, then the limited partner must make his contribution when demanded by the general partner. The general partner on the other hand agrees that he will keep all of the funds received by him in a special bank account in trust (sometimes these funds are held by the attorney for the production and sometimes they are held by the general partner) and the funds may not be used until the amount necessary to produce the show has been raised.

The general partner further agrees that after the partnership is formed he will open a special bank account or accounts in the name of the partnership in New York City in which all of the capital and all of the gross receipts of the partnership (and no other funds) will be deposited. The funds in these accounts may be used solely for the business of the partnership.

Books of Account

The general partner agrees to keep or cause to be kept full and faithful books of account in which all the partnership transactions will be fully and accurately entered. The books of account as well as the box office statements received from the theatre (or theatres) are available for inspection and examination of the limited partners or their representatives. The general partner further agrees to deliver to the limited partners a complete statement of production expenses not later than sixty days after the official opening of the play, a monthly unaudited statement of operations, and such other financial statements as may be required by the New York Theatrical Syndication and Financing Act and regulations. The limited partners are furnished with all information necessary to prepare their federal and state income tax returns.

General Partner's Services

The general partner agrees to render the services customarily and usually rendered by theatrical producers, and to devote as much time as necessary to the production. It is understood that the producer may engage in other businesses, including other theatrical productions.

The agreement will state that the general partner has complete control of production of the play and the exploitation of all rights in the play. The limited partners' liability is limited, but so are the limited partners' rights with respeect to management of the production.

General Partner's Fee and "Cash Office Charge"

For his services the producer is paid a producer's fee which is usually in the amount of 1, 1½, or 2 percent of the gross weekly box office receipts or a fixed amount generally ranging between $200 and $750 each week. The producer will also reimburse himself for office facilities furnished to the production; this includes office space, secretarial services, telephone service, stationery, and the like. The amount which the producer takes as reimbursement is known as the "cash office charge" and is usually an amount between $250 and $600 each week. The cash office charge does not cover long distance telephone calls, and if there are unusual expenses which would cause the producer's cost to exceed the amount set forth as the cash office charge, the producer would most usually be entitled to reimburse himself for these additional charges.

The producer will generally receive the cash office charge and his producer's fee beginning two or three weeks prior to the first rehearsal and continuing through the week after the close of the play. Of course, if the producer's fee is based upon a percentage of gross box office receipts, he would not receive the producer's fee until there are box office receipts.

Fee and Cash Office Charge If More Than One Company

In the event that there is more than one company, the fee and cash office charge is also payable for each additional company for the period beginning two or three weeks prior to the first rehearsal of such additional company and continuing until one week after its close.

Additional Limited Partners

The agreement will very often provide that additional persons may become limited partners either before or after the aggregate limited contributions have been obtained. If after, and the general partner needs money above the original amount intended as the total capitalization, he may not take additional limited partners and reduce the respective shares of the original limited partners, so the general partner must pay such additional limited partners from the general partner's share of the net profits, just as the general partner would pay for a bond deal from his share of the profits.

Advances and Loans

The agreement will usually provide that the general partner has the right to make or receive loans to the partnership, and these loans will share a certain advantage. If all of the production money has been expended and additional funds are needed to get the show on or to keep the show running, then the general partner may make a loan to the producing company or obtain a loan from someone else, which may be repaid in full prior to the return of any of the contributions of the limited partners. It is most usual, however, for the agreement to provide that the partnership may not incur any expenses in connection with any such loan or advance, and that the percentage of the net profits payable to the limited partners must not be affected by such an arrangement.

Additional Services by Producer

The Limited Partnership Agreement should contain a provision that if
the producer finds it necessary to perform any services that would otherwise be performed by a third person, then he may — if he so desires —
receive reasonable compensation in the amount that the third person would
have received for such services. It may happen, for instance, that the
producer has to fill in and direct the show, or act as stage manager, or serve
in some other vitally important capacity, and unless this provision appears
in the agreement, he could not be paid for such services no matter how well
performed and no matter how important to the company.[7]

Share of Profits

As was previously stated, it is most usual for the limited partners to
share the profits equally with the producer after they have recouped their
total investment. The agreement usually states this in the following way:
each limited partner shall receive that proportion of 50 percent of the net
profits which his contribution bears to the aggregate limited contributions,
excluding, however, from such limited partners all persons who may be
entitled to compensation as limited partners only from the share of the
general partner in such net profits and excluding from such aggregate
limited contributions, the contributions as limited partners so made by such
persons. Simply stated, this means that each limited partner shares the 50
percent of the net profits with the other limited partners, pro-rata in
accordance with the size of the investment of each limited partner. The
excluded limited partners for their excluded contributions, as we have
stated, would receive compensation from whatever part of the general
partner's profits the general partner has agreed to pay them.

In lieu of returning any part of the capital contribution of a limited
partner to cover the contingency previously referred to — in the event that
the play is finally capitalized for less than the estimated production
requirements — the percentage of the net profits is accordingly increased so
that each limited partner will receive that proportion of 50 percent of the net
profits which the contribution made by the limited partner bears to the
reduced aggregate limited contributions, excluding the same limited
partners (and their contributions) who are compensated from, the producer's share of the profits. This means simply that if the capitalization of
the show is less than anticipated, then the limited partners' specific dollar

amount will purchase a larger percentage than originally anticipated. Each limited partner still shares part of the 50 percent of the net profits, and his share is pro-rata in accordance with the size of the investment; however, if the total budget decreases, his same dollar amount invested is then a proportionately larger percentage of the smaller reduced capitalization. It will be remembered that this was discussed previously under the heading "Use of Funds — Smaller Capitalization Finally," where it was pointed out that $3,400 purchases 1 percent of the net profits of a $170,000 production and the same $3,400 purchases 1.09 percent of the net profits of a $155,000 production.

Limited Partners' Limited Liability

The agreement specifically states that limited partners will not be personally liable for any debts, obligations, or losses of the partnership except from the capital contributed by them.

Payments in Cash

Unless agreed to, the limited partners have no right to demand and receive property other than cash in return for their contributions.

Return of Contributions

Contributions of the limited partners are returned to them after opening of the play after the partnership has accumulated a cash reserve in the amount of the sinking fund (plus a reasonable amount for initial expenses in the event that the original company is sent on tour, and plus an amount for any additional company or companies which the producer wishes to organize to present the play), and after the payment of all expenses and provision for contingent expenses. If an investor, instead of investing cash, has given an obligation to Actors' Equity Association or to a similar organization, then in lieu of paying that particular investor's share to him, the partnership will set aside the amount of each distribution until there is a sum sufficient to release the bond to the limited partner, and will then substitute the amount for the limited partner's obligation and release the bond security to such limited partner.

Distribution of Profits

The agreement will provide that after the Limited Partners' contributions have been returned to them, after accumulating the cash reserve in the amount of the sinking fund plus any reasonable amount for additional companies, and after payment of all expenses and provision for contingent expenses, the net profits are to be paid monthly to the limited and general partners in accordance with their respective interest in the profits. The monthly financial report prepared by the accountants for the partnership is used to determine whether or not any contributions are to be repaid or net profits distributed.

Distribution upon Closing

Upon the closing of all companies and abandonment of further intention of producing the play, the assets of the partnership are liquidated as promptly as possible. The cash proceeds are used first for the payment of all debts, taxes, and obligations, for the creation of reserves for all contingent obligations, and then for the repayment of the capital contributed by the limited partners if they have not been repaid. The balance is then divided among the limited and general partners in the proportion that they share in the net profits.

The agreement will probably provide that all physical assets of a salable nature belonging to the partnership must be sold at public or private sale, but that no assets other than the physical assets have to be sold. Any limited and/or general partner may purchase the physical assets at such sale.

After the completion of the run of all companies under the management of the partnership, the general partner has the right to sell or otherwise dispose of the production rights and the partnership's interest in the subsidiary rights other than the motion picture rights. The limited and/or general partners may be the purchasers at any such sale provided that the amount paid by them as purchasers is a fair and reasonable price. The agreement will sometimes provide that if there is a dispute as to the fairness and reasonableness of the offer, the president of the League of New York Theatres will make the determination.

Return of Contributions or Profits to the Company

Most Limited Partnership Agreements provide that if any contribution or distribution of profits is returned to the partners and funds are thereafter needed by the partnership, the general partner may demand the return of any part of the profits or contribution distributed. The general and limited partners must first repay any profits received by them, and, if such profits are insufficient, then the limited partners must return their capital contributions. The return to the partnership of profits and contributions by each partner is in proportion to the respective amounts received as profits by the parties.

Abandonment

The partnership agreement will provide that the general partner has the right, whenever he deems it necessary, to abandon the production at any time prior to its opening for any reasonable cause. In such event the production will liquidate all of its funds or accounts and the gross receipts will be distributed in the same manner that they would be distributed if there were no abandonment of the production. This provision is an essential part of any agreement, because although the producer agrees that he will produce the show and fully intends to do so, show business, like no other business, has unpredictable possibilities which could preclude proceeding with a production.

If the general partner, after the first public performance of the play, determines that continuation of the run is not in the best interests of the partnership and should be abandoned, he has the right to make arrangements with any person to continue the run of the play on such terms that he feels are to the best interests of the partnership.

Substitute Limited Partner

A limited partner may assign his interest in the partnership to someone else who would be then known as an assignee. It is not unusual for a partnership agreement to provide that the assignment may only be made once and only with the producer's approval and may further provide that an assignee may not become a substitute limited partner in the place of his assignor. Under the partnership laws of the state of New York, there is a provision that one may become a substitute limited partner in accordance with certain procedures. The producer must be in a position to choose his limited partners and would not want to end up with a limited partner who is undesirable to him, hence the limitation appears in most agreements.[8]

Additional Company to Produce Here or in Great Britain

Use of Company Funds

The partnership agreement may provide that the general partner may organize an additional company or companies to present the play in the United States, Canada, or Great Britain (if the rights to produce the play in Great Britain accrue to the partnership). Under such circumstances the net profits are not distributed until there is further accumulated in the bank account in addition to the reserve (sinking fund) provided for, a sum which, in the opinion of the general partner, will be sufficient to pay the production expenses of each such additional company. In the event that there is more than one company being presented at the same time, the reserve (sinking fund) provided for shall be maintained for each separate company before the repayment of contributions or distribution of net profits.[9]

General Partner's Involvement in Other Company

It is not unusual for the agreement to also provide that the partnership may enter into an agreement concerning the disposition of the British production and subsidiary rights of the play with any partnership, corporation, or other firm in which the general partner may be any way interested, provided that such agreement must be on fair and reasonable terms.

There is also likely to be a provision that the general partner may be associated with any person, firm, or corporation which produces or co-produces a second company of the play and may receive compensation for doing so, without any obligation to account to the partnership or to the partners of the original producing company, provided that the original company receives from any such person, firm, or corporation the customary fees and royalties payable to it as the producer of the original company.

The general partner may have the right in the contract, at his discretion, to make arrangements to license the road rights to any other party or parties he may designate, provided that the partnership receives reasonable royalties, or other reasonable compensation, and the partnership assumes no obligation in connection with any loss or expenses of the company to which the license is granted. The limited or general partners are not disqualified from participating in the company to which the rights are licensed by investing their funds, or otherwise, as a separate enterprise. A general partner may render services to the entity licensing the rights in connection with the exploitation of such rights.

General Partner's Acquisition of Rights After Termination of Partnership

If, after the termination of the partnership, the general partner purchases the production rights of the play for the United States or Canada, either with or without the physical production of the play, and with or without the partnership's interest in the proceeds of the subsidiary rights of the play, then the amount which the general partner pays for such rights must be the fair and reasonable market value, or an amount equal to the best offer obtainable, whichever is the higher price.

Motion Pictures

It is not unusual for the agreement to contain a provision to the effect that the parties acknowledge that one or more of the limited partners may be a motion picture company, or person nominated or otherwise controlled by a motion picture company, and that such company may acquire the motion picture rights in the play. In such event the partnership must be free to deal with the motion picture company without liability on the part of the motion picture company to account to the partnership or to the general partner or limited partners for any profits it may derive from, or in connection with, the rights which it acquires.

Execution of Agreement

There are certain provisions in the agreement which are designed to simplify the execution of the agreement and the filing of the necessary documents. For example, there is a provision that the agreement may be executed in counterparts, all of which taken together shall be deemed to be one original. This avoids the necessity of all partners actually signing the same copy of the document. Each of the partners agrees that the original of the agreement (or set of original counterparts) may be held at the office of the partnership; that a Certificate of Limited Partnership be filed in the office of the county clerk and a duplicate original (or set of duplicate original counterparts) held at the office of the attorney for the partnership; and that each partner shall receive a conformed copy of the partnership agreement. In addition, the limited partners give any one of the general partners a power of attorney in his place to make, execute, sign, acknowledge, and file: (1) the Certificate of Limited Partnership and to include in the certificate all information required by the laws of the state, (2) such amended Certificates of Limited Partnership as may be required, and (3) all papers which may be required to effectuate the dissolution of the partnership after its termination.

Arbitration

The limited partnership agreement will almost always contain an arbitration clause which provides, in effect, that if there is a dispute in connection with the making or validity of the agreement, or its interpretation, or any breach of the agreement, then such dispute is determined and settled by arbitration in New York City (if that is the location of the parties or at least the party with the most bargaining power) pursuant to the rules of the American Arbitration Association. Any award rendered by the Arbitration Association is final and conclusive upon the parties and a judgment may be entered in the highest court of the forum, state or federal, having jurisdiction. Such a provision cannot, however, affect the rights of the limited partners under the federal securities laws (later discussed), which govern the offering of a security (a limited partnership interest is considered a security) to the public for sale.

CERTIFICATE OF LIMITED PARTNERSHIP

The Certificate of Limited Partnership previously referred to is the document that is filed in the county clerk's office in the county where the partnership will have its office and do business. The partnership agreement usually provides that the partnership will come into existence when the certificate is filed.

The certificate and any amendments to the certificate must be signed by all of the partners, both general and limited. The limited partnership agreement contains a specific provision designed to simplify the signing of the certificate by the limited partners, for if there are forty or fifty limited partners, it could be a troublesome chore to obtain all of their signatures. For this reason, the Limited Partnership Agreement contains a provision that each limited partner appoints a general partner as his attorney to sign the Certificate of Limited Partnership, any amendments, and the Certificate of Dissolution of the partnership. So the general partners will sign as general partners, and one general partner will sign for all the limited partners pursuant to this power of attorney.

Contents of Certificate in New York State

The certificate will contain the following information:
1. The name of the partnership.
2. The nature of the business of the partnership which is usually stated to be: to act as theatrical producer and to turn to account all rights held in the play.
3. The principal place of business.
4. The date that the partnership commences business and the date of termination.
5. The time when the contribution of each limited partner is returned to him.
6. The name and place of residence of each member, general and limited partners being respectively designated, the amount of cash and a description of and the agreed value of any other property contributed by each limited partner, and the percentage of individual profits to be received by each limited partner.
7. Additional contributions, if any, agreed to be made by each limited partner and the times at which or events on the happening of which they will be made.
8. If a limited partner may substitute an assignee as contributor in his place, then this must be set forth together with the terms and conditions of the substitution.
9. The right, if given, of partners to admit additional limited partners.
10. The right, if given, of one or more of the limited partners to priority over other limited partners as to return of contributions or as to income and the nature of such priority.
11. The right, if given, of the remaining general partner or partners to continue the business on the death, retirement, or insanity of a partner.
12. The right, if given, of a limited partner to demand and receive property other than cash in return for his contribution.

Publication of Certificate in New York State

Immediately after the certificate is filed, a copy of the certificate or a notice containing the substance of the certificate must be published once a week for six successive weeks in two newspapers in the county in which the original certificate is filed. The county clerk will designate the newspapers;

in New York County one is always the *New York Law Journal*. These publishing costs can be reduced considerably by filing the certificate with only one limited partner and adding all the others in an amendment, since an amendment — unlike the certificate — does not have to be published. This can mean a savings amounting to thousands of dollars.

CHAPTER 6

Co-Producers and
Associate Producers

EITHER BEFORE OR AFTER the option is acquired, the producer may decide to produce the play together with a co-producer. Producing a show is a large venture and it may be advisable to have assistance in the raising of the money in handling the business details, and in the many areas of decision.

What one gives the co-producer and what one receives in exchange depends upon the relative bargaining power of the parties.

Co-Producer a General Partner

Bear in mind that a co-producer will ultimately also be a general partner of the limited partnership. As a general partner he may bind the partnership. Furthermore, each general partner, as stated, in obligating the general partnership obligates at the same time all of the general partners personally to the payment of a debt. The partners, as between themselves, may agree to share the obligations of the partnership in any fashion, but a creditor of the partnership may seek payment in full from any one of the general partners.

Co-Producers Operate as a Joint Venture

Before the limited partnership comes into existence, the producer and co-producer will be operating as an entity — usually a "joint venture." A joint venture is a kind of a partnership and each of the joint venturers is a general partner, and thus personally liable for all of the acts of the joint venture.

Joint Venture Agreement

Basic Terms

The Joint Venture Agreement will state that the co-producers own a property which they wish to produce, that they are going to endeavor to raise the money for the production, and that when the money is raised they will be the general partners of a limited partnership which will produce the show. It will set forth the basic terms which will be incorporated into the Limited Partnership Agreement. There will also be set forth the amount of the budget, the method of sharing profits and losses by each of the partners, whether or not the partners' profits are related to the amount of money that each producer raises, how the producers' fees are to be shared, how the cash office charge is shared, and so forth.[1]

Sharing of Profits by Co-Producers

The co-producers may agree that they will share equally in the profits of the company irrespective of which partner is responsible for the raising of most of the money for the show. On the other hand, sometimes co-producers wish to relate the share of the profits more directly to the amount of money which each one raises. If one is going to relate the sharing of the profits to the amount of money that each co-producer raises, one ought also to relate the other important contributions to the production to the sharing of the profits. For example: the partner who discovered the property could claim a larger percentage of the profits for this contribution, the party influencing the star could claim something extra for that, and so on. The next logical step is an attempt to balance all of the items that each of the co-producers contributes, and to relate the share of the profits to the relative importance of each contribution. Very often when co-producers sit down and try to balance the contribution that each one makes to a production, they discover that the importance of each contribution is difficult to measure. As a result they end up sharing equally in the profits and losses, with all parties agreeing to contribute their best efforts to the production in all ways.

Who Makes Decisions

The Joint Venture Agreement will also set forth how decisions are to be made and what happens if there is a deadlock. It is very important that there be some quick resolution in the event that there is a disagreement. In the case of an artistic decision, two co-producers may provide that in the event of a dispute between them, the director will make the final determination. they may also provide that in the event of a business dispute, the question will be settled by the attorney, the accountant, or anyone else whose business judgment both producers would respect. Other possibilities exist for settling such disputes and are as various as one's imagination.

Who Signs Checks and Agreements—Billing
Credits—Arbitration

The argeement should also set forth who may sign checks and who may sign other obligations of the joint venture. The ever-prevailing question of credits must be dealt with in this agreement — that is, whose name comes first. It is usual to provide that wherever the name of one co-producer appears, the name of all co-producers will appear in type of the same size, prominence, and boldness. Billing credits are usually in alphabetical order in the absence of other more pressing considerations. An arbitration clause may be included which, as we know, means that in the event of a dispute, rather than going to court, an impartial person would make the determination.

Personnel Agreed Upon

The Joint Venture Agreement should also set forth the personnel the producers have agreed upon who will be employed by the show, namely the attorney, the accountant, the general manager, and any other personnel agreed upon at this stage.[2]

Termination of Joint Venture

The joint venture will cease upon the organization of the limited partnership unless the parties abandon the play and decide to terminate it sooner.

ASSOCIATE PRODUCERS — MONEY

An associate producer is sometimes part of a production, and almost always means that he makes a contribution of money. Associate producers rarely have any say-so in the business, although a smart producer will always consult with the associate, even if he ignores the associate's advice or suggestions.

The associate, in addition to getting billing credit, will generally get a percentage of the producer's profits. It is not unusual to give the associate 1 percent of the producer's share of the profits for each 4 percent (it could be for each 3 percent or 5 percent — 4 percent is usual) of the producing company purchased by an investment for which the associate producer is responsible.[3]

FRONT MONEY

Amount Needed and Uses

It may be necessary or advisable to take a co-producer or an associate producer to assist with front money. Usually one may expect to need a minimum of $15,000 front money for a Broadway show, and if the producer is putting a big musical together, it is not difficult to spend between $35,000 and $50,000 in front money. Front money is that money used for the production prior to the receipt of the total capitalization and release of the investors' funds. It is generally used to acquire the property, to engage a star and director, to print scripts, to make a payment to the general manager and the attorney, and other such usual pre-production expenditures.

Producer Reimbursed for Front Money Not Used
to Raise Money

Front money expended is reimbursed to the producer after the play is financed to the extent that the front money was not used to raise money. One may not reimburse oneself for money spent to raise money. Thus the cost of auditions and the like must be borne solely by the producer and may not be recouped as a pre-production expense.

Agreement Should Set Forth Facts

Sometimes a co-producer will contribute all of the front money if, in exchange, the other producer furnishes the property. The facts should be set forth in the Co-Production Joint Venture Agreement as to who is responsible for the front money, and what the party receives for it.

Front Money Arrangements

An arrangement for front money must not be confused with the assignment of profits in exchange for raising capital for the production. Front money is risk capital and, as stated, can be used prior to the capitalization of the show. If the show is not produced, then the front money investor loses the money spent by the producer, and to that extent has a tax loss. The person furnishing the front money will usually get 1 percent of the producer's share of the profits for each 1 percent of the producing company that that particular amount of money would buy from the limited partner's share of the profits.

A front money investor might also be given associate producer billing in addition to the percentage interest. Of course, if the front money is left in the production after the budget is raised — that is, if the amount of the budget is reduced by the amount of the front money and that front money was not used to raise money — the front money investor will receive a share for the amount of the front money from the limited partner's profits, as well as what he receives from the general partner's share. If the front money investor wants his money returned to him at the time the show is fully financed, then he is left only with his share of the producer's profits, since he leaves none of his money in as an investment as a limited partner.

CHAPTER 7

Raising Money — Necessary Filings — The Securities and Exchange Commission and Attorney General

THE SECURITIES AND EXCHANGE COMMISSION AND ATTORNEY GENERAL FOR A PRODUCTION IN NEW YORK STATE

IF FUNDS WILL BE RAISED from the public outside of the state of New York,[1] the production must file certain documents with the Securities and Exchange Commission and with the attorney general of the state of New York before any fundraising occurs. If funds are to be raised solely in the state of New York, then filing with the SEC is unnecessary, but one must still file with the attorney general.

If the offering exceeds $1½ million, a full registration is in order in accordance with what is know as Form S–1. The full registration is a detailed, complicated chore and requires careful preparation, for it is important that there be no misleading statements in the documents filed with the SEC.

If the total offering price does not exceed $1½ million, then instead of a full SEC registration in accordance with what is know as Form S–1, it is possible to file for an exemption from registration pursuant to Regulation A. The fact that the offerer is "exempt" from registration does not mean that the offerer is exempt from filing. The filing which must take place is a simpler and less complicated kind of filing than the full registration and usually may be accomplished in less time.

It bears repeating that if funds are being raised outside the state in which the business is to be conducted and if the funds are being raised from the public, then one must either file a full registration or, if the offering is for less than $1½ million, an exemption from registration. The SEC presumptions favor a conclusion that an offering is being made to the public, if there is any doubt as to whether or not it is a public offering.

The penalties for non-compliance with the Securities Act are severe: in addition to possible criminal penalties, for example, a producer may be held responsible for the total budget if there is non-compliance. This means that he may raise money, open the show, close the show, lose the entire investment for the investors, and then have to reimburse the investors for the total budget. For this reason, if there is any doubt as to whether a filing should be made, it is wise to resolve the decision in favor of filing.

The SEC is careful to point out that they do not actually approve of the facts as submitted to them. What the SEC does is accept or reject a filing. If it is not accepted, appropriate changes must be made in the documents submitted so that the documents will be accepted. They must accept the documents before an offering may be made to the public. However, the SEC makes the fine distinction that acceptance of a filing does not constitute "approval" of the filing.

A person should bear in mind that no sales material of any kind may be given to a prospective investor unless it is filed and accepted by the SEC. Each prospective investor must be given an offering circular or a "prospectus," as it is sometimes called.[2]

REGULATION A
SEC EXEMPTION FROM REGISTRATION

Documents to be Filed

In order to obtain an exemption from registration, certain documents must be prepared and filed with the SEC: (1) Form 1 – A — Notification under Regulation A; (2) the offering circular; (3) a copy of the Limited Partnership Agreement; (4) a consent and certification by the attorney; (5) any other pertinent documents or agreements.

Form 1–A—Notification Under Regulation A

The Notification under Regulation A, like all of the other documents, is submitted to the SEC in quadruplicate.

This document must set forth the name of the producer, the name of the producing company which will be organized to produce the play, the date that the company will be organized, the state in which it will be organized, and the state in which the principal business will be carried on.

The offerer must set forth any predecessors, affiliates, and principal security holders of the issuer as well as their addresses and the nature of the affiliation. The name of any person owning 10 percent or more in the producing company must be set forth as well as the amount of such interest.

The name and residence of each director, officer, and promoter of the offering company must be set forth.

The Prospectus or Offering Circular For a Regulation A Exemption

The prospectus which is prepared, filed, and used in an exemption from registration, as well as the prospectus which is used for a full filing pursuant to S – 1, are both intended to detail the terms of the agreement between the investor and the producer. Hence, one may discern a good deal of repetition in the discussion of the prospectus in that it restates the Limited Partership Agreement terms, which we have already discussed in detail. In addition to the Limited Partnership Agreement terms, the prospectus is intended to inform the prospective investor of the inherent risks in investing in theatre. [3]

The offering circular which must be filed with the SEC is patterned after a form which was arrived at as a result of discussions between the SEC and the League of New York Theatres. The present form of offering circular leaves much to be desired from a theatrical point of view, but it is a vast improvement over the circular previously used, which was created for the purpose of protecting investors from dishonest promoters of oil wells, non-existent steel companies and the like, but did not have any relationship to the theatrical business and its own peculiar attendant insecurities.

Front Cover

In the present form of the offering circular, in addition to setting forth the amount of money which is being raised, the name of the company, and the name of the play, the following must appear on the outside front cover page in capital letters and in type as large as that generally used in the body of the circular:

THESE SECURITIES ARE OFFERED PURSUANT TO AN EXEMPTION FROM REGISTRATION WITH THE UNITED STATES SECURITIES AND EXCHANGE COMMISSION. THE COMMISSION DOES NOT PASS UPON THE MERITS OF ANY SECURITIES NOR DOES IT PASS UPON THE ACCURACY OR COMPLETENESS OF ANY OFFERING CIRCULAR OR OTHER SELLING LITERATURE.

The Offering

The circular will set forth the name of the producer and the fact that he will be the general partner. It will state what financial contribution, if any, is made by the general partner and how the profits and losses will be shared. It will state the minimum amount that each limited partner may invest and the maximum amount that will be raised. If the partnership may be formed before the total budget is raised, then this must likewise be set forth.

The name of the attorney for the production is usually set forth.

The Risk to Investors

The offering circular must set forth the fact that the risk of loss is especially high in this business and the investor should be prepared for the possiblility of a total loss. It will state the fact that during the last season a certain percentage of plays resulted in loss to investors; depending upon the season, this will vary between 70 percent and 80 percent. Information must be furnished as to how long the play must run at capacity to return to the limited partners their initial contributions. The percentage of plays which have run this long during the last season must also be set forth.

There will usually be about ten separate risk factors which must be included in the offering circular. These clearly emphasize the fact that investment in theatre is a risky business. And, of course, it is. Because of the risk, however, if a play is successful the returns are commensurate with the risks.

Subscriptions

The agreement sets forth to whom the investment is to be given and the fact that the funds will be held until an amount sufficient to present the play has been raised. It is usual to state that if the amount necessary to present the play has not been raised by a certain date, all funds will be returned to the investors.

It usually says that an investor may consent to the producer using his funds prior to the total budget being raised. If this is stated, it is also pointed out that there is no advantage to the investor in giving this permission and, in fact, there may be a disadvantage. [4] The producer reserves the right to pay any investor an additional percentage of the profits so long as it is paid from the producer's share of the profits.

Overcall

A Limited Partnership Agreement, as noted in the discussion of such agreements, will sometimes set forth the fact that the limited partners must contribute an additional 10 percent, 15 percent, or 20 percent above the initial investment if called upon by the producer to do so. If this is the case, it must be set forth in the offering circular.

The Producer

Detailed facts are set forth concerning the producer. The SEC is careful to make sure that only ascertainable facts are set forth and that there are not any misleading statements or superlative adjectives. Information must be given about all previous plays produced by the producer during the previous five years and it must state the names of the plays, the opening and closing dates, the number of performances, and the percentage of gain or loss per dollar invested.

The Play

A brief outline of the play or other details about the play must be set forth.

The Author

Details about the author and his previous works must be set forth. If this is the first play produced by the author, then it must be so stated. The payments to the author will also be detailed here.

The Director

Information about the director and past works must be set forth, if the director has been hired. The offering circular must also state the fee payable as well as any royalty payments.

The Cast

The names and information about any important cast members who are signed must be set forth together with the details concerning their salaries. [5]

Theatre

If a contract for the theatre has been entered into, all of the details must be set forth. If not, it must be stated what the estimated capacity of a probable theatre will be and what the estimated costs will be.

Scenic Designer

Appropriate information about and the compensation of the scenic designer must be set forth if he has been signed.

Compensation of General Partner

This section must state the amount of the producer's fee, the amout of the cash office charge, and the fact that the producer will receive 50 percent (or whatever percentage is to be received) of the net profits of the company, as well as any other compensation to which he would be entitled. It is wise to set forth the fact that if the producer does perform any services of a third person, then the producer may, if he so desires, receive reasonable payment in the amount that the third person would have received for these services. In the absence of such a provision, if the producer with directing ability found it necessary to direct the show to save it, he could not be compensated for the directing.

Use of Proceeds

A detailed production budget must be set forth showing the proposed expenditure of the funds raised.

Estimated Weekly Budget

The total weekly costs at capacity must be set forth as well as the number of weeks that the play must run at full capacity to return the original investment.

Net Profits

Net profits are defined and the offering circular here sets forth any payments from the gross weekly box office receipts which are deducted in the computation of net profits. Since the limited partners will receive net profits, they should want to know if a large percentage of the gross box office receipts will be payable to a star, author, or director and thus deducted from the gross receipts in computing what constitutes net profits.

Return of Contributions—Share of Profits

The circular must set forth how the profits are shared, which is usually 50 percent for the limited partners and 50 percent for the general partner. It will also state when the contributions will be returned to the partners.

Production and Subsidiary Rights

It will briefly be stated what rights in the play the production owns and the extent of the interest in subsidiary rights.[6]

Other Financing

The circular must state whether or not any one has advanced anything of value toward the production of the play.

Financial Statements

Since the partnership will later be formed, there are no financial statements available to furnish to prospective investors and this will be stated. A statement will also be made that the limited partners will be furnished with all financial statements required by the New York law. The name of the accountant and attorney will be stated.

Production Personnel

The offering circular will sometimes set forth the names of the general manager, the press agent, and the production supervisor or stage manager.

In addition to the notification, the prospectus, and the Limited Partnership Agreement, the submission will include a document signed by the attorney consenting to being the attorney and any other exhibits that are pertinent, such as the contractual arrangements.

SEC FULL REGISTRATION PURSUANT TO FORM S–1

The registration statement consists of a facing sheet of the form, the prospectus containing certain specified information, certain other information required which is largely inapplicable to a theatrical financing, and the exhibits.

The Facing Sheet

The facing sheet sets forth the name of the issuer — that is, the name of the limited partnership and the general partner or general partners, since it is the limited partnership, through the general partners, which is offering the securities (limited partnership interests). In addition, the nature and amount of securities being offered is indicated. Thus, for example, if the partnership is capitalized at $1,750,000, $1,750,000 in limited partnership interests would be stated. If the general partner is entitled to 50 percent of the net profits of the company and the limited partners the other 50 percent, then the price per unit is, for convenience, figured on the basis of 50 units. In a partnership capitalized at $1,750,000, each 1 percent interest in the limited partnership would cost $35,000. The filing fee and the name and address of counsel to the issuers are indicated and a statement is added that the approximate date of the proposed sale is as soon as possible after the effective date of the prospectus (the date of clearance with the SEC).

The Prospectus

The prospectus (also referred to as an offering circular), being the basic sales document used in connection with the sale of securities to the public, must contain all of the relevant facts concerning the offering, and no sale can be made unless a prospectus is shown to the potential investor prior to the sale. The prospectus must be prepared with great care and accuracy since misstatements, even though unintentional, may be serious.

Although no sales may be made until after the prospectus has been accepted for filing by the SEC, while the SEC is processing the offering a "red herring" prospectus may be distributed to potential investors. After the prospectus is initially filed with the SEC, a legend in bold red ink is printed across the top of the first page as follows:

PRELIMINARY PROSPECTUS — ISSUED

A registration statement relating to these securities has been filed with the Securities and Exchange Commission, but has not yet become effective. Information contained herein is subject to completion or amendment. These securities may not be sold nor may offers to buy be accepted prior to the time the registration statement becomes effective. This prospectus shall not constitute an offer to sell or the solicitation of an offer to buy nor shall there be any sales of these securities in any State in which such offer, solicitation or sale would be unlawful prior to registration or qualification under the securities laws of any such State.

This red herring prospectus (which may be used with a full registration but not with an exemption from registration) may be sent to potential investors to advise them that an offering is being processed and that sales will be made in the future. It is important that a detailed record be kept of when and to whom the "red herring" is distributed, as such information will be requested by the SEC.

Contents of the Prospectus

The prospectus will contain all of the facts of the partnership agreement, information about the persons involved in the production, and facts which the SEC Regulations require and which are designed to give the investors complete information so that there is a full and fair disclosure.

Introductory

Initially there is stated a set of statistics concerning the speculative nature of the offering: approximately 80 percent (this figure may vary from year to year) of the plays produced in the past year resulted in loss to investors; based on estimated expensed, this play would have to run "X" (the number is inserted depending upon the facts) number of weeks at capacity merely to recoup the capitalization and "X" percent (the percent amount is inserted depending upon the facts) of the plays produced in the past year failed to run that long; of those that did, most did not play to capacity. The investor is reminded that there is no ready market for the partnership interests being offered, that no assignee of a limited partner may become a substituted limited partner, and that there is no right to withdraw from the partnership except in the event the entire capitalization is not raised by the outside date set forth in the Limited Partnership Agreement.

Some general statements are made concerning the nature of the partnership: the limited partners furnish all of the capital of the partnership and bear all of the losses up to the amount of their partnership contributions, in return for which they are each entitled to their proportionate share of 50 percent of the net profits of the partnership; if there is to be an overcall, that is stated; the general partner, who makes no cash contribution to the partnership, receives 50 percent of the net profits, a percentage of gross receipts as a management fee (usually from 1 to 2 percent), and a weekly office expense charge for each company presenting the play (usually from $300 to $600 per week); limited partners take no part in the control of the business or affairs of the partnership, and the general partner makes all decisions relating to the conduct of partnership business. The investor is advised that to an extent the success or failure of a play depends on the ability of the producer to secure suitable talent and a suitable property and that considerable competition exists among producers in the acquisition of talent and properties. He is further reminded that ultimately it is the professional drama critic and the audience who determine whether the production will be a commercial success or failure.

The Producer

The name and principal place of business of the producer is indicated. In addition, a brief outline of the producer's background in the theatre and his past record is set forth. The record indicates, in table form, the plays he has produced during the last ten years, their opening and closing dates in New York, the number of performances in New York, and the profit or loss to the investors per dollar invested.

Acquisition of Property

A few sentences briefly stating the nature of the play appear here, with an indication of the size of the cast which will be required and the number of major roles.

The date and parties to the Dramatists Guild Minimum Basic Production Contract, or other rights acquisition agreement, are set forth in addition to the royalties payable to the authors (which would include the bookwriter, lyricist, and composer if it is a musical). In addition, if the play is based on a book or a movie or some other underlying work, the date and parties to the underlying rights agreement are given together with the royalty payable to the owners of the underlying rights. A general outline of the Dramatists Guild Minimum Basic Production Contract, or other rights acquisition agreements, with respect to the right of the partnership to share in subsidiary rights income is also set forth. There is a statement that the contracts are on file and available for inspection at the offices of the attorney for the partnership, and that copies are on file with the SEC in Washington, D.C. Finally, reference is made to the fact that, upon formation of the partnership, the general partner will assign the contracts to the partnership.

Estimated Cost of Production and Aggregate Contributions Being Offered

A statement is made as to the estimated total cost of producing the play (usually the capitalization of the partnership). Reference is made to an overcall, if there is to be one, and a statement is made that if funds are required in addition to the capitalization of the partnership, the general partner may make loans to the partnership, without interest, which are repayable prior to the return to the limited partners of their contributions.[7]

An explanation of the share of net profits to which each limited partner would be entitled is again included and also an indication of the minimum amount which may be invested by each limited partner. "Net profits" are defined usually as the excess of gross receipts over all production expenses, running expenses, and other expenses, as defined in the Limited Partnership Agreement.

Return of Contributions if Partnership Not Formed

A limited partnership contribution is payable at the time of execution of the partnership agreement. All contributions are held in a special bank account in trust until employed for production or pre-production purposes or until returned to investors. (This clause is essential in the Limited Partnership Agreement, as it is a requirement of the New York state attorney general's regulations.) If the entire capital is not raised by a specific date, each limited partner will receive the return of his contribution unless it was expended pursuant to his written consent and he specifically waived the return of his contribution. It should be stated that his contribution will be returned "without interest." Monies advanced by the general partner personally for partnership expenses are deemed a cash contribution to the partnership if the general partner elects not to have the money reimbursed to him.

General Nature of Offering

Plan of Offering Interests to Public

The prospectus will state how the contributions will be offered to the public. That is, it will usually say the offering will be made through the mails, by telephone and personal solicitation by the producer. It will almost always state that the producer intends to solicit motion picture and record companies for contributions to the capital of the limited partnership.

Subscription to Limited Partnership

This section of the prospectus will state that, in order to subscribe, the limited partners must sign copies of the Limited Partnership Agreement and deliver this together with the amount of the investment to the producer. The producer has the right to accept a subscription or not.

Restriction on Right of Limited Partner to Withdraw from the Partnership

The offering circular will state that, upon signing the partnership agreement, the party is obligated to become a limited partner of the partnership and has no right to withdraw from the partnership or reduce his contribution. If the total budget is not raised, then, of course, the contributions will be returned to the prospective limited partners.

Right of Assignee of a Limited Partner

There will be set forth the fact that an assignee of a limited partner will not have the right to become a substituted limited partner. It may also state that the partnership is not bound by any assignment of a limited partner unless the general partner consents to the assignment, or whatever the proposed limited partnership agreement provides on this item.

Use of Proceeds

There is here set forth a pre-production budget stating how it is estimated that the proceeds will be used. It will also usually state that the estimate is not necessarily based on any bids of third parties, and the general partners are not limited in their use of the funds as set forth, but may make changes in the allocation which may be deemed necessary or advisable. There is likely to be a statement also that the estimate includes some expenditures which have already been made and others to which the general partner is committed.

Purpose of Partnership

The prospectus will state the purpose of the partnership, and the language used will probably be to the effect that the purpose is to manage and produce the play and to exploit and turn to account all rights at any time held by the partnership in connection with the production of the play.

Commencement of Partnership

It will be stated that the general partner will form a partnership in accordance with the partnership law of the state of New York, and will open up a partnership special bank account in which all of the funds of the partnership will be deposited. The partnership monies will be used solely for the business of the partnership. There may also be a reference to the effect that the monies invested prior to the formation of the partnership are to be held in a special account in trust, as described in another section of the offering circular.

Contracts and Assignments Thereof

There will be here set forth all agreements which have been and will be entered into in connection with the production of the plays, as well as agreements which are anticipated. It is stated that the producer will assign to the partnership all of the contracts entered into in connection with the play.

Sources of Partnership Income

The prospectus will state that the partnership income will come from turning to account all rights in the play.

If there is a pre-production recording or other contract, all of the terms of such contract will be set forth.

Expenses of Conducting Business

"Production expenses" and "running expenses" are defined. There is also attention called to the fact that running expenses, in addition to certain stated items, will also include any percentage of the net profits or of the gross receipts which are payable to an author, member of the cast, scenic designer, costume designer, director, choreographer, or any other person offering services for the play. It will also include the percentage of the gross receipts paid as the producer's fee, as well as the payment to the producer for the weekly cash office charge.

Disposition of Partnership Income; Return of Contributions; Profits and Losses

The prospectus will here set forth the terms outlined in the limited partnership for the repayment to the investors of their contributions pro rata after payment of all expenses and establishment of a cash reserve in a stated amount. There is also herein set forth the fact that losses are borne entirely by the limited partners, in proportion to their respective contributions, until net profits have been earned, and after net profits have been earned the general partners and limited partners share losses in the same proportion that they are entitled to share in the net profits. There is also the statement contained in the Limited Partnership Agreement that contributions and profits paid to the partners may have to be returned to the partnership if required.

Net Profits

It is here pointed out that the producer may enter into contracts providing for payment of shares of the net profits, and the remaining net profits are then divided between the limited and general partners. It is not unusual to have to pay a percentage of the gross receipts or net profits to the star, the theatre, or the director, and sometimes the choreographer and designer.

As of the date of the prospectus, there is set forth the specific percentage payments of gross weekly box office receipts and net profits which are deducted prior to computing the net profits payable to the partners.

Effect of Federal Income Taxes

The offering circular may state that in the opinion of counsel for the partnership, the net profits are treated, for federal income tax purposes, as ordinary income, and any losses as ordinary losses deductible from ordinary income.

Additional Funds

The offering circular may state that the general partner, if additional funds are needed, may lend money to the partnership or borrow money from others for this purpose. Such loans may be repaid prior to the repayment of contributions to the limited partners. Also, union and theatre bonds and guarantees may be furnished instead of using partnership funds for this purpose, and the amount of such bonds and guarantees may also be repaid prior to repayment of the limited partners' contributions.

Additional Companies [8]

If the Limited Partnership Agreement contains provision for the partnership to produce other companies of the play, then these facts must be set forth. It may state that funds of the original company may be used for this purpose.

Theatre Tickets

A complete detailed list of everyone entitled to purchase house seats is set forth in this section of the offering circular.

Control by General Partner

It will here be stated that the general partner has complete control of the production and that he agrees to render such services as are customarily rendered by a theatrical producer. He may, of course, engage in other businesses, including other theatrical productions.

Remuneration of General Partner

There is here set forth the fee payable to the producer. It is not unusual for the producer's fee to be an amount ranging between 1 and 2 percent of the gross box office receipts.

Reimbursement of General Partner

There will be here set forth the amount which the general partner has laid out for the production for which he will be reimbursed after the partnership is formed.

Interest of General Partner in Certain Transactions

There is here set forth the fact that the general partner will furnish office facilities and what these will consist of, as well as a statement that he will be reimbursed by payment to him of a specified amount known as the cash office charge. If the Limited Partnership Agreement authorizes the partner to deal with the partnership or to function in any way so that his interests are adverse to the interests of the partnership, then these facts must be set forth.

Abandonment of Production

The general partner may abandon the production at any time prior to the opening for any reason whatsoever, and this fact is set forth in the offering circular.

The Creative Elements

The names and biographical credits of the author, composer, lyricist, director, choreographer, and star are detailed as well as information about any other creative personnel who are signed for the production.

Termination of Partnership

There is here set forth details as to when the partnership will terminate and the fact that if the limited partner dies the partnership may continue, with his executors or administrators having the same rights that he would have.

Underwriting

Any facts concerning arrangements for underwriting all or any part of the investment must be set forth here in detail.

Miscellaneous

The name of the attorney for the production is set forth. It is also stated that there are no financial statements available, since the company has not yet been formed, but that upon formation of the company, the limited partners will be furnished with financial statements as required by law.

Other SEC Information Required

There is a large mass of information that must be accumulated and furnished to the SEC for their purposes which does not appear in the prospectus. Much of this information is intended to inform the SEC about the conditions surrounding offerings other than theatrical offerings, and is particularly applicable to corporate offerers. For this reason, many of the items are inapplicable to a limited partnership, and especially inapplicable to a theatrical production, so the information is furnished by stating that the items are inapplicable. The exact information required is carefully prepared by the attorney for the production, although a detailed itemization is beyond the scope of this book.

There are two other SEC exemptions from registration that should be briefly noted. Rule 240 provides that an offering of not more than $100,000 for any twelve-month period may be made, provided that there are not over one hundred (100) purchasers. The offering must not be sold by any means of general advertising or general solicitation, and no commission or similar remuneration may be paid for solicitation of prospective buyers in connection with the sale. Furthermore, there is limitation on the resale of such securities and the Issuer must exercise reasonable care to assure that purchasers are not acting as underwriters. The issuer of the securities must file notices of sale with the Securities and Exchange Commission as provided in the rule.

Rule 146 is a private offering exemption from filing. The Rule 146 exemption is called a "safe harbor" exemption but in order to get to the harbor, the route is very complicated and difficult. The offerer must obtain detailed financial information about each person to whom the offer is made and must make a determination that the person to whom the offer is made understands the nature of the investment and can afford the risk and the loss involved. The sale may be made to not more than thirty-five (35) persons. If the prospective purchaser does not have sufficient knowledge and experience, it may be necessary for him to have a representative do this for him. Rule 146 is almost never used in theatrical offerings for a number of reasons.

THE ATTORNEY GENERAL

If the money is going to be raised only in the state of New York, an SEC filing may be avoided. In all cases, however, there must be a filing with the office of the attorney general.

New York, like all of the others states in the union, has what are known as "blue sky laws." In addition to the New York law, there are the New York state theatre financing regulations which govern a theatrical financing. It may be necessary to file in other states in which money will be raised. The production attorney will make this decision as to where filings are necessary.

If a filing has been made with the SEC, the filing with the attorney general is greatly simplified, since the attorney general will accept the offering circular filed with the SEC with one or two minor additions which will have been included at the time the SEC filing is made.

If there is no SEC filing and money will be raised solely in the state of New York, and if the offering is for less than $100,000, the producer may file and use a prospectus (an offering circular) and a Limited Partnership Agreement, or may choose to simply file and use a Limited Partnership Agreement setting forth all of the terms of the agreement with the limited partners. If more than $100,000 is being raised, an offering circular must be filed and used. If it is possible to avoid the use of an offering circular, I usually recommend it, as the attorney general's offering circular, like the SEC form, must contain some provisions likely to discourage investment.

If the offering is to be made to less than twenty-six persons, it is possible to avoid filing with the attorney general if each of the investors expressly waives in writing the right to have offering literature filed and the right to receive information that would be contained in such an offering circular.[9]

CHAPTER 8

The League of New York Theatres and Producers

THE BROADWAY PRODUCER must deal with a number of different craft unions and associations. The producers and theatres owners founded their own association on January 30, 1930, which is known as the League of New York Theatres and Producers. The League has offices at 226 West 47th Street in New York City. It is interesting to note that whether a person owns one theatre or seventeen theatres, and whether he is the producer of one show or seven shows, he is entitled to only one membership in the League. [1]

Purpose of the League

The objectives of the association, as stated in their bylaws, are to conserve and promote the general welfare of the legitimate theatre and the common interests and welfare of theatre owners, lessees, or operators and producers of plays, and to afford an organization which enables them to act for their common purpose and interest. The primary duty of the League is to act as bargaining representative for theatre owners and producers with the various craft unions and associations. Each contract is negotiated and entered into for a specified limited period. There are usually some changes, sometimes minor, when each contract is negotiated.

Dues

The dues paid by producers and theatre owners is $75 per week during each week that a show is running in a first-class theatre in New York City.[2]

Collective Bargaining Agreements Negotiated

The League has negotiated and signed collective bargaining agreements with many associations and craft unions which can, for our purposes, be divided into three categories. There are the agreements between the unions and the theatre owners or lessees. There is another group of contracts between the unions and the producers. There is a third category of agreements which are entered into by the unions with both the theatre owners or lessees and the producers. Bear in mind that those contracts between the theatre owners and unions are, of course, as important to the producers as the contracts which the producers make directly with the unions, for these contracts directly affect the producer.

Agreements for Theatre Owners or Lessees

The contracts negotiated by the League for the theatre owners or lessees are with the following:
— Theatrical Protective Union, Local No. 1, IATSE, which represents the basic house crew of a theatre covering the carpentry, electrical, property, and other related work including "taking in" and "taking out," handling, assembling, and dismantling all equipment used in the show. This would cover the curtain men, sound men, fly men, as well as the carpenters, electricians, property men, and the like.
— Treasurers and Ticket Sellers Union, Local No. 751, which, as the name implies, covers treasurers, assistant treasurers, and other box office personnel involved in ticket selling. Ticket Takers and Telephone Operators Union Local No. 751 is aligned with Treasurers and Ticket Sellers.
— Legitimate Theatre Employees Union, Local No. B–183, which covers the employment of ushers, directresses, chief ushers, front doormen, the ticket takers, and the backstage doormen.
— Theatre, Amusement, and Cultural Building Service Employees, Local No. 54, which covers building service employees such as porters, elevator operators, cleaners, and matrons.
— Local Union No. 30, International Union of Operating Engineers, affiliated with the AFL–CIO, which covers the employees engaged in the

operation and maintenance of heating boilers, heating systems, mechanical refrigerating systems, air circulation (which is part of the mechanical refrigerating system), standpipes, and fire pumps.

Agreements for Producers

The contracts with the producers negotiated by the League include the following:
— Actors' Equity Association, which covers actors and stage managers.
— Theatrical Wardrobe Attendants Union, Local No. 764, which covers the wardrobe crew consisting of wardrobe supervisors and dressers.
— The Society of Stage Directors and Choreographers, which, as the name clearly states, covers directors and choreographers.
— The Dramatists Guild Minimum Basic Production Contract, previously discussed in detail, is also negotiated by the League for the producers.
— The United Scenic Artists, which covers set designers, lighting designers, costume designers, and assistant designers.

Agreements for Both Theatre Owners and Producers

The contracts negotiated by the League which are entered into by both the theatre owners and the producers are the following:
— Association of Theatrical Press Agents and Managers, Union No. 18032 AFL–CIO, which, as the name states, covers press agents (which would be hired by the producer or the theatre owner, but most usually just the producer), company managers (which would be hired by the producer), and house managers (which would be hired by the theatre).
— Associated Musicians of Greater New York, Local No. 802, American Federation of Musicians, which, as the name states, covers the musicians. The number of musicians required in a particular theatre will vary, depending upon whether the show is a drama or a musical. If the production is a drama, the number of musicans employed will depend upon the amount of live and taped music used in the production. If the production is a musical, the number of musicians employed depends upon the size of the house — though, of course, musicians in excess of the contractual minimum may be employed if deemed necessary for artistic considerations.

Employer and Employee Also Sign Agreement—Term of Employment

The League has entered into a bargaining agreement with all the above listed associations and unions. Those with a bargaining agreement will still have a separate agreement which must be entered into between the employee and the employer. The theatre generally hires employees under a one-year contract during a season, which is usually the period from Labor Day to Labor Day. A producer will enter into an agreement with an employee for a particular production.

The contracts entered into with the theatres will be discussed separately from those entered into with the producers and those entered with both the producers and the theatres.

Terms in Common

Union Sole Bargaining Agent

All of the contracts have some things in common. For example, all of the agreements — with one exception — have language to the effect that the producer (producer is referred to as "manager" or "management" in many of these agreements) recognizes the union as the sole and exclusive bargaining agent for all employees who perform work under the jurisdiction of the union. The one exception where there is not a recognition clause makes it quite implicit even though it is not specifically stated.

Employee Must Join Union—No Strikes or Lockouts

All of the agreements state in similar language that an employee doing the kind of work covered by the union contract must become a union member within a specified time, usually within thirty days after this employment. The contracts will almost always provide that there will be no strikes or walkouts, nor will there be any lockouts.

Scope and Jurisdiction

All agreements have a clause setting forth the scope of the agreement and the jurisdiction of the union. Of course, the language differs with each agreement, since each union or association has a different jurisdiction — that is, some are applicable only to legitimate theatre while others cover revues, night clubs, ballet, etc., as well. The geographic jurisdiction varies also with the different unions and associations.

Rates—Pension and Welfare

The schedule of rate payments differ as do the hours of employment. There are provisions for welfare payments and/or pension payments in all of the agreements.

Business Agent May Enter Theatre

Some contracts provide for a payment of dues (checkoff) by the theatre and producer directly to the union. It is most usual to find a provision that the business agent of the union (or other representative) may be admitted to the theatre at all times for the purpose of verifying conditions.

Grievance Procedure and Arbitration

All of the contracts have a provision for grievance procecure and/or arbitration to settle any disputes. The contract dates vary from one to ten years. In several cases there is provision for vacation benefits to employees.

Pension and Welfare Tables

Tables 1, 2, and 3 will be helpful with respect to certain items contained in all contracts so that a comparison can be made.

DEPARTMENT OF SPECIAL PROJECTS

In 1973 the League formed a Theatre–Industry Committee. The Committee decided that the League must expand to deal with the various problems that confront the legitimate theatre. In late 1975 a Department of Special Projects was created. Special Projects was directed to address, among others, the following priorities: urban environment; computerized ticket selling and marketing; and public relations.

Urban Environment

The League, recognizing the importance of the ambience of the Times Square area to the theatre-going public, is taking an active stance on the current laws, rules, and regulations affecting the theatre and theatre dis-

TABLE 1—CONTRACTS WITH THEATRE

	Local #1 — Carpenters, Electricians, Property	Local #751 — Treasurers and Ticket Sellers	Local B-751 — Mail and Telephone Order Clerks	Local B-183 — Ushers, Directresses, Front & Back Doormen	Local #54 — Building Service Employees, Elevator Operators, Cleaners, Matrons, etc.	Local #30 Heat & Air-Conditioning Maintenance
Contract Dates	August 1, 1979 to July 31, 1982	September 5, 1976 to September 1, 1979	January 23, 1977 to January 21, 1980	September 9, 1978 to September 6, 1981	September 4, 1978 to September 7, 1981	December 22, 1976 to December 21, 1979
Pensions	7% gross earnings	8% gross earnings	—	$.90 per day per employee paid monthly	5% gross earnings	$14.20 per employee per week
Welfare	5% gross earnings	3% gross earnings	6% gross earnings	6% gross earnings	$420.00 per employee semi-annually	$15.00 per employee per week
Vacation	7% gross earnings paid yearly by separate check	6% gross earnings	5% gross earnings	5% gross earnings	24 weeks' work first year gets 1 week's paid vacation	6% gross earnings

TABLE 2—CONTRACTS WITH PRODUCER

	Actors' Equity Association	Local #764 — Wardrobe Supervisors & Dressers	Society of Stage Directors & Choreographers	Local #829 — United Scenic Artists
Contract Dates	June 27, 1977 to June 28, 1980	September 3, 1976 to September 2, 1979	August 13, 1977 to May 15, 1980*	March 20, 1978 to December 31 1989
Pensions	8% gross earnings up to $1,500.00	5% gross earnings	$367.50 initial contribution; $21.00 weekly contribution; $10.50 each additional company	11% of contract fee not to exceed $1000.00**
Welfare	$16.50 per actor per week	5% gross earnings	$210.00 initial contribution; $10.50 weekly contribution; $5.25 each additional company	—
Vacation	4% to a maximum of $26.20 weekly	7% gross earnings	—	—

* Some clauses in this contract were negotiated in 1962 and are to remain in effect until August 13, 1982.

**The maximum contribution will be increased in 1981, 1982, and 1983 by the contractual cost of living formula.

TABLE 3—CONTRACTS WITH THEATRE AND WITH PRODUCER

	Association of Theatrical Press Agents and Managers Union No. 18032	Local #802 American Federation of Musicians
Contract Dates	January 1, 1977 to December 31, 1979	September 11, 1978 to September 13, 1981
Pensions	7 percent gross salary	5 percent gross payroll*
Welfare	$325.00 semi-annually per employee**	$6.20 per week per employee
Vacations	6 percent of gross weekly salary	6 percent of gross weekly salary

* First paid out of money allocated from the 5 percent of gross NYC amusement tax no longer paid to the city, or such greater amount as is so allocated to the union.
** If cost of benefits purchased by contribution is increased, employer will pay additional cost.

trict. The Department of Special Projects works daily with the federal, state, and city agencies with jurisdiction and responsibilities in the Broadway area. Special Projects encourages the enforcement of laws and regulations on the books as well as the maintainance of the region. Specific concerns have been to urge the development of statutes or ordinances dealing with loitering, the licensing of massage parlors, peep shows, and liquor licenses for topless bars. In addition, Special Projects has endorsed a rigid enforcement of existing laws concerning prostitution, peddling and vending, building code violations, and littering. Special Projects and the League have undertaken efforts to improve the physical appearance of the Broadway area by providing trash receptacles in heavily traveled areas and developing decorative planting projects for public spaces.

Special Projects has also researched real estate developments projected for the Broadway area and has taken positions pro or con on behalf of the League. These include the redevelopment of Eighth Avenue, Manhattan Plaza, Manhattan Project–Theatre Row, a proposed convention center, a proposed major hotel development, and the proposed Broadway Mall project.

Computerized Ticket Selling

Special Projects is working with the Shubert organization to encourage the installation of a new computerized ticket system developed in conjunction with Control Data and its Ticketron division. The Shubert organization has started going "on line" with its theatres throughout the country. The computerized system will allow patrons to purchase tickets at the box office, remote outlets, or by telephone. The computerized systems have high speed scanners and printers at all outlets to provide the best seats for the desired performance. Radio City Music Hall is now using a computerized ticket system for their legitimate, film, and concert attractions, and many theatre owners are recognizing the advantages of these new systems.

Public Relations

Special Projects has taken strong affirmative action in the field of public relations. A major effort has been and is being made to promote the importance of the Broadway theatre to New York City, the state, and the entire country. Politicians and public officials at every level of government are provided data and urged to consider laws directly or indirectly involving the Broadway theatre. Special Projects undertakes to produce statistical information to demonstrate the economic and cultural importance of the Broadway theatre to the American economy and way of life. In the 1978–79 Broadway season $137 million in ticket sales were tallied. It is estimated that in that same season $149 million in theatre-going related expenditures were generated, having a theatre related economic impact in the New York Metro Area of some $458 million. In the same season the economic impact of Broadway and its major road companies on the U.S. economy was placed at $1.457 billion. A study completed in 1977 by the New York State Commerce Department revealed that the Broadway theatre was by far the major tourist drawing card for the city. Broadway theatre was cited as the major attraction by 37 percent of the respondents, followed by museums with 18 percent, and shopping with 15 percent.

Special Projects has taken these statistics and joined with the city and state of New York to promote tourism and the Broadway theatre. Several distinctive campaigns have been mounted featuring the cast of major Broadway hits and the special allure of the city and Broadway. The "I Love New York" campaign has been chief among these.

The Tony Awards focus the attentions of millions of Americans on the Broadway theatre each year. Special Projects involves itself with the promotion of the awards show as well as its planning. From promotional brochures to the creation of a Broadway theatre museum, to educational projects in New York school districts, and lobbying on behalf of the Broadway theatre, the League's Special Projects department is expanding the League's abilities to serve Broadway's theatre owners and producers.

Funding for Special Projects is shared by the producer and theatre owner on a prorated basis. A musical is assessed at $600 per week and a dramatic play is assessed at $400 per week.

Contracts with the Theatre

Hiring Personnel

IN HIRING THE CREW, a producer ought to try to find a group that is compatible socially, as well as on a working basis. There are certain persons in the business who most usually work together. A certain electrician may work with a particular carpenter most of the time as a team, so a producer would hire both together. This is desirable since it is to the advantage of a production to have persons on the show who know the working habits of their fellow workers. Liking the people one works with is also most helpful, especially in theatre when oftentimes the work is under extreme pressure and in close quarters.

THEATRICAL PROTECTIVE UNION, LOCAL #1, IATSE

Jurisdiction

As I have mentioned, this union has jurisdiction over carpenters, electricians, and property men, and includes "taking in" and "taking out," handling, assembling, and dismantling of any and all equipment, property, chairs, seats, furniture, hardware, all electrical fixtures and appliances, staging, scenery, masking, unloading, loading of vehicles, and the like. The minimum basic house crew for each theatre consists of a head carpenter, head electrician, head property man, and curtain man, and in the Mark Hellinger, the Minskoff, the Uris, and the Winter Garden, the basic crew in addition includes an assistant electrician.

Term of Employment

Although the employment is for the term of the agreement with the union, the employee need not be paid during the period that the theatre is dark, subject to any other specific provisions of the contract.

Work Week

The work week commences on Sunday and ends with the following Saturday night's performance. All men work on a weekly salary basis with a few minor exceptions which are specifically set forth in the agreement.

Take-In and Take-Out

There are detailed terms covering the take-in and put-on of an attraction as well as the take-out of an attraction. The take-in provisions include, for example, the fact that all men must be called for not less than a minimum call of eight hours on a take-in and put-on of a show during the first day, and all calls after that must be for not less than a minimum of six hours. The men must receive one hour off for meals between 12 noon and 1 p.m., and between 6 p.m. and 7 a.m. or be paid double the hourly rate for such hours. [1]

Regular Work Week Hours

The contract states that during the regular attraction the work week for heads of departments and assistants consists of eight performances: six evening performances occuring during the hours of 7:30 p.m. to 11:30 p.m. Monday through Saturday evenings, plus two matinee performances occuring during the hours of 1:30 p.m. to 5:30 p.m. on Wednesdays and Saturdays. The hours are slightly less for other persons. The heads of departments must work as well as direct the department. A carpenter cannot operate the curtain but may assist the curtain man in one-scene shows.

Minimum Hours and Repertory

All calls, unless otherwise specifically provided for in the contract, shall be for a minimum of four hours' duration.

When any theatre operates under repertory conditions — that is, two or more shows playing within the repertory season — the pay scales will be 10 percent above the normal rates. Giving two one-act plays as part of a single performance is not repertory.

Extra Performances and Sign Work

The agreement contains specific provision for nine or more performances per week and seventh day performances, as well as regular Sunday, special Sunday, holiday performances, and midnight performances.[2] It is also provided that the men must be paid a full weekly salary even if an attraction operates on a fixed policy of less than eight performances per week. There are special provisions covering work on theatre signs.

Vacation and Temporary Closings

Employees on vacation must be replaced by the union during their vacation. They must be paid one-half of their regular salary during a period of voluntary closing, which is considered the interruption of a show in order to permit a star a leave of absence, or for some other similar reason.

Fireproofing and Inspections

There are specific provisions that the respective head of a department must be employed on at least a four-hour call for fireproofing of scenery, drops, props, equipment, or material; that the three heads of departments and the curtain man must likewise be employed on a similar call for annual fire inspection; and that the head electrician will be given a six-hour call to obtain or renew the standpipe license or permit for the theatre.

Discharge for Cause—Severance Pay

Except in the case of discharge for drunkenness, dishonesty, or incompetence, heads of departments and assistants employed for at least one year are entitled to severance pay in the event of termination of their employment. They are entitled to one week's pay at the rate being received at the time of termination for each year of service, with a maximum of fourteen weeks' pay.

Rehearsals and Construction Work

There are detailed provisions concerning rehearsals at rehearsal halls and theatres, as well as detailed terms concerning closing performances.[3] The rates of pay for theatre rehabilitation and construction work are set forth in detail. This includes work in the pit, platforms, stage work, flooring, rigging, loading and unloading of cars, etc.[4]

Dark Houses, Safe Conditions, and Photos

The agreement also covers work in dark houses and the reduction of manpower as a result.[5] There are provisions that the working conditions will be safe. Specific provision is also made for the taking of all commercial pictures, television taping, and filming.[6]

Treasurers and Ticket Sellers Union, Local #751

Jurisdiction

As the name implies, this union governs the hiring of treasurers and ticket sellers within the five boroughs of the city of New York. The League members must negotiate special terms, wages, and hours for theatres outside this area.

Wage Rates

The wage scale provided in the agreement is as follows:

Sept. 3, 1978 to
Sept. 1, 1979

TREASURERS, for week of six
(6) days (Monday to Saturday
inclusive) not less than $456.27
ASSISTANT TREASURERS, for
week of six (6) days (Monday
to Saturday inclusive)
not less than $400.74

SUNDAYS, Box Office is to be open from 12:00 Noon to 10:00 P.M. A
minimum of four (4) members of the Box Office Staff shall receive, in
addition to their weekly salary for two performances, and a minimum of
three members of the box office shall receive not less than one-sixth ($1/6$) of
weekly salary for one performance, without any offset or deduction for
taking a substitute day off during the week.
MIDNIGHT PERFORMANCES, not less than one-sixth ($1/6$) of weekly
salary.

The above scales provide for up to 8 performances from Monday through
Saturday. One-eighth (⅛) extra shall be paid for any performance in excess
of eight during that period.

Advance Sale — Extra Attractions
Other than Current Attraction

TREASURERS, when performance
given on Sunday (regardless
whether tickets sold in advance
or not) for one performance,
not less than $76.04
for two performances,
not less than $114.07
ASSISTANT TREASURERS,
when performance given on Sunday (regardless whether tickets
sold in advance or not) for one
performance, not less than $66.79
for two performances,
not less than $100.18

Advance Sale and Benefits

For handling the advance sale of a current attraction on weekdays and for a weekday matinee, the salary may not be less than one-sixth of the weekly wage for each day. The parties must also be paid a salary, prorated at the weekly rate, for advance sale and for benefit performances during a period that the theatre is normally dark.

Refunds

If more than $400 has to be refunded, the treasurer and assistant treasurer must be retained for that purpose and must be paid at the rate of one-sixth of the weekly salary for each day, but in no event longer than one week unless the employer decides to retain the staff. After the amount of the refund is reduced to less than $400, further refunds may be handled without additional compensation at any box office which is staffed by members of the union. If the theatre has a following attraction, then the treasurer and assistant treasurer must make refunds with no extra compensation to them, providing that the continuity of employment is not interrupted.

Contract for Season

A standard individual contract is entered into with each employee which names the theatre at which he is employed and the period of employment, which may not be less than a season (as hereafter defined) except in cases of extra box office help. There is also an exception in that the employment may be for less than a season if the lease of the employer terminates before the expiration of the season and/or the employer loses control of the theatre. In such event the contract of employment is for that portion of the season that the employer is in control of the theatre. The employer must designate the box office staff not later than August 1 of each year that the theatre is open, and if the theatre is dark, he must designate the box office no later than September 1, regardless of when the theatre thereafter opens. Although the hiring is seasonal — even during the season (see below), unless otherwise specifically provided in the contract — the employee is not paid if the theatre is closed.

Season, Box Office Staff, Subscription, and Benefits

"Season," as it is used in the contract, means such time as the theatre is open from September 1 to August 31 the following year. The box office staff of each theatre consists of a box office treasurer and at least three assistants, except that during a refund week it consists of those staff members under contract. There is negotiation procedure outlined in the agreement for determining whether theatres seating over one thousand should be required to employ yet another assistant treasurer at assistant's salary. No person other than the treasurer or his assistants may handle ticket sales to the public or a broker. Extra help may be engaged to handle subscriptions and benefits at places other than in the box office. All reservations at the theatre must be handled by employees covered by this agreement. The employer or his representative, the producer or his representative, the treasurer or his assistant treasurer and ticket sellers are the only ones permitted in the box office.

Minimum Hours

Treasurers and assistant treasurers must be called to service at least one week prior to opening of the play, and one day must be added to the one week for each paid preview in advance of the public opening. The treasurer outlines the hours of the box office employees and these may not exceed eight hours in any one calendar day, of which one hour must be a meal period. Work for advance sales less than a full week is prorated. Time and a half is payable for certain holidays as set forth in the agreement, and the employees receive an additional one-sixth of their weekly salary for "settlement" at the end of a run.

Bonding of Treasurers and Assistants

Box office treasurers and assistants must be bonded and the bond is paid for by the employer. The money and tickets for which the treasurer and his assistants are responsible can be handled only by them.

Termination of Employment

Either party, by written notice, may terminate the contract of a box office employee during the first week of employment. This, however, may not be done where that box office employee was employed for the previous season for the same employer and did not receive notice of termination before May 31; he is automatically reengaged for the following season.

Transfer of Theatres and Closing Notice

House staff employees may be transferred from one theatre to another during the season, providing that the continuity of the operation is designated in the individual contract of employment. If the attraction has run more than four weeks, then closing notice given by the employer to the box office employees before the closing of the box office on Monday night shall be effective to constitute one week's notice of closing as of the following Saturday night. If the employer fails to give notice, he must pay one week's compensation in lieu thereof. If the attraction has run four weeks or less, then notice of closing is not necessary. However, if the attraction closes during a calendar week, the box office staff is entitled to a full week's compensation.

Discharge for Cause

An employee may be summarily dismissed for cause without prior notice. Cause means intoxication on duty, dishonesty in the discharge of duty, disorderly conduct in the performance of duty, or inability to secure a bond. There is provision in the contract for review of a summary dismissal.

Notice if Theatre Sold

If the theatre is sold, the box office employees' employment may be terminated on two weeks' notice or two weeks' pay in lieu of the notice.

Miscellaneous and Riot, Fire, Strikes, etc.

There are specific provisions in the contract for negotiations in the event that the theatre is leased for less than a year by the same employer or by a different employer for other than legitimate theatre purposes. Employees are not paid during the period that a production is closed because of fire, accident, strikes, riots, act of God, the illness of the star or a principal featured performer, or action of a public enemy which could not be reasonably anticipated or prevented.

Ticket Cannot Be Sold for More Than Stated Price

The contract specifically states that neither the employer nor the employee may accept any charge or fee in excess of the amount designated on the ticket as the ticket price.

LEGITIMATE THEATRE EMPLOYEES UNION, LOCAL # B–183

Jurisdiction

This union agreement controls the hiring of ushers, ticket takers, directors, head ushers, and doormen. The union shop provision is to the effect that the union will supply the employer with applicants in the operation of "legitimate" theatre or theatres and vaudeville or motion picture theatre or theatres having a "reserved seat" policy, as distinguished from a "grind" policy in the city of greater New York. If the union cannot supply help, then the employer may engage help in the open market.

Term of Employment

If an employee is retained for four weeks, the employee may not be replaced before the following Labor Day except for just cause. If there is a dispute as to what constitutes just cause which the theatre and the local union cannot settle, then the League of New York Theatres and the general office of IATSE (the parent union) will settle the matter.

Prior employees must be recalled for the following season unless they are given notice of termination at least thirty days before Labor Day.

Although the hiring is for the season, the employee need not be paid during a period when the theatre is closed unless otherwise specifically provided for in the contract.

Wage Rates

The weekly and daily wage rates are as follows:
(minimum wages per performance in parenthesis)

	Effective
	Effective
Ushers	$105.27 (13.16)
Directors	111.93 (13.99)
Head Ushers	126.27 (15.78)
Ticket Takers	159.72 (19.97)
Doormen	167.97

Eight Performance Week

The scale of employment is based on an eight performance week (except doormen), and employees substituting for regular employees are paid a proportionate share of a week's work. Performances in excess of eight are at the rate of time and a half, except where a show opens with a policy in excess of eight performances.

Doormen's Week

Doormen's work week is six days but not exceeding forty hours in a week. Over forty hours per week is paid at the rate of time and a half with a minimum overtime call of seven hours. Doormen receive no extra compensation for extra performances.

Overtime (Other Than Doormen)

Extra time required for ushers, head ushers, directors, or ticket takers in excess of the regular hours is paid at the hourly rate, with a minimum of one hour. All midnight performances are paid at the rate of time and a half.[7]

Program Insertions and Cancelled Performances

Employees are paid $2 extra per week whenever they insert printed material (other than cast changes or show publicity) in the theatre programs. In the event of a cancellation, employees on a regular eight-performance week will be paid for eight performances even though they may work less.[8]

Time Employees May Leave Theatre

With the exception of opening night, one-half of the employees (excluding doormen) are permitted to leave work twenty minutes after the curtain goes up. If a theatre has only one ticket taker, this does not apply to him.

Special Uniforms

If the producer requires that an employee wear any special uniform, then such apparel must be furnished by the producer. White collars for ushers must also be furnished by, and laundered at the expense of, the producer.[9]

Notice of Discharge

An employee on a weekly salary must be given two weeks' notice in writing of discharge, and employees wishing to terminate must do the same. If the theatre closes or the policy of the theatre changes, only one week's notice is required. If an attraction closes after having run less than four weeks, no notice is necessary, nor is it necessary for an employee discharged for drunkenness or dishonesty.

THEATRE, AMUSEMENT, AND CULTURAL BUILDING SERVICE EMPLOYEES, LOCAL #54

Jurisdiction

This agreement covers custodians, roundsmen, elevator operators, twenty-six-hour custodians, and matrons.

Wage Rates

The minimum weekly wages are as follows:

Head custodian (If the theatre has only one porter, he shall be
considered head custodian) shall receive:
A minimum weekly wage of $209.50 for the period commencing
Labor Day 1979.

Custodians shall receive:
A minimum weekly wage of $196.00 for the period commencing
Labor Day 1979.

Roundsmen shall receive:
A minimum weekly wage of $196.00 for the period commencing
Labor Day 1979.

Elevator operators shall receive:
A minimum weekly wage of $196.00 for the period commencing
Labor Day 1979.

Head twenty-six-hour custodians shall receive:
A minimum weekly wage of $137.90 for the period commencing Labor
Day 1979.

Twenty-six-hour custodians shall receive:
A minimum weekly wage of $128.32 for the period commencing Labor
Day 1979.

Matrons shall receive:
A minimum weekly wage of $127.32 for the period commencing
Labor Day 1979.

Basic Crew

The basic crew employed in a theatre is the same number of employees
employed in the theatre on the first day of August, 1955, or, if closed on that
date, the last open date before then. New theatres opened since then have a
basic crew consisting of the number of employees used on the opening of
the theatre. [10]

Discharge for Cause

An employee may not be discharged except for intoxication while on
duty or an act of dishonesty. The contract contains provision for investiga-
tion and review of a discharge. [11]

Sunday Performances

The entire crew (normal complement of workers) must be employed in the event of a Sunday performance or performances. If the Sunday is the seventh consecutive day of work, the employee receives time and a half.[12]

Hours of Work

Standard Week and Overtime

Custodians work a standard forty-hour week consisting of six days not exceeding eight hours per day. Overtime for work in excess of eight hours per day, or forty hours per week, is at the rate of one and one-half the regular straight time hourly rate. If a custodian is required to work in excess of three evening performances a week, then he must be paid time and a half for all hours worked during such performances. The regular head custodian of the house must be at the theatre when the box office is open to the public, even though the house is not in operation.

Twenty-Six-Hour Custodians' Standard Week and Overtime

Twenty-six-hour custodians work a standard week of twenty-six hours consisting of six days not exceeding four hours each day performed between the hours of 7 a.m. and 1 p.m. with one additional hour each matinee day at the conclusion of the matinee performance. The overtime rate for twenty-six-hour custodians is one and a half the regular rate and is paid after four hours of work per day, or after six days per week, or after twenty-four hours per week, except when there are matinee pick-ups, in which event overtime commences during that week after twenty-six hours.

Matrons' Standard Week and Overtime

Matrons' standard work week consists of eight performances per week within a six-day period. The maximum time of each performance is four hours. All time worked in excess of eight performances per week or four hours per performance is considered overtime and is paid at the rate of time and a half.

Uniforms and Equipment Supplied

The uniforms, work clothes, and equipment required to be worn or used by the employees is supplied and maintained by the employer.

MAIL AND TELEPHONE ORDER CLERKS UNION, LOCAL B-751

Jurisdiction

This agreement covers all mail clerks, telephone operator and head mail clerks, and head telephone operators employed in any and all theatres.

Wage Rates

The minimum weekly wages effective January 22, 1979 are as follows:

Mail Order Clerks	$206.52
Telephone Operators	$213.57
Head Mail Order Clerk and Head Telephone Operator	$238.76

Scope of Work

The mail order clerks and telephone operators assist the treasurer and assistant treasurer in servicing mail and telephone ticket orders. If three or more mail clerks or three or more telephone operators are employed, one of them will perform the functions of a "head" as agreed to by the treasurer of the theatre and the business representative of the union.

Hours of Work

The basic work week for heads shall be five days or 36¼ hours per week. Time and one-half will be paid after 36¼ hours. The mail order clerks basic work week is five days, 7 hours per day, for a total of 35 hours per week, excluding meal hours. The basic work week for telephone operators is six days. Approximately 6 hours per day for a total of 36 hours per week. All time worked in excess of six hours in a day or 36 hours per week or on a seventh day will be paid for at time and one-half. Overtime is computed in one-hour segments.

The basic work week for all employees excludes Sunday. Work on Sunday is paid at time and one-half, in addition to the basic weekly salary.

Holidays

Employees who work on any of the following holidays will receive one-half a day's pay for such work, in addition to their other compensation: New Year's Day, Lincoln's Birthday, Washington's Birthday, Memorial Day, Independence Day, Labor Day, Columbus Day, Election Day, Veteran's Day, Thanksgiving Day and Christmas Day. If an employee is not required by management to work on any such holiday, the employee shall be given credit for the day.

Safety

At no time shall an employee be required to work in a theatre alone.

Termination

An employee may be dismissed only for just causes and then only upon notification to the Union in writing within twenty-four hours after the dismissal specifying the reasons for the discharge. Except for the closing of a show during preview weeks or the week of the official opening, one week's notice of layoff or one week's pay in lieu thereof will be paid to laid-off employees.

LOCAL UNION #30 OF THE INTERNATIONAL UNION OF OPERATING ENGINEERS

Jurisdiction

Local #30 is the collective bargaining agent for employees engaged in the operation and maintenance of the heating and air conditioning systems in the theatres.

Work Week

The work week consists of five straight time days and a sixth day at the rate of time and a half. All work in excess of eight hours in any day or in excess of forty hours during a week is at the rate of time and one-half.

Wage Rates

The minimum wages of the employees covered by this agreement, effective December 22, 1978, is an hourly rate of $7.08 times 40 = $283.20 plus eight hours for the sixth day at time and one-half or $10.62×8= $84.96. The weekly salary for a forty-eight-hour week is $368.16.

Holidays and Vacations

The employer agrees that employees will be paid for New Year's Day, Independence Day, Labor Day, Memorial Day, Election Day, Lincoln's Birthday, Washington's Birthday, Thanksgiving Day, and Christmas Day. Employees required to work on a holiday must be provided with eight hours work at double the regular rate, plus time and one-half for everything in excess of eight hours. The employer further agrees that a replacement will be hired to replace each man while he is on vacation.

Season

Employees are employed on a seasonal basis from October 15 (unless the theatre opens later) to April 15, which is the guaranteed employment period. An operator must also be hired during the air conditioning season to operate the equipment.

CHAPTER 10

Contracts with the Producers

ACTORS' EQUITY ASSOCIATION

Casting

U SUALLY THE STAGE MANAGER and the casting director (if one is hired) take charge of the casting, so that the director, author, and producer are insulated from seeing persons totally impossible for the parts. The good possibilities are brought back for the director, author, and the producer to see and a decision is then made. The decision, as it should be, is largely the director's, but the entire cast must be approved by the author (and composer and lyricist if it is a musical) and the producer, who does the hiring.

In most instances the negotiations for the cast are carried on by the general manager for the production. Equity requires that there be an open call at which any Equity member so desiring may audition for any part.

Star and Director

Probably the most that a star will be paid is $15,000 per week. A star might also get a smaller amount as payment against a percentage of the gross box office receipts, and perhaps also a percentage of the net profits, so that the star on good weeks could end up getting paid something more than the flat $15,000 per week.

If a director or star gets a percentage of the net profits, although it is a share of the "net" profits, it nevertheless comes off the top and is considered an operating expense. It is thus not payable from just the producer's share of the profits, but from the profits before they are shared by the investors and producer.

Three Standard Contracts

The Actors' Equity Association Contract covers the hiring of the cast and stage managers. There are four basic contracts: (1) a Standard Minumum Contract for principal actors, (2) a Standard Minimum Contract for chorus, (3) a Standard Stage Manager's Contract, and (4) a Standard Run of the Play Contract. The minumum contract for principals and the minumum contract for the chorus are almost indentical, with a few minor differences.

Contracts Include Agreement with League and Equity Rules

The Actors' Equity contracts are very simple one-page documents. The Standard Minimum Contracts and the Run of the Play Contracts are on 8½- by 11-inch paper. The type is small but easily readable. However, each of these agreements states on it that all of the provisions contained in the basic agreement entered into between Equity and League, and the Equity rules governing employment, is part of the agreement as if it were set forth at length. The Equity rules governing employment are set forth in a small pamphlet of ninety-two pages with twenty-nine mimeographed pages of changes effective June 27, 1977, which will be incorporated into the rules. The rules are very detailed and set forth most of the provisions governing the employment of an actor. [1]

Deputies

One of the members of the cast is elected as the deputy to represent the Equity members in dealing with the producer in connection with any breach of the agreement or other employment terms. If a chorus is employed, then there is a deputy for chorus singers and deputy for chorus dancers. [2]

Minimum Salaries

The minimum salaries which became effective June 25, 1979, are as follows:[3]

	Point of Origin	*Away from point of organization out-of-town expense payment*	
Actors			
1979 $400	Plus Cost-of-living Increase	$245 per week	Plus Cost-of-living Increase

Rehearsal expense money is the amount of the minimum salary, no matter what the actor's contract salary is.

Stage Manager — Dramatic
1979 $560   Plus Cost-of-living $245 per week   Plus Cost-of-
                  Increase   Living Increase

Stage Manager — Musical
1979 $665   Plus Cost-of-Living $245 per week   Plus Cost-of-
                  Increase   Living Increase

1st Assistant Stage Manager — Dramatic
1979 $460   Plus Cost-of-Living $245 per week   Plus Cost-of-
                  Increase   Living Increase

1st Assistant Stage Manager — Musical
1979 $515   Plus Cost-of-Living $245 per week   Plus Cost-of-
                  Increase   Living Increase

2nd Assistant Stage Manager — Dramatic
1979 $400   Plus Cost-of-Living $245 per week   Plus Cost-of-
                  Increase   Living Increase

2nd Assistant Stage Manager — Musical
1979 $430   Plus Cost-of-Living $245 per week   Plus Cost-of-
                  Increase   Living Increase

Origin Point

The contract has designations for either New York, Los Angeles, Chicago, or San Francisco as the points of origin for a show. In the case of any other city, Equity has the right to designate the point of origin. While performing in the city designated as the point of origin, New York conditions apply. In all other cities, road conditions apply. The point of origin remains the same after it is designated. [4]

Rehearsal Payments

The producer agrees to pay rehearsal expense money for a period of four weeks for a dramatic production and five weeks for a musical production and revues for principal actors, and up to six weeks for the chorus in musical productions and revues.

If the producer wishes to extend a rehearsal period he may do so by paying for each of the first three days, one-sixth of the weekly rehearsal expense money amount; the last seven days of any rehearsal period is paid at 1/7 of the New York or road company minimum, whichever is applicable. The producer may extend a rehearsal period up to an additional ten days. [5]

Before or During Rehearsals

The producer must notify the actor and Equity in writing of the first date of rehearsal. If the beginning rehearsal date is not fixed in writing, the actor may terminate at any time prior to the commencement of rehearsals without penalty; the actor may also terminate, whether or not he has received notification of the first rehearsal date, without penalty at any time prior to two weeks before rehearsals commence. However, if the actor gives notice of termination within two weeks of the fixed first rehearsal date, he must pay the producer a sum equal to two weeks' compensation. Likewise, the Standard Minumum Contract may be terminated by the producer before the opening by giving written notice to the actor and paying him a sum equal to two weeks' compensation plus rehearsal salary due. [6]

Certain Extra Payments for Chorus

Dance captains must be paid not less than an additional $75.00 per week. [7] If a member of the chorus is required to play a part, speak lines, sing a song, or do a dance that is individual in its character and which is understudied, then such person must be paid an additional $12.50 per week. If such assignment is not understudied, then the person will be paid not less than $10.00 per week in addition. [8]

Televising, Recording, and Motion Pictures

There are detailed provisions set forth in the rules for television, recordings, and motion pictures. [9] It is provided that each actor engaged in a television, motion picture, or sound recording of a play, in full or in part, must be paid a minumum of one week's salary for each day or part of a day employed on such production.

If one week's salary for each day or part thereof is less than the minumum rate required by the American Federation of Television and Radio Artists, or by the Screen Actors Guild, then the actor must receive not less than the AFTRA or SAG minimum. If an actor is employed to make a television spot commercial of one minute or less duration using material from the play, then Equity will waive the one-week payment required; however, the actor must receive no less than the AFTRA or SAG minimum for such work. Close circuit or paid television is not covered by the rules and the producer agrees that there will be none, without prior negotiations and agreement with Equity as to the payments and working conditions. The producer may make a non-commerical filming or recording (to be used in the production) using the chorus only by paying one-half the weekly salary for each day or part thereof. The foregoing (both commercial and non-commercial) is applicable whether the televising, recording, or filming is done at the theatre or elsewhere.

Show Album

On the show album, the producer must use the actor who sings or verbalizes the part in the show. A producer must give the actor at least one week's notice of the making of a recording. A day's recording session is limited to eight out of nine hours with a one-hour break after no more than five hours, and must be completed not later than 6:30 p.m. when it occurs on a day of an 8:00 p.m. performance. [10] The stage manager must be used for the recording session.

Broadcast of Part of a Production

If the producer gives permission for a broadcast of any part of a production, the producer must pay a minimum of one-eighth of a week's salary to each actor for any day or part thereof that the actor is engaged in the broadcast or in rehearsing for the broadcast, or the American Federation of Television and Radio Artists' minimum for such broadcast, whichever is greater. [11]

Number of Performances

Eight performances constitute a week's work and may be given only during a period of six out of seven consecutive days. [12] A week's work consists of eight performances in no more than six days, even on road tours. The actors must be paid a week's compensation even if less than eight performances are given in any week, and they must be paid a sum equal to two-eighths of the weekly compensation for each performance in excess of eight during each week. If admission is charged (except bona fide benefits endorsed by the Theatre Authority or Equity), then they are counted and considered as performances for which the actor is to be paid.

If more than two performances are given or begun in any one day, the third performance is paid for as an extra performance even though the total number of performances given during that week is eight or less. [13] Any performance begun before 2 p.m. and/or after 11:00 p.m. is counted as an extra performance and is paid for at the rate of two-eighths of the actor's weekly salary. Actors must have at least one full day of rest in each calendar week free of rehearsals and performances. These days off will be no further apart than nine consecutive performance days.

Performances Lost

There is specific provision in the contract for the payment of actors in the event of performances lost as a result of an act of God, riot, public enemy, fire, accident, etc. [14]

Rehearsal Hours and Recesses

During Rehearsal Period and Prior to New York or Road Tour Opening

During the rehearsal period there must be a recess of 1½ hours after each 5 consecutive hours of rehearsal. The chorus and principals working with chorus must be given a 5-minute break during each hour.[15]

During each calendar week of rehearsal period, the actors must be given one day off, except during the last seven days prior to the first public performance when none is required.

Rehearsal hours prior to the New York or road tour opening must not exceed 7 out of 8½ consecutive hours a day which includes the 1½-hour recess above referred to.[16]

Final Week of Rehearsals Prior to First Public Performance

The maximum rehearsal time above described does not apply during the final week of rehearsals prior to the first public performance. During that week the rehearsals must not exceed ten out of twelve consecutive hours a day including recesses, except for the final day before opening. If the company does not rehearse for the full week before opening on the twelve consecutive hour basis, then when it returns to New York it may use that number of unexpected days of the week prior to the New York opening on a twelve consecutive hour basis, provided that there is still unexpired rehearsal time.

After First Performance But Prior to New York Opening — Maximum Hours

After the first public performance outside New York City, and before the New York opening, rehearsals including recesses and performances must not exceed twelve hours on any one day while the company is out of town. If there is unused rehearsal time, there is provision — with certain limitations — for using it upon the return to New York.[17]

Rest Periods

The company must receive a regular rest period of twelve hours at the end of the day (ten hours for principal actors on days before matinee days). The rest period preceding the call on the day of the first paid performance must be no less than nine hours.[18]

After New York Opening — Half-Hour Call

After the official opening in New York City, the company may not be called sooner than the one-half hour call on the day following the scheduled day of rest, except in emergencies or in case of a replacement of a star or major featured principal on the day of his first performance in the part.

After New York or Road Tour Opening —Chorus Hourly Limit

After the New York or road tour opening, chorus rehearsals — except those necessary for emergency cast replacements — are limited to eight hours weekly for routine rehearsals, or twelve hours weekly for understudy rehearsals or new material or numbers. In no event can the total rehearsals for the week exceed twelve hours unless overtime is paid.[19]

After New York or Road Tour Opening —Principals' Hourly Limit

After the New York or road tour opening, principal actors' rehearsals, except rehearsals necessary for emergencies and cast replacements, are limited to eight hours weekly, or twelve hours weekly for understudy rehearsal; however, during the first two weeks after the New York or road tour opening and for emergencies or in cast replacements, rehearsals may be five hours per day (two hours on matinee days).

Overtime Pay for Rehearsals

If the actors rehearse more than the hours stipulated, they must be paid an additional $8.50 per hour, or part thereof.[20]

Overtime Pay for Travel

Overtime pay for travel is $13 per hour. On a day of travel, rehearsal and travel time combined must not exceed ten hours excluding rest periods.[21]

If No Pre-Broadway –Hourly Limits After New York Opening

If a show is scheduled to open without a pre-Broadway tour, but gives preview performances prior to the official opening in New York, then for a period of up to two consecutive weeks after the first public performance, rehearsals and performances may not exceed ten out of twelve consecutive hours each day.

Terms of Employment

The Standard Minimum Contract and the Run of the Play Contract both provide that an actor must be guaranteed no less than two weeks' consecutive salary plus any rehearsal expense money due.[22]

Guarantees—Minimum and Run of Play Contracts

The Standard Minimum Contract for principals and chorus both provide that the actor will be paid a minimum of two weeks salary. This salary must be paid after the date of the first public performance or the opening date specified in the contract, whichever occurs first.

The Standard Run of the Play Contract is distinguished from the Standard Minimum Contract in that under the Run of the Play Contract, the actor is guaranteed a minimum of two weeks employment during each theatrical season. At the time the contract is entered into, the producer and actor agree that he will be employed (if the show runs, of course) during a certain number of seasons, and the contract sets forth the number of seasons. If the contract is for more than one season, the producer guarantees that the actor will be paid a minimum of two weeks employment for each season contracted, unless notice is given as provided in the contract. The notice provided for must be delivered to the actor and to Equity not later than five weeks after the first public performance in New York City (which date cannot be later than fifteen weeks after the opening performance) or five weeks after the opening of the road tour (if the contract is for a road tour), and the notice must state that the producer does not intend to present the play during any season following the current season. If the notice is delivered, together with payment for all of the seasons contracted after the second season, then the producer does not have to pay the guarantee for the second season. The notice, however, must be given simultaneously to all actors in the cast holding Run of the Play Contracts for more than one season or year.

If a play continues its run, an actor signed to a Run of the Play Contract must be paid his salary for every week during the season(s) that he is signed for, but in no event for less than two weeks. This is so even if the actor is replaced in the part.

The producer and actor may agree to a layoff during the months of July and August, providing that the producer gives at least four weeks' written notice of such layoff to the actor and designates a reopening date not later than September 1, or fourteen days after the layoff, and also guarantees the actor at least two weeks' employment upon the reopening.

The advantage of a Run of the Play Contract is obvious in that the producer can know for certain that an actor will be with him if it is an extended run. On the other hand, the actor can know that he will be paid for each week of the season he is signed for if the play runs. The price that the producer must pay is the guarantee for the minimum number of weeks in each season. If, for example, a producer wanted to make certain that a particular performer would be with the show if it ran for five years, then, if the show closed without the notice (discussed above) having been given to the actor, then he must receive a minimum of two weeks' salary for each of the five years or a minimum of ten weeks' salary. If the show closes after the notice has been given and the payment is made with the notice, the producer could save the guarantee for the second year and would only be obligated to pay the total of eight weeks' salary; that is, two weeks for the first year and for each of the third, fourth, and fifth years.

If should be noted that an actor signed on a Run of the Play Contract is entitled to be paid for the run of the play unless his employment is terminated in accordance with some provision of the contract.[23]

Converting Standard Contract of Principal Actor to Run of the Play

It is possible to sign a principal actor to a Standard Minimum Contract and convert the contract to a Run of the Play Contract.

Increased Salary and Written Notice

If the actor, at the time he enters into the Standard Contract, gives the producer the right to convert to a Run of the Play, then, at the time of the conversion, the actor's salary on the Run of the Play Contract must be an increase of at least 10 percent weekly or $75 weekly, whichever is greater. In order to exercise this option and convert, the producer must deliver personal written notice to the actor before the fifth consecutive performance of the actor in the play.

No Probation and Five-Week Guarantee for Principal Actor

The rider which gives the producer the option to convert must also provide that the five-day probationary period in the contract is deleted, so that there is no probationary period for the actor. Also, the rider granting the option to the producer must provide that the actor is guaranteed not less than five weeks' employment, rather than the minimum two weeks' employment that would otherwise be provided for if this rider were not added to the Standard Contract. [24]

Chorus Six-Month Run of the Play Contract

There is also provision for hiring a member of the chorus on a six-month Run of the Play Contract. The rider, which is added to the contract, must provide that: (1) the rider will apply to the road tour or point of organization and run only through the tryout period included; (2) neither party may give notice of termination of the contract before two weeks from the opening of the play (the opening at point of organization for dance captains); (3) the rider must be signed by the parties before the first day of rehearsal; (4) if the member of the chorus obtains a contract to play the part of a principal during the six-month rider, then the chorus member may terminate his employment upon two weeks' notice; (5) the rider may only be used if the chorus member is paid at least $25 per week above the minimum, not including payment for any extras or other duties for which extra compensation is provided. [25]

Extensions of Chorus Six-Month Run of Play Contract

If, during the twenty-sixth week of the period or any time thereafter, the producer requests in writing that the chorus member agrees to a further extension for an additional six months and the chorus member does not consent, then the producer has the right to discontinue the additional $25 payment. If the chorus member consents, the producer must pay an additional increment of no less than $15 for a second or subsequent six-month rider. This provision also applies to subsequent twenty-four-week periods after the first and second twenty-four-week periods.

Conversion to Chorus Six-Month Run of Play Contract

The producer may also sign a chorus member under a contract which gives the producer the option to convert to a six-month run of the play rider, provided that the producer exercises the option prior to the first day of rehearsal. If this rider is used, the chorus member is paid at least $25 more per week than the minimum salary, not including payments for any and all other duties.[26]

Extra Chorus Payment

A member of the chorus designated to swing a number in a production who is not hired solely as a swing performer must receive $10 per week in addition to the regular weekly salary. (A swing performer is a chorus member who may be called upon to perform in a number as a replacement if a chorus member is out.) The chorus member may perform in several numbers and swing on another number if he is needed.[27]

Number of Chorus

The rules make specific provision as to the number of chorus members that must be retained. Following the first day of rehearsal this number may not be reduced in any way.[28]

No Pay For Actors' Fund

The rules provide that an actor must perform without compensation for one performance during the first three months of the play's run, and for one performance every twelve months thereafter for the Actors' Fund Benefit. There are specific terms covering the notices, rehearsal, and procedure for an Actors' Fund Benefit.[29]

Paid Previews Before Opening Count Toward Minimum Guarantee

If a show gives paid previews immediately preceding the opening — that is, where there are no intervening days, rehearsals, or unpaid previews — and if the play closes within two weeks of the opening, then the producer may claim the pro-rata salaries paid to the actors for the previews as a credit and offset against the minimum guarantee provided for in the contract of employment. The producer need not pay rehearsal expense money if the actor is not required to rehearse more than four hours on the day of a paid preview. Any sums paid to the actor for rehearsals, whether at full salary or as rehearsal expense money, or any sum paid for unpaid previews or for paid previews not immediately preceding the opening performance, may not be credited against the minimum guarantee specified in the contract. The point is that credit is given only for salary payments immediately preceding opening and only in the event that there are no intervening days.

If an actor is paid rehearsal expense money in addition to payment for the preview, the producer may have an additional day of rehearsal for each such preview for payment of only rehearsal expense money. Payment for such previews, however, may not be used as a credit against the minimum contract guarantee.[30]

Individual Termination After Opening

The producer or the actor may terminate the contract at any time upon or after the date of the first public performance of the play by giving two weeks' written notice to the other party. If a company is closed in accordance with the notice of closing to the entire company, the company notice will supercede any individual notice then outstanding.

Termination by the Company After Opening

The producer may close the play and company upon one week's written notice or upon payment of one week's contractual salary in lieu thereof, provided that he has paid the Equity actors for all of their services rendered to the date of closing and in no event less than two weeks' salary plus rehearsal expense money.

Termination by Actor After Opening

If the actor wishes to terminate the contract after the play has opened, the producer has no responsibility for the return transportation. The chorus member's successor must not be engaged at a lesser salary than that of the chorus member replaced unless the chorus member terminated solely for the purpose of fulfilling another engagement.

Payment Where Actor Does Not Work Out Notice

If the actor is not allowed or required to work out any notice given to him under the contract, he must be paid immediately and may accept other employment. If the producer gives individual notice of termination, the producer must pay the actor the cost of transportation and baggage back to the point of organization whether he returns immediately or not.[31]

Termination—Run of the Play Contracts

Notice of Closing

The producer must give all actors signed to a Run of the Play Contract one week's individual notice in writing of the closing of the production and company or pay one week's salary in lieu thereof.

Run of the Play Contracts, with certain exceptions hereafter noted, terminate on the date stipulated in the individual contract of employment without further notice. A principal actor engaged under a Run of the Play Contract may agree to continue with the production after the expiration of the season (i.e., employment ending June 30) contracted for without entering into a new contract, but from and after June 30 he will be deemed to be employed under all the terms and conditions of the Standard Minimum Contract. The parties, if they decide to extend the term of employment beyond September 1, must execute a new contract by that date, otherwise the contract may be terminated by either party giving two weeks' written notice to the other party. If the producer gives notice to the actor at any time between June 30 and September 1, he may replace the actor at a lesser salary only if the actor's Run of the Play Contract was for a period longer than five months. Signing a Run of the Play Contract does not bind the actor to tour unless it is specifically stated in his contract by rider.[32]

Exceptions to Foregoing Closing Provisions

There are certain exceptions to the foregoing. They include:

1. Termination of rehearsals as a result of fire, accident, riot, strikes, illness, or death of the star or prominent member of the cast, act of God, or act of a public enemy. Under such circumstances the actors must be paid one-seventh of the out-of-town living expenses for a maximum of two weeks. If the layoff has continued for two weeks, the producer may pay half the contracted salary for two further weeks and may terminate the contract without penalty.
2. Where an actor absents himself from rehearsal for seven days due to

illness, the producer may terminate the contract at the end of the seven days. Equity may consent upon appeal to reduce this period.

3. If the play is abandoned before opening, the producer must pay the actor an additional two weeks' salary.

4. If an illness or an injury other than injury in the course of the actor's employment prevents the actor from performing and the illness continues or appears that it will continue for ten days or more, Equity may at the request of the producer modify or terminate the actor's contract on such terms as it considers just.

5. An actor may be discharged for inability to perform due to intoxication or similar cause. There are provisions for arbitration as to whether it was for just cause.

6. If an actor's part is cut out, the producer may terminate the contract by the payment of a sum equal to four weeks' contractual salary in addition to any other sums due for services rendered, plus four additional weeks' salary to the extent that the play runs more than four weeks after the actor's part is cut out or the contract terminated.

7. Where the producer gives notice to an actor who was hired for more than one season and notice is given not later than five weeks after the first public performance or five weeks after the opening day of the road tour that he will not present the play during any season following the current one, he may terminate if at the same time he pays the actor any and all sums due him under the guarantee for each season contracted for beyond the second season.

Closing Notice

A closing notice given at or before the end of the performance on Monday night is considered to be one week's notice effective at the end of the following Saturday night, and notice effective at the end of the second Saturday following is deemed to be two weeks' notice. If a show is playing a schedule of Tuesday through Sunday, then notice given on Tuesday is effective at the end of the following Sunday night performance as one week's notice, and effective the Sunday after that would be considered two weeks' notice. Except as just stated, a week's notice is considered to be seven calendar days. A notice of closing must be posted for the entire notice period unless it is initialed by every member of the cast. If the notice is posted after the half-hour call (half-hour before curtain time) it must be promptly called to the attention of the cast.[33]

Hiring "As Cast" and "Understudy as Cast"

If the part to be played by a principal actor is not specified, then he is only required to appear and perform in the part in which he makes his first public appearance. If a principal actor is employed to appear "as cast," then — except in revues — he is not required to appear and perform in any part or parts other than the part or parts he appeared in during the first two weeks of the run of the play. When hired "as cast," the producer must designate at least one-half of the roles "as cast" on the actor's contract. An actor hired "as cast" may terminate during the rehearsal period without penalty by giving the appropriate termination notice. If the principal actor is employed to "understudy as cast," then — except in revues — he may not be required to appear and perform in any part or parts other than the part or parts he was assigned to understudy up to the date following the first two weeks after the opening of the play in New York City, or four weeks after the out-of-town opening, whichever is sooner. An actor may not be required to understudy unless his contract specifically provides that he will understudy, and if the actor and producer have agreed to a specific understudy part or parts in the original contract of employment, then such provisions as set forth in the contract would be applicable. Hiring "as cast" shall not be applicable to revues. [34]

Juvenile Actors

Juvenile actors are paid the same as other actors. A juvenile under the age of fourteen may, at the time he signs his contract, agree to a six-month Run of the Play Contract and the contract may also provide that the producer has an option to extend the contract for an additional six-month period at a 10 percent salary above the actor's original contract salary. This option must be exercised in writing at least four weeks prior to the expiration of the initial six-month period. [35]

Extras

An "extra" is defined as one who may not be identified as a definite character either singly or within a group — i.e., an actor who provides atmosphere and background only. An extra may not be required to change makeup but may, however, be required to make a single costume change. Extras cannot be rehearsed for more than two weeks before the first public performance and may not speak except in "omnes" (in a group), may not sing, dance, understudy, and may not tour except with a pre-Broadway tryout of eight weeks or less.

Extras are paid no less than half the minimum salary of an actor. During a pre-Broadway tour, they must be paid one-seventh of out-of-town expenses per day for each day they spend out of town in addition to their regular salary. Extras receive hospitalization and medical coverage. After the New York opening the extra may be rehearsed for two weeks, the same as principal actors. After the two weeks, extras must be paid $11 for any hour or part of an hour. An extra gets a one-week guarantee of salary from the date of opening of the play, and one week's notice of termination of the contract; no probationary period is provided for in the contract. [36]

Understudies

Dramatic Plays

In dramatic plays all parts for which contracts are issued, except star and bit players, must be covered by understudies.

Extra Payment for Performance –Principal Actor

No understudy can perform in a role which he covers without additional compensation, except that a principal actor understudying a principal actor may perform the part he understudies without additional compensation when the understudied actor is on vacation. If the actor is paid not more than $125.00 over the minimum, he will be permitted to understudy up to five roles. If the actor is paid more than $125.00 over the minimum, he will be permitted to understudy up to seven roles. For each role understudied after seven, the actor must be paid $62.50.

One-eighth of an actor's own contractual salary will be paid to the understudy for each performance of the role understudied. A cast member understudying a star billed over the title, if receiving less than $100 over the minimum, will be paid at least $75 for each performance given in place of the star. [37]

Chorus—Extra Payment Under Contract

If a member of the chorus understudies a principal, he must be paid not less than $15 per week in addition to his weekly salary. If a member of the chorus understudies another member of the chorus (involving understudy rehearsals), he must be paid a minimum of not less than $10 per week in addition to his other salary.[38]

Understudies Present at All Performances

Understudies must be present at each performance unless the producer consents otherwise.

Time of Hiring and Commencement of Performance as Understudy

Understudies must be hired no later than one week before the first paid public performance for road tours and two weeks after the first paid public performance for pre-point of organization tryouts or previews where the show is opening cold at the point of organization.[39]

Understudy parts assigned to chorus must be assigned with new contracts or riders and with salary adjustments no later than three weeks after the first public performance of the production or at the time of the official New York opening.

Where the contract of a chorus member is amended so that additional compensation is agreed upon based on the assignment of the understudy work, the producer may, within two weeks of the first public performance in New York, withdraw said understudy work and additional compensation and assign it to another chorus member. This does not apply, however, where the understudy work and compensation is part of the original contract of employment.[40]

An understudy cannot be required to perform until one week after he is engaged. The producer must use his best efforts to provide the understudy with scripts and/or sides and music no later than two weeks after the New York opening. Understudies may be in only one company at a time.

Termination of Principal Actor and Replacement

If a principal actor's employment is terminated, a contract for replacement must be negotiated and signed between the producer and the understudy or other replacement no later than two weeks after the principal's last performance in the production.

Stage Managers and Payment

There must be at least one stage manager and one assistant stage manager on a straight dramatic show and at least one stage manager and two assistant stage managers on a musical show. The stage manager must be engaged and paid the contractual salary at least two weeks before the beginning of rehearsals. The assistant stage manager is paid the contractual salary from the time of the first rehearsal call. When a stage manager or assistant stage manager is called to perform services in productions either prior to the week before rehearsals begin, or after the production is closed, he must be paid no less than one-fifth of the applicable minimum weekly rate for each day. Stage managers and assistant stage managers must be members of Equity in all companies in which an Equity member is employed.

A replacement stage manager in a musical must also be hired one week prior to the date he is to take over the production. All stage managers and first assistant stage managers in musicals are not permitted to act or understudy, except in an emergency. [41]

Layoffs

If the actor has worked for two weeks, the manager may lay off the company during Holy Week and/or for no more than seven consecutive days during the fourteen-day period before Christmas Day, providing that the actor receives two consecutive weeks of employment after the layoff. The producer must give four weeks' written notice in the event of such layoff. During the layoff, the actor need not give any services except a run-through rehearsal on the day of reopening. If there is a change in cast or illness of a star or prominent member of the company, then Equity may allow additional rehearsals. If the company is outside point of organization, then the minimum salary plus out-of-town expense money must be paid during the layoff. [42]

Death of Star or Illness

The contract sets forth detailed terms and provisions in the event of the illness or death of a star, or if there is no star, in the event of the death or illness of the first featured actor who is playing a leading role.

Part Cut Out of Show

If the actor is on a Run of the Play Contract and if the part is cut before the official opening, the producer may terminate the contract by payment of an amount equal to four weeks' contractual salary in addition to all sums due for services rendered, plus four additional weeks after the actor's part is cut out or terminated. In no event may an actor on a Run of the Play Contract whose part is cut out receive less than payment for the guarantee period specified in his contract of employment. [43]

Billing

The contract provides that wherever houseboards are maintained, and within the limitation of the existing facilities, the names of the principal actors in the cast must be listed on the houseboards in front of the theatre in letters no less than one-half inch in height. Where there is no houseboard outside the theatre, the producer must agree to place one prominently inside the lobby. There is also provision for removal of an actor's name and pictures in the event that he leaves the cast, and a specific provision for notification of the producer of any breach of the billing clause. If a breach of this clause is not corrected within seven business days, the producer must pay a sum equal to one-eighth of the actor's salary for the first week of the breach, two-eighths for the second week, three-eighths for the third week, etc. [44]

Billing if Understudy Plays Part

There are specific provisions set forth for program billing in the event that an understudy takes the place of a principal actor. [45]

Clothes and Makeup

All wardrobe must be furnished for all actors. All wigs, hats, gowns, footwear, and wardrobe must be furnished for all actors and must be new if they are modern and conventional wear. All costumes or clothing furnished by the producer must be freshly cleaned when delivered and cleaned thereafter when necessary, but at least once every month and within one week before the show goes on tour. Ordinary and conventional makeup is furnished by the actor, but anything that is unusual must be furnished by the producer. If the actor must use body makeup, the producer must furnish a regular linen towel service for removal of the makeup.

The chorus must be furnished with their costumes, including footwear. The producer must furnish one pair of toe shoes for each member of the chorus who must dance on toe.

If the principal actor wishes to wear his own clothes instead of those supplied by the producer, he may do so only with the producer's consent. Under no circumstances may a chorus member wear his own clothes. A principal actor will not rent or lend any wardrobe to a producer for use in any production unless the terms of the rental or loan are stated in his contract of employment and approved by Equity.[46]

Transportation and Baggage

There are detailed rules concerning transportation of the actor and baggage, including specific provisions covering rail, bus, and air transportation. The rules are very detailed concerning the times, the amount of baggage, when the parties may travel, overtime travel, and the like.[47]

Photographs and Publicity

There are specific provisions set forth in the rules for the taking of photographs and publicity with stated limitations upon picture calls.[48]

Alien Actors

If a producer wishes to import alien actors for a production, he must obtain the approval of Actors' Equity Association, which approval may be applied for in three different ways.

Individual Actor—or Less Than the Entire Cast

If a producer wishes to import an actor or actors for a production, he must first submit the application, a copy of the script, and other pertinent information to Equity.

Upon receipt of the application, the Equity Alien Committee has ten days to consider the application and render its decision.

If the producer is dissatisfied with the Alien Committee's decision, he may appeal, and present his case to the Equity Council at its next meeting, at which time the council will render its decision.

If the producer is still dissatisfied, the matter may be submitted to an impartial arbitrator who will, within one week's time, render a decision binding on both parties. The arbitrator is instructed to use as a criteria certain definitions contained in the Actors' Equity agreement and rules governing the employment of non-resident aliens.

An alien actor may qualify if he meets all the criteria set forth in one of two categories — if he is a star performer or an actor providing unique services — or if he is part of a unit company or special character cast.

Star Performer

The producer must submit documents testifying to the current widespread acclaim, international recognition, playbills with star billing, receipt of internationally recognized prizes or awards for excellence, and documentary evidence of earnings commensurate with the claimed level of ability.

Actor Providing Unique Services

The producer's application must document that the actor whose services are sought will be providing unique services that cannot be performed by any existing members of Equity; that there are no persons in the United States capable of performing such services; and that a diligent search has been made in the United States to find such an actor.

Unit Company

If a producer desires to bring over a repertory company, then the application is made to Equity. Equity will approve of the application providing that it is a true repertory company. They must do at least two shows in repertory and the company must appear for a limited run — that is, not over twenty weeks in each city in which they appear.

Special Character

It is possible to make an application to Actors' Equity to approve of an entire cast based on the fact that the play is of such a unique character that by design or by the nature of the play, the entire alien cast must be kept intact to preserve the particular quality of the play; that it is impossible to do the play here with local actors. Whether or not a play is of such a special character is determined solely by the Counsel of Actors' Equity, which is the governing board of this group.[49]

THEATRICAL WARDROBE ATTENDANTS UNION, LOCAL #764

Jurisdiction

This agreement is applicable to every New York production and every production originating in New York, and governs the employment of wardrobe supervisors, assistants, and dressers. Each show must have a minimum wardrobe crew of one wardrobe supervisor, except on: (1) "one-man shows" and (2) on special shows where no wardrobe other than the performers' street clothes are worn, and no wardrobe changes requiring the assistance of any other person are to be made.

Wardrobe supervisors and assistants may not perform dressers' duties, and dressers engaged in a production may not perform the duties of supervisors or assistants except in places of extreme emergency, limited to one performance. A performer may not assist another performer in dressing nor may the stage manager or his assistants perform the duties of a dresser.[50]

Wardrobe, Stars, Duties Defined

Wardrobe is considered to be all clothing, hats, shoes, etc., worn in the production, whether personally owned by the performers or purchased or rented. The term "stars" is defined to mean performers whose names appear above the title of the show or carry the label "starring" or "also starring" before their names. The duties of employees covered by the contract include maintaining, cleaning, dying, pressing, sorting, handling, distributing, hanging, packing, repacking, repairing, altering, transporting, and the general supervision of all items, costumes, wardrobes, and costume — wardrobe accessories, as well as the dressing of, and making changes for all performers. The duties also include making, executing, fitting, and remodeling of such items as well as the control, disposition, and organization of costumes and wardrobe for their efficient and artistic utilization.

Star's Dressers

Stars may personally select their own dressers, but any dresser so selected, whether on the payroll of the production, the star, or both the production and the star, is subject to the provisions of this agreement and must be or become a member of the union. Star dressers shall have the right to negotiate additional pay for any extra services required. A letter or contract shall be signed between management and the star dressers.[51]

Changes in The Law—May Reopen Negotiations

The agreement provides that if the Labor Management Relations Act of 1947 as amended is further amended or repealed, or in the event that there are new rulings or legislation covering permissable union security forms other than presently allowed, or should the NLRB issue a decision or advisory opinion declining to exercise jurisdiction over the League of New York Theatres or over the business of its members, then the union shall have the option on ten days' written notice of reopening the agreement for the limited purpose of negotiating modifications to the extent authorized by any such change in the law.

Rates of Pay—Hours of Work and Overtime

The schedule of minimum rates of pay provided in the agreement is as follows:

	9-4-78/9-2-79
Wardrobe Supervisors	$311.05
Assistant supervisors	285.14
Per diem — on tour	31.11
Overtime hourly rate	
Wardrobe supervisors	11.66
Assistant supervisors	10.88

Seventh Day

Wardrobe supervisors Assistant supervisors	Time and one-half of one-sixth of gross weekly salary

Sunday performances
2nd & 3rd performances
Performances in excess of
Eight (8)

	$15.00 additional for each performance
Wardrobe supervisors Assistant supervisors	Time and one-half of one- eighth of gross weekly salary

Holidays

    Wardrobe supervisors
    Assistant supervisors

Lincoln's Birthday Washington's Birthday Memorial Day July 4th Thanksgiving Day Christmas Day New Year's Day	Double-time of one-sixth of gross weekly salary
Labor Day Columbus Day Election Day Veterans Day	Time and one-half of one-sixth of gross weekly salary

Dressers:

Per performance	$25.50
Per week	$203.98
Per diem — on tour	$31.11

Holidays

(Per performance) Lincoln's Birthday Washington's Birthday Memorial Day July 4th Thanksgiving Day Christmas Day New Year's Day	$51.00

Hourly rate for above
    Holidays $14.56

(Per performance)
Labor Day
Columbus Day $38.25
Election Day
Veterans Day
Hourly rate for above
    Holidays $10.91

Broken time per four (4)
hour call $29.10

Dressers per hour $ 7.28

Overtime per hour —
Time and one-half $10.91

Overtime per hour — Doubletime
(12:00 midnight – 8:00 a.m.) $14.56

Packing during performance
(additional) $12.74

All broken-time calls are for a minimum of four (4) hours.
All daytime picture calls are for a minimum of four (4) hours
except as otherwise specifically set forth.

Eight Performance—Six-Day Week and Overtime

Six days constitute a regular work week and the seventh day is a rest
period. Any work performed on the seventh consecutive day shall be paid
for at time and one-half (one-sixth of the weekly salary in the case of
wardrobe supervisors and assistant supervisors). When employees are
required to render services for more than eight performances of an attraction within any regular work week, the employee gets paid time and
one-half of his regular rate for each such additional performance. For a
single performance on Sundays, dressers shall be paid the regular straight
time rate unless it is seventh-day work or performance in excess of
eight.[52]

Dressers

Dressers' Work Time

Dressers are required to report thirty minutes before curtain time. If
there is a change in the advertised curtain time, the producer must notify the

wardrobe personnel of the actual time for the next performance within the first hour of the previous performance. Dressers are required to give their services for the payments above set forth provided that the performance does not exceed 3½ hours, including the thirty minutes prior to curtain time.

Dressers' Hours and Overtime

Where the work of hanging costumes at the end of the performance does not exceed fifteen minutes after curtain time and where the performance time does not require an excess of 3½ hours work, then no overtime payment need be made. Where under such circumstances there is in excess of 3½ hours work, excluding fifteen minutes after curtain time as above referred to, all time worked en excess of 3½ hours is paid for at overtime rates. A full hour's overtime must be paid for any fractional hours worked. This does not, however, apply to opening night in New York.[53]

Dresser Minimum

Any dresser ordered to report for a performance or for maintenance work who reports at the specified hours is guaranteed the minimum call as set forth in the schedule.

Dressers Accompany Wardrobe

Dressers are required to accompany all wardrobe removed from the theatre for any reason whatsoever, from the time of removal until the return of the wardrobe to the theatre. If no dresser is available, the wardrobe supervisor or assistant acts in the dresser's place and is paid at the broken time rate set forth in the schedule. This does not apply to wardrobe removed from the theatre for washing, cleaning, or repairing.

Rehearsals

Wardrobe personnel are not paid additional during put-ons, rehearsals, and run-throughs if there is no commercial tie-up involved.

Number of Employees and Minimum Hours

After the New York opening, the necessary number of wardrobe per-

sonnel agreed upon between the business manager of the union and the
producer is required and each must receive a a minimum call of four
hours.[54]

Closing—Wardrobe Supervisors and Assistants

When a production closes out of town, wardrobe supervisors and
assistants are paid from the time of closing of the show until their return to
New York.

Rest Periods

All employees who are part of the maintenance crew in the theatre when
a performance is not being given must get rest periods of five minutes for
each hour or twenty minutes for every four-hour period.

After Midnight

If a performance commences before midnight and runs after midnight,
all wardrobe employees must be paid at the double-time rate for such
performances. They receive waiting time at the broken time rate from the
fall of the curtain on the previous (regular) evening's performance unless
no regular performance was given that day.

Wardrobe Supervisors Packing for TV

Wardrobe supervisors receive additional compensation at the rate of
one-sixth of their weekly salary for the service of packing and returning the
wardrobe to proper condition for use in a production when a wardrobe is
sent to a television studio for use in a television show. If no dresser is
available, the wardrobe supervisor or assistant will act in the dresser's
place.

TV at Theatre

If a production is televised from the theatre during the regular performance, all employees are paid at the prevailing television rate in addition to
their regular pay.

Publicity Pictures

Wardrobe supervisors, assistants, and dressers are paid an hourly rate as provided in the contract for their services involved in the taking of all commercial or publicity pictures. This does not apply to non-commercial pictures. Commercial pictures are defined as those where the pictures are exploited in connection with an advertised product or when the producer derives compensation for such pictures.

As a continuity of employment, pictures may be taken (on an hourly basis) one hour before or after a performance and in such instance all the wardrobe personnel must be employed.

For taking of all pictures after the performance (whether commercial pictures or pictures for general publicity), those employees involved are paid at the overtime rate in addition to their regular pay.

Working Conditions

The League agrees to use its best efforts to see that a suitable wardrobe room with a window or other means of proper ventilation is provided as well as proper sanitary conditions, toilet facilities, washbasins, etc. Personal clothing of the members of the wardrobe crew must also be safeguarded. All sewing and other equipment furnished by the employees must be insured against fire and theft at the producer's expense, or, in lieu thereof, the producer is required to reimburse the employees for any loss or damage to their equipment.

Equipment Furnished

The producer agrees to furnish sewing machines for proper repairs and irons and/or ironing boards, and if the employee is required to furnish any such equipment, a weekly rental as agreed upon between the employee and the producer is charged.

Making a Costume

If a costumes made, produced, or executed by a wardrobe employee, whether it be a duplicate or not, the employee is paid additional compensation in addition to the regular salary at an agreed upon sum.[55]

Travel and Transportation

Wardrobe employees are furnished first-class transportation the same as for other members of the stage crew, which includes first-class sleeping accomodations for travel between 8:00 p.m. and 8:00 a.m. The producer must, in addition, pay the cost of, or reimburse the wardrobe employees for, transportation of hand luggage up to $3 each way. When traveling by plane, management will reimburse the employee for the premium payment incurred in purchasing flight insurance of up to $60,000.[56]

Bus Travel

If bus travel is arranged, all wardrobe employees must be provided with the same sleeping acocomodations as the production road crew. If the bus travel, either by day or night, is more than three hours on days when two performances are given, or more than six hours on days when one performance is given, or more than eight hours on a day when no performance is given, then each wardrobe employee must be paid an additional $5 per hour. All provisions applicable to bus travel by Equity members or stage road crews are also applicable to wardrobe employees.[57]

Layoffs and Reductions and Dismissal for Cause and Replacement

All contract wardrobe employees must be given two weeks notice in writing by the producer of any layoff or dismissal, and one week's notice of closing. Dressers must be given one week's notice of layoff, dismissal, or closing. Except in the event of a closing, written notice of any layoff or dismissal must also be given to the union. Contract wardrobe employees must give the producer two weeks' notice in writing for resignation, and dressers must give the producer one week's notice of a resignation.

No reduction in the number of dressers is permitted after one week of performances in New York City unless there has been a sufficient reduction in wardrobe to warrant it.

Dismissal for Cause

Replacement of laid-off, dismissed, or resigned wardrobe employees is mandatory. An employee may not be discharged without just cause, which means intoxication, dishonesty, or failure to abide by any of the terms of the agreement between the League and the union.

If the producer wishes to lay off the entire company for Christmas or Holy Week, the producer must give the wardrobe personnel at least two consecutive weeks of employment prior to the layoff and two consecutive weeks of employment after the layoff. Wardrobe employees on tour for any such layoff period are paid full expense money or a week's salary, whichever is greater.

Termination and Renegotiation

The parties agree that at least sixty days prior to the expiration date they will meet and confer to negotiate the terms of a new agreement.

SOCIETY OF STAGE DIRECTORS AND CHOREOGRAPHERS

Directors—Extra Payment for Rewriting

Nowadays directors pick up extra money by participating in the writing of the show. Although a director may not get program writing credit, he may get as much as 1½ or 2 percent of the gross reciepts for the writing, in addition to the directing fee. The minimum director's fee, as will be noted, is $4,410 plus 1½ percent of the gross receipts; however, if he is a good, big-name director he is more likely to be paid between $5,000 and $8,000 and between 2½ percent and 4 percent of the gross receipts as a directing fee. He may also receive up to 10 percent of the net profits of the company. In addition, the director who helps with the writing would share in the writer's receipts from the movie sale as well as from the sale of the other subsidiaries, and this could mean big money.

Jurisdiction

The collective bargaining agreement of the Society of Stage Directors and Choreographers governs, as the name implies, employment of directors and choreographers in first-class productions in the United States. First-class productions do not include vaudeville-type shows, concert-type shows, readings, night clubs, theatre restaurants (Las Vegas, however, is considered first class where so classified by Actors' Equity as part of a road tour), ballets, symphonic and musical importations, and any production not under the jurisdiction of Actors' Equity. In exchange for recognition of the Society for first-class productions, the Society has agreed that it will not attempt to seek recognition to bargain with the producers for other than the first-class presentations just noted. A theatrical production, to be covered by this agreement, must also be presented on the speaking stage in a first-class theatre.[58]

The Society agrees to admit members on a non-discriminatory basis and agrees that its constitution and by-laws will provide that any initiation fee or similar charge will be reasonable and be required of all applicants and members. The current initiation fee is $500, with annual dues of $75 as well as 1½ percent of the member's annual gross.

Producer/Director or Producer/Choreographer

The contract does not cover a producer not previously a member of the Society when such producer is acting as a producer/director or a producer/choreographer, nor will such person be induced, coerced, or otherwise required to become or remain a member of the Society. Any producer/director or producer/choreographer who was previously a member of the Society remains a member and the contract would be applicable.[59]

One Waiver of Royalties Permitted

A producer may not request that a director or choreographer waive any of the terms of the agreement without the consent of the Society; however, a reduction of royalties of up to four weeks (which need not be consecutive) may be made without the consent of the Society provided that the agreement in writing for the reduction is signed by the producer and the director or choreographer and is filed with the Society within one week after the reduction is agreed upon.[60]

Twenty-Year Waiver on Bargaining Certain Issues

The Society has agreed that it will waive bargaining for a period of twenty years with respect to the director's or choreographer's right to participate in subsidiary rights, with respect to the existing relations between producer, director, choreographer, and dramatist, and with respect to duty, authority, and control of any production. This waiver will expire on August 12, 1982.

Cost of Living Adjustment

The agreement which became effective on August 13, 1977, provides that one year after its effective date, and annually thereafter, minimum fees shall automatically be adjusted to reflect the increase in the cost of living which may have taken place during the previous year (no mention is made of a possible decrease in the cost of living). The index used is the Consumer Price Index for the city of New York (1957–1959=100) published by the Bureau of Labor Statistics, United States Department of Labor. The index for the city of New York as of August 13, 1962, is the base index. Cost of living adjustments operate prospectively and apply only to Minimum Basic Contracts executed on or after the date of the adjustment. Cost of living adjustments must not be pyramided. In no event shall these adjustments apply to contracts which provide fees in excess of the minimum.

Director and Choreographer Terms

Fees

The minimum fee payable to a director of a first-class production is not less than $4,410, and for a choreographer $3,570. Not less than 25 percent of the fee in either case is paid directly to the director or choreographer on signing of the contract and is nonreturnable, and the balance of the fee is payable in three equal payments at the beginning of the first, second, and third weeks of rehearsal, or not later than one week before the first performance, whichever is sooner. If a production is abandoned, there is no liability for fee payments after the date of abandonment; however, those fees accrued prior to the abandonment must be paid to the director or choreographer and may be retained by him.

Royalties

In addition to the contract fee, the director of a first-class dramatic production must be paid a royalty of not less than 1½ percent of the gross weekly box office receipts, and the director of a musical must be paid a royalty of not less than three-quarters of 1 percent of the gross weekly box

office receipts. The choreographer of a first-class musical must be paid
one-half of 1 percent of the gross weekly box office receipts. In all instances
the weekly payments must be made no later than ten days after the week for
which the weekly payments are due. [61]

Gross Box Office Receipts Defined

Gross weekly box office receipts are defined in the agreement as the
receipts from the box office less:
1. All admission taxes levied by any governmental agency on gross
   receipts.
2. Pension and welfare deductions exercised as a result of the New
   York City tax abatement program.
3. Theatre party commissions and discounts, and cut rate sales.
4. Subscription fees.
5. Actors' Fund benefits.
6. Any deductions similar to the ones listed above.

In bus and truck operations where a guaranteed lump sum is paid to the
producer, the lump sum less booking commissions is the basis for the
computation of royalties in lieu of gross box office receipts. Any sum
received by the producer in excess of the guaranteed lump sum shall also be
included in computing royalties. [62]

Option to Direct Future Companies and Payments

The director and the choreographer are given an option to direct all
future companies presenting the play in the United States in which the
producer is interested. If the director of choreographer accept the employment with the additional company, then he will receive for each additional
company one-half of the original fee. In addition, a director will receive no
less than 1½ percent of the gross weekly box office receipts for a dramatic
production, and no less than three-fourths of 1 percent of the gross weekly
box office receipts for a musical production; the choreographer will receive
no less than one-half of 1 percent. If the director elects not to direct the
additional company, then he will receive no fee but will receive no less than
three-fourths percent of the gross weekly box office receipts for a drama
and three-eights percent of the gross weekly box office for a musical. If the
choreographer does not elect to exercise his option, he will not receive any
fee, but will receive no less than one-fourth of 1 percent of the gross weekly

box office receipts derived from any and all such companies. The director or choreographer has ten days within which to decide whether or not he wishes to do the additional production.[63]

Length of Employment

A maximum of eight consecutive weeks in the case of a drama and ten consecutive weeks in the case of a musical, after the first public performance out of town, is the limit of the director's or choreographer's obligation prior to the official New York opening. If additional time is required during out-of-town tryouts, the director or choreographer must continue to work if he is available and uncommitted by virtue of any other professional engagement.[64]

Strike–Lockout–Fire–Flood–etc., and Suspension Rates

If a production is suspended because of strike, lockout, fire, flood, act of public enemy, or act of God, the period of suspension is not considered part of the consecutive employment periods above referred to. When a suspension occurs prior to the date the production opens in New York, if the director or choreographer is available he will continue to serve, and if unavailable, additional directorial or choreographer's royalties are reduced as follows: (1) production not in rehearsal — no royalties; (2) production in rehearsal for at least two weeks — one-third of royalties; (3) after out-of-town opening — two-thirds of royalties.[65]

Out-of-Town Expenses

Effective August 13, 1978, directors and choreographers are paid not less than $52.50 per day for out-of-town expenses. Effective August 13, 1979, the per diem shall be increased by the cost of living increases of the Consumer Price Index for the city of New York from July 1 to June 30 of each year.

Billing Credits

The agreement provides that the director and choreographer must each receive billing in all programs and houseboards. The director's credits must appear on a separate line in an agreed size, type, and position on which no other credit will appear. For each company choreographed by the choreographer, he shall receive billing in all programs and houseboards.[66]

Dismissal for Cause

A director or choreographer may not be dismissed (except where the director or choreographer is guilty of breach of contract) without full payment as provided in the contract.

After Opening Supervision

The director and choreographer must supervise and maintain the quality of the production after opening. Each of them must see the production at least once every eight weeks unless prevented from doing so by other contractual obligations. If additional direction or rehearsal is necessary, the director and choreographer must do so without additional compensation. If either the director or choreographer neglects to supervise and maintain the quality of the production as set forth in the contract, then that director or choreographer would forfeit one-half of his or her royalties until the work is done.[67]

Terms Applicable Solely to Choreographer

The choreographer's agreement has certain provisions in it which are not applicable to a director.[68]

Assistant

For an example, it is provided that the choreographer may have an assistant of his choice during the entire rehearsal period and during part or all of the out-of-town tryout period. The length of the assistant's employment and compensation must be negotiated by the assistant and the producer, as the assistant is not covered by the provisions of the agreement between the producer and the Society or between the League and the Society. The choreographer may waive this requirement.

Dance Captain

The choreographer has the right to designate a captain or replacement for him among the dance company, who — after the show has opened in New York — will have authority to call necessary rehearsals and rehearse understudies and replacements to maintain the quality of the dancers' performance.

Approval of Rehearsal Pianist

The choreographer will select or approve a dance rehearsal pianist who will be at the choreographer's disposal for the rehearsal, road, and tour period. The duration of the dance captain's employment and compensation, and the duration of the rehearsal pianist's employment and compensation, will also be negotiated by the respective parties and the producer, as neither of them is covered by the provisions of the collective bargaining agreement between the League and the Society.

The choreographer has first call on the services of the pianist. However, when the pianist is not occupied with dance routines, the pianist is available to the rest of the company.

UNITED SCENIC ARTISTS, LOCAL #829

Jurisdiction

The United Scenic Artists, Local #829 Agreement applies and is limited in its application to scenic designers, costume designers and lighting designers, and assistant designers employed by or engaged in a theatrical production produced for Broadway. If an individual designs the scenery and/or the lighting and/or the costumes he must have a separate contract for each.

Definition of Services

Scenic Designer

The scenic designer designs the production and completes either a working model of the settings to scale or completes color sketches or color sketch models of the settings and necessary working drawings for the constructing carpenter. The designer also supplies the contracting painter with color schemes and designs, and selects or approves properties required for the production, including draperies and furniture, and designs and supervises special scenic effects for the production, including projections. The designer will also supply specifications for the constructing carpenter, supervise the building and painting of sets and the making of properties, and, at the request of the producer, discuss estimates for the set construction with the bidding contractors. In addition, the designer will be present at pre-Broadway and Broadway set-ups, technical and dress rehearsals, the first public performances and openings out-of-town, the first public performance and opening in New York, and will conduct scenic rehearsals for these as may be required. [69]

Costume Designer

The costume designer designs the costumes and will submit a costume plot listing costume changes by scene for each character in the cast; provide color sketches of all costumes; and supply the contracting costume shop complete color sketches of all costumes or outline sketches with color samples attached. The designer will participate in not more than three estimating sessions with costume shops of the producer's choice. If the designer is required to obtain more than three estimates for the same costumes, extra compensation agreed upon by the designer and producer and subject to the union's approval will be paid. [70] The designer selects and coordinates all contemporary costumes including selections from performers' personal wardrobes when the situation arises. The supervision of all necessary fittings and alterations, the selection and approval of all costume accessories (such as headgear, gloves, footwear, hose, purses, jewelry, umbrellas, canes, fans, bouquets, etc.), and the supervision and approval of hair styling and selection of wigs, hairpieces, mustaches, and beards are responsibilities of the costume designer. The designer should be present at pre-Broadway and Broadway technical and dress rehearsals, the first public performance and openings out-of-town, the first public performance and opening in New York, and will conduct costume rehearsals when required. [71]

Lighting Designer

The lighting designer designs the lights, provides a full equipment list and light plot drawn to scale showing type and position of all instruments, and provides a color plot and all necessary information required by the contracting electrician. A control plot showing allocation of instruments for lighting control must be provided by the designer. The lighting designer will supervise and plot special effects and supervise hanging and focusing of the lighting equipment and the setting up of all lighting cues. Up to three estimates may be obtained by the designer for the producer. If the producer requires the designer to obtain more than three estimates, extra compensation will be paid as agreed upon between designer and producer subject to the union's approval. The designer will be present at pre-Broadway and Broadway set-ups, technical and dress rehearsals, the first public performances and openings out-of-town, the first public performance and opening in New York, and will conduct lighting rehearsals as may be necessary. [72]

Minimum Scenic Design Fees

Effective March 20, 1978, designers in all design categories employed by a producer shall be paid not less than the following rates for dramatic and musical productions and for any other type of theatrical productions other than so-called concert presentations, which will be discussed separately. The rates for scenic designing a dramatic single set is $2,750; a dramatic multi-set is $4,000; and a dramatic unit set with phases is $5,000. The scenic designing of a musical single set is $2,750; a musical unit set with phases is $5,000; and a musical multi-set is $9,000.

A unit set is a set that stays in view of the audience at all times. One may bring in items or remove items from the basic set, but if the basic set remains in view it is a unit set. Each change is called a "phase."

Minimum Lighting Design Fees

The minimum lighting design fee for a dramatic single set is $1,700; a dramatic multi-set is $2,500; and a dramatic unit set with phases is $3,200. For the musical single set the minimum fee is $2,000; a musical unit set with phases is $3,000; and a musical multi-set is $4,500.

Minimum Costume Design Fees

Costume design fees are determined on two different scales. The fee for a design for a dramatic play is determined by the number of characters in the play and whether the setting of the play is considered "modern" or period. "Modern" is defined as five years either way of the current date. For a dramatic play with one to three characters the minimum fee is $1,500 with the fourth to seventh additional character at an additional fee of $125 each. For a dramatic play in a modern setting with eight to fifteen characters the minimum fee is $2,500. If the play is period it is an additional $500. The sixteenth through twentieth character is again an additional $125 each, regardless of period or modern setting. A design for modern dramatic plays with twenty-one to thirty characters demands a fee of $3,500, with an additional $750 for a period setting. Again, an additional $125 is charged for the thirty-first through thirty-fifth character, regardless of period or modern setting. The design fee for a dramatic play with thirty-six or more characters in a modern setting is $4,500. If the play is period there is an additional fee of $1,000. A fee for a design for a musical play is based upon the number of persons who appear on stage in costume. The minimum for the musical play in which one to fifteen persons appear on stage in costume is $3,000; beyond fifteen persons it is an additional $150 each up to twenty persons. A musical with twenty-one to thirty persons who appear on stage in costume has a minimum fee of $6,000 with each additional person on stage, to a total of thirty-five, at an additional $150 fee each. A musical with thirty-six or more persons appearing on stage in costume has a minimum designer fee of $9,000. [73]

Payment of Designers' Contracts

An individual agreement must be signed by the producer and the designers for scenic design, for costume design, for lighting design, and for assistant designers. All individual agreements must be signed and filed in triplicate with the union for its approval before work can commence. When the individual agreement is filed with the union, the producer deposits with the union a cash bond in an amount equal to 25 percent of the design rate payable to the designer, or $1,000, whichever is greater. The remaining 75 percent will be deposited with the union when painting or construction of sets commences in the shop, or on the first day of full cast rehearsal, whichever occurs first.

The union will pay the designer his fee from this bond according to the following timetable:

1. Not less that 25 percent of the design rate or $1,000, whichever is greater, on the filing of the individual agreement.

2. 25 percent of the design rate when painting or construction of sets commence or on the first day of full cast rehearsal, whichever occurs first.
3. 25 percent of the design rate on the first public performance.
4. The balance shall be paid on the official New York opening or road tour opening, whichever is applicable.[74]

Out-of-Town

The producer will provide the designers and any assistants with round trip transportation expense whenever they are required to travel outside New York City. The producer will pay designers and assistants not less than $50 per day for living expenses for each day they are required to be outside New York City in connection with the production.[75]

Postponement

On the opening date of a production these payments shall be made as if the production had been carried out and opened on the originally named date so long as the designer has completed the necessary working drawings and color sketches or plots (sets, costumes, or lighting). If the opening is postponed for four weeks or more, the designer shall perform the remaining services only so far as his contractual commitments permit.[76]

Abandonment

If a production is abandoned prior to the first public performance, and the designer has completed the necessary working drawings and color sketches or plots (sets, costumes, or lighting), the designer shall receive three-quarters of the originally agreed upon payment.

If a production is abandoned and the designer has not completed the designs agreed upon, the designer and producer shall negotiate the remaining payment due, but in no event will the designer receive less than one-half of the originally agreed upon payment.[77]

Duties and Obligations

The specific requirements of each of the designers varies.

The scenic designer must either construct a working model of the settings to scale or complete sketches; supply the contractors with color schemes or color sketches; design, select, or approve properties required for the production, including draperies and furniture; design and/or supervise special scenic effects for the productions, including projections; supply specifications for the constructing carpenter to build and paint the sets; participate in three estimating sessions; attend the first out-of-town and the New York openings and dress rehearsals; and attend public performances from time to time for the purpose of conducting "normal check."

The lighting design contract provides that the lighting designer must furnish a full equipment list and light plot drawn to scale showing type and position of all instruments necessary to accomplish the lighting; provide color plot and all necessary information required by the contract electrician; provide color plot showing the allocation of instruments for lighting control; supervise and plot special effects; supply specifications and solicit estimates of the same; supervise the hanging and focusing of the same; supervise the hanging and focusing of the lighting equipment and the setting up of all lighting cues; attend the first out-of-town and New York openings as well as dress rehearsals; conduct the lighting rehearsals for each performance; and attend performances from time to time for the purpose of conducting a "normal check" of the lighting.

The costume designer must submit a costume plot of the production, listing costume changes by scene for each character in the cast; complete all sketches of costumes designed for the production; supply the costume shop with complete color sketches or outline sketches with color samples attached, including drawings or necessary descriptions of detail and its application; solicit estimates from three different costume shops; be responsible for selection of all contemporary costumes or selection from the performers' personal wardrobe where appropriate; supervise all necessary fittings and alterations; design, select, and/or approve all costumes accessories, such as headgear, gloves, footwear, hose, purses, jewelry, umbrellas, canes, fans, bouquets, etc.; supervise and/or approve hair styling and selection of wigs, hair pieces, moustaches and beards; attend dress rehearsals and the first out-of-town opening; and attend public performances from time to time for the purpose of conducting a normal check of the costumes.

Transportation and other expenses

The producer will reimburse the designer and assistants for all authorized out-of-pocket purchases made for the production and for authorized work transportation involved in New York and out-of-town.

No Design Alterations and Additional Payments

The producer agrees in the contract that he will not alter, or make substitutions for, the work created by the designer without the designer's approval. If additional work is needed over and above what was originally contracted for, the designer must be paid additional sums of money for the additional work.[78]

Strikes —Fire —Acts of God

There is a provision that the designer's obligations are subject to delays due to strikes, acts of God, fire, or other causes beyond the control of the designer, and that the designer is not responsible for damages which result through the failure or inability of contractors, builders, painters, or other persons who are hired to carry out the execution of the plans.

Title to Designs

The title to all drawings, designs, and specifications remain the property of the designer, who, however, may only use them for exhibition or use other than sale for use in another production. The producer and designer may agree to share in the proceeds of any sale of these designs to a gallery.[79]

Kickbacks Forbidden

The designer agrees that he will not accept any compensation, commission, gift, or any other remuneration or payment of any kind from any persons, firms, or corporations employed or engaged to carry out any work in connection with the production. This is intended to prevent the designer from receiving a kickback for referring work to contractors.

Concert Presentations

A concert presentation, whether musical or dramatic, is defined in the agreement by way of example. The productions of *Darrow* (Henry Fonda) and *Will Rogers U.S.A.* are not concert presentations, while the Hal Holbrook production of *Mark Twain* is considered a concert presentation.

When a bona fide pre-existing concert presentation is brought to

Broadway no fee shall be required. If any additional work is required a mutually negotiated fee will be agreed upon.

However, if the concert presentation is prepared solely for the purpose of making its appearance on Broadway, or Broadway prior to road show, the following fees shall apply: where work is actually required in any design category, a minimum of $1,500 shall be paid for that category for concert presentations in the Broadway, 46th Street, Imperial, Lunt-. Fontanne, Majestic, Mark Hellinger, Minskoff, Palace, St. James, Shubert, Uris, Winter Garden, and new or renovated theatres of comparable size; a minimum of $900 for each category in all other theatres. Pension and welfare contributions will be paid on all work performed.

A standing committee of six members, three selected by the union and three selected by the League, will review on an on-going basis a production's designation as a "concert presentation."[80]

Assistants

Assistants to lighting, costume, and scenic designers will be hired by the producer at the request of the designer. The work of the assistant will be to assist the designer in his work. A separate agreement must be filed with and approved by the union for each assistant. The assistant's fees, including required pension and welfare payments, must be filed with the union similar to the designer's fees. All designer's assistants will be employed at not less than these weekly rates; for scenic assistants, $352.50; lighting assistants, $330.00; and costume assistants, $330.00. If an assistant is on the road for less than five days he or she shall be paid for each day at a rate which is prorated at one-fifth or his weekly salary plus the $50.00 per diem.[81]

Billing

The producer will give the designers billing on the theatre houseboards, the theatre program, in the initial New York City newspaper display advertisements, and in other New York City newspaper display ads of similar content prior and subsequent to the New York opening. Billing will also be given to designers on window cards and three sheets where billing is given to any other creative participant in a production other than the author, starring actors, directors, and star choreographers. If the producer gives billing to more than two of the four categories mentioned, billing must be given to the designers.

The size of billing and format will be negotiated between the producer and designer. Under no circumstances will the billing be less than clearly legible in relation to the use of the medium. The designers' credits will be of equal size with each other and will be grouped together and placed in the traditional position in relation to the director or choreographer of a musical show and to the director of a dramatic show.[82]

Subsequent Productions

The original designer will have the right of first refusal for any subsequent reproduction of the company by the original producer. The designer has a minimum of two weeks to accept.

If the original designer declines to perform the work, the producer shall select a substitute designer subject to the approval of the original designer. The fee of the original designer will be reduced by the amount of the fee paid to the substitute designer.[83]

Importation

Importation, whether domestic or foreign, of scenery or scenic designs, lighting or lighting designs, or costume or costume designs are permitted. If work is not required to make the scenery, costumes, or lighting ready for Broadway, a designer need not be employed. The standing committee, described in the section on concert presentation, will determine if work will be required. The committee will also determine the fee to be paid to the designer employed to perform the necessary work. The producer must notify the League at least ninety days prior to the anticipated importation.[84]

Other Uses or Designs

The producer will not assign, lease, sell, license, or otherwise use, directly or indirectly, any of the designs and/or settings, costumes, or lighting for use in motion pictures, television, television cassettes, live broadcasts, simulcast, tapes or film, film cassettes, or any other use without the prior written approval of the designer and without negotiating with the designer for such use. Where the designs or any settings or parts of settings, costumes or parts of costumes, or lighting are used for reproduction for television broadcasting (whether live, filmed, or any other process), the producer will, prior to such use, deposit in the office of the United Scenic

Artists a cash bond. For any single use in any closed-circuit television or subscription television (whether by closed-circuit or air broadcast) the amount of the designer's fee for those designs actually used will be negotiated on a case-by-case basis; in commercial (free air broadcast) television, 50 percent of the designer's original design fee for those designs actually used; and in non-commercial (free air broadcast, such as PBS), 35 percent of the designer's original design fee for those designs actually used. The television rights granted under this provision are limited to a single broadcast and no rights are granted beyond this initial broadcast (except for PBS, when the broadcast rights are limited to one week following the initial broadcast), nor is any right granted to reproduce this television broadcast or showing by means of Kinescope, film, electronic tape, or other means, except upon written agreement with the designer and upon the payment of a fee for each broadcast. If used for promotional purposes and no one connected with the production is paid (other than actors at the applicable actors' minimum), no payment shall be made to the designer.[85]

Cost of Living

Effective January 1, 1981, January 1, 1982, and January 1, 1983, respectively, the minimum design rates, assistant rates, per diem and daily rate shall be adjusted by the percentage increase in the Consumer Price Index for the metropolitan New York area for the period November to November of the preceding year. For example, if the CPI for the period November 1979 to November 1980 increased by 5 percent, then the rates mentioned above would be increased by 5 percent effective January 1, 1981.

Reopening

On January 1, 1984, and on January 1, 1987, the agreement will be subject to reopening solely on the issues of minimum design rates, assistant rates, per diem, and daily rates. All other terms and condition of the agreement will remain fixed until December 31, 1898, and shall not be subject to any reopenings.

CHAPTER 11

Contracts with the Producers and Theatres

ASSOCIATION OF THEATRICAL PRESS AGENTS AND MANAGERS, UNION #18032

Jurisdiction

THIS ASSOCIATION IS COMMONLY KNOWN as ATPAM and covers the employment of press agents and managers. Managers include house managers employed by the theatre, and company managers who are employed by the production.

In fact, the agreement specifically provides that a contract of employment must be entered into with each employee and that a press agent, a house manager, and a company manager must be employed at all times that a production is playing within the union's jurisdiction.

The agreement states that the jurisdiction of the union is intended to include not only stage productions, but variety and vaudeville attractions, summer theatre, burlesque, road show picture presentations, theatrical entertainment, opera, musical presentations, concerts, ballets, carnivals, circus, sport expositions, and similar exhibitions and events. [1] The jurisdiction is not confined to the New York metropolitan area.

Wage Rates

The minimum weekly wage scale for the period commencing January 1, 1979, to December 31, 1980, is as follows:

House Managers/Company (All Cities)	$467.00
Press Agents	585.00
Company Managers (Dramatic Tour)	644.00
Company Managers (Musical Tour)	703.00
Press Agent (Tour)	703.00

Doubling Prohibited

An employee may not double. For example, one employee may not be both the house manager and company manager.[2]

Work Week

The work week consists of six working days from Monday to Saturday inclusive, with not more than eight performances during the six days. For each additional performance during a week, the house manager and company manager must receive an additional one-sixth of their respective weekly salaries. If a production is performed seven days a week in New York City (defined in the contract as the five boroughs of the greater city of New York) then the company and house manager must be paid for the seventh day at two-sixths of contractual weekly salary, in addition to any other compensation.

Time of Salary Payments

Salaries payable to managers and press agents must be paid no later than 6 p.m. on Friday of the week in which the services have been rendered, and expense statements must be paid at the same time if the statements are rendered sufficiently in advance for the payment to be made.

The employer must pay all transportation charges. All plane travel is to be made on scheduled first-class flights on major airlines. Non-scheduled flights are not permitted.

Summary Dismissal

An employee may be summarily dismissed for intoxication on duty or dishonesty in the discharge of his employment.

Production of Radio, TV, Motion Picture, or Industrial From Theatre

The house manager and company manager must receive one week's salary in addition to their regular salary when a radio, TV, motion picture performance, taping, or recording of substantially the entire production originates in the theatre. When a radio, TV, motion picture performance, taping, or recording of a portion of the entire production originates in the theatre — exclusive of radio or TV news programs, such as critical reviews — the house and company manager must be paid one-half week's pay, in addition to their regular salary. Such partial taping or recording must require not more than three days. The company manager and press agent must receive one week's pay in addition to their regular salary when a television performance of all or part of the production originates outside of the theatre. The house manager must receive not less than one week's regular salary whenever an industrial show performs one or more performances in the theatre during the week.[3]

Recording of Albums

The company manager and the press agent must receive one week's regular salary for each production album recorded.[4]

Closing Run of Less Then Four Weeks

An employer may close a play and terminate the employment of all members of the union engaged for the play or the theatre without any notice to the employees if the play runs for four weeks or less. They must, however, be paid the minimums; a company manager for a musical must be employed for at least five weeks prior to the Monday of the week in which the first public performance takes place (four weeks for a dramatic production), and a house manager must be employed at least one week prior to the day in which the first public performance takes place and for at least two weeks. This does not affect the tenure of the house manager, who is, as stated, entitled to tenure after one week's employment.[5]

Closing Run of Over Four Weeks

If the play has run more than four weeks, the employer must give one week's notice of closing. If the production closes on a Saturday night, the company manager and house manager must be paid at least one day's additional pay for the purpose of finishing the detail work in connection with the closing of the show. If either the company or house manager is called upon to render more than one day's service, he must be paid for each additional day an amount equal to one-sixth of his weekly salary.[6]

Fire—Strike—Riot—Etc.

If the show cannot be performed because of fire, accident, strike, riot, the public enemy, act of God, the illness of the star or a principal or featured performer, or if the employee cannot perform on account of illness or other valid reason, then the employee is paid only up to the date of the closing of the attraction if such be the case, or to the date of the employee's incapacitation.

Termination of Employment—Notice—Company Manager or Press Agent

If an employer wishes to terminate the employment of a company manager or press agent prior to the closing of a show, he must give the company manager or press agent at least two weeks' notice in writing if he has been employed for twelve weeks or less, and must give four weeks' notice in writing if the employment has been for more than twelve weeks but less than twenty-four weeks. A company manager or press agent who wishes to terminate his employment must give the employer at least two weeks' notice in writing.[7]

Midnight and Extra Performances—Pay and Commercial TV

House staff employees and company managers must also receive additional pay in the amount of one-fourth of the regular weekly salary for midnight performances. Extra performances are also covered in the agreement, and there is a provision that house and company managers must be paid for pay TV and commercial TV.[8]

Managers—Specific Terms

Minimum Term of Employment —Company Manager

A company manager for a musical production must be employed at least five weeks (four weeks for a dramatic production) prior to the Monday of the week in which the first public performance (paid or otherwise) takes place.[9]

Minimum Term of Employment —House Manager

A house manager must be employed at least one week prior to the day in which the first public performance takes place. The house manager must be on service at all times when the theatre is open to the public. A house manager must receive at least two weeks' salary, even if the production closes within the first week of its engagement. If a house manager is hired, he must continuously remain until the attraction is postponed or abandoned, and until he is given proper notice in accordance with the agreement.[10]

Limited Engagement —Company Manager

If a limited engagement in New York City is booked and played as a road tour after the original engagement in New York City, then the company manager must be paid his contracted salary as a company manager on tour throughout the New York engagement, rather than his salary as part of a New York engagement.

Sunday —Extra Pay —House and Company Managers

House managers and company managers are entitled to receive additional compensation for Sunday performances at the rate of one-sixth of the regular weekly salary for one or two performances. These additional payments are not made if Sunday is part of the regular six-day week.

House Staff Employees

House Staff Defined

House staff means the house manager and house press agent, if there is a house press agent. A house manager must be employed but a house press agent is optional.

Seasonal Employment

House staff employees are hired for a season (unless the lease, if the premises are leased, terminates before the end of the season) which runs from Labor Day to the Saturday night preceding the following Labor Day. Although the hiring is seasonal subject to other specific contract provisions, a house staff employee is not paid during a period that the theatre is dark. A house staff employee under contract for seasonal employment may accept other employment while his theatre is dark, provided that his new engagement does not interfere or conflict with his contract for seasonal employment.[11]

Dismissal During First Week

A house manager employed for the first time may be dismissed by an employer during the first week without the consent of the union, but after the first week the house manager has tenure and cannot be dismissed, except in accordance with the terms of the agreement.

Automatic Renewal

A house staff employee is automatically engaged for the following season unless he is otherwise notified in writing not later than May 31 of the current season.

Severance Pay

A house manager is entitled to receive four weeks' severance pay if he has up to three years of employment with the same management or same theatre, and six weeks' severance pay if over three years. Ten weeks' work in any season is considered a year of employment. The employee cannot receive credit for more than one year during any season. There is no severance pay if the employee is discharged for just cause.

Ownership Change —Severance Pay

If the ownership or the control of the theatre changes and the house staff is not continued, the employee must be paid severance pay due at time of sale or lease. The employer agrees, however, that he will exercise every reasonable effort to continue the same house manager on the job for the balance of his contract. Notice of any sale or rental of the theatre must be given to the union.

Theatre Owner Guarantees House Manager and Staff

The contract of employment for a house manager must be guaranteed by the theatre owner or operator, and if it is a four-wall rental of the theatre, then the house staff must be guaranteed payment by the theatre owner.

Press Agents

Minimum Term of Employment

A press agent must be employed four weeks prior to the Monday in which the first paid public performance is given when the attraction opens cold in New York City. If the attraction opens out of New York City on a pre-Broadway tour, a press agent must be employed at least five weeks prior to the first paid public performance.

If an attraction goes on tour after a New York City engagement, the employer must employ a press agent at least five weeks prior to the day of the first public performance on tour. This does not relieve the producer of the obligation to employ a press agent until the end of the New York engagement. [12]

Part Time

If the employer engages a press agent on a part-time basis prior to the times above set forth, then the press agent must be paid a one-half week's salary for part-time work during the fifth, sixth, seventh, and eighth weeks before the week in which the opening occurs in New York City, and one week's salary for part-time work for any four-week period prior to the eighth week before the week in which the opening occurs in New York City. A press agent may not be discharged unless he has received the equivalent of two weeks' full salary for such part-time work. The part-time arrangements are applicable only in New York City and, of course, are not applicable if the press agent is required to devote full time during any of the weeks. Oddly enough, the agreement provides that the union is the sole judge as to whether or not the employment is part time or full time.

Opening Postponed—Abandonment

If the opening is postponed or abandoned, the union and the employer will make arrangements for compensation to the press agent during the period that he does not render services, but the press agent must have received at least two weeks' full salary before the week in which the attraction was scheduled to have opened. [13]

After Opening Closing

If the press agent does not have a Run of the Play Contract, and the producer wishes to close the show, he may terminate the press agent's employment during the first week after the opening of the play and pay him for each day's compensation at one-sixth of the regular weekly salary on the condition that the play actually closes on the Saturday following the notice to the press agent. If notice is given before noon, the press agent need only be paid up to and including the day preceding the notice. If notice is given after noon, he must be paid up to and including the day that the notice is given to him. If the play continues beyond the Saturday, the press agent resumes work and receives a salary for the period of the layoff.

Temporary Closing

If a production is temporarily closed and reopens in the same city within four weeks, then the same press agent must be employed at least one week prior to the reopening. If the closing is longer than four weeks, the same press agent must be hired at least four weeks prior to the Monday of the week of the first paid public performance (the number depending upon whether the show is opening cold in New York City or out-of-town pre-Broadway), the same as above stated for a new production. [14]

Exclusive Services

The employer and press agent may mutually agree that the press agent's services are exclusive. An associate press agent's services are limited to engagements within the city of New York or pre-Broadway tours. No press agent on tour after the New York engagement, or after six weeks of a pre-Broadway tour, may handle more than one attraction, nor may a press agent handle more than one production on pre-Broadway tour at the same time.

Advertising Agency

After the press agent is hired, the producer will have to give considera-tion to the selection of an advertising agency. The advertising agency, as distinguished from the press agent, handles all of the paid advertising; the agency works in conjunction with the press agent. The agency does not cost the producer any additional money for placing the advertising, as an advertising agency is paid a percentage of the billing by the periodical or newspaper in which the advertising is placed. The agency is, of course, paid for art work.

The advertising agency will help with all of the art work and the ad layouts, will work up the logo, will advise where and when and how much to advertise, and will do this for the producer together with the advice of the press agent, who is, in fact, in charge of the entire advertising campaign.

ASSOCIATED MUSICIANS OF GREATER NEW YORK, LOCAL #802 AMERICAN FEDERATION OF MUSICIANS

Hiring of Musicians

All musicians are hired by the theatre; that is, they are signed by the theatre even though the payment of the musicians may be shared by the theatre and producer as discussed in the chapter on the theatre license agreement. A contractor selects and hires the musicians and signs the contract with the theatre. Very often the composer or conductor has someone that he would like in the orchestra, so this will influence the actual selection.

Jurisdiction

The League of New York Theatres has entered into a collective bargain-ing agreement with the musicians union which sets forth the minimum rates of pay as well as other provisions of employment.

Minimum Number of Musicians — Musical

The minimum number of musicians required in a musical show is set by contract. The following minimum number of musicians will be employed at the following theatres until the Sunday following Labor Day 1981 (all figures include the leader): [15]

Broadway, Mark Hellinger, Majestic, Imperial, Shubert, and Palace — 26

Lunt–Fontanne, Winter Garden, St. James, and 46th Street — 25

Minskoff and Uris — 24

Alvin — 20

ANTA, Martin Beck, and Billy Rose — 16

Broadhurst — 15

Biltmore, Longacre, Helen Hayes, Ambassador, Barrymore, Morosco, Music Box, Eugene O'Neill, Lyceum, Belasco, Cort, Plymouth, Royale, and Brooks Atkinson — 9

Circle in the Square, Golden, Booth, and Ritz are to be determined by the executive board of the union in consultation with the producer involved, with a maximum limitation of six. Every musical show must have an associate conductor who shall receive 30 percent additional over and above the minimum scale.

Minimum Number of Musicians — Dramatic

If a dramatic show includes less than four minutes of music, whether recorded or live, no musicians need be employed. However, if four to twenty-five minutes of recorded music is used, four non-playing musicians are required. If four to twenty-five minutes of live music is used, some combination of playing and non-playing musicians totaling four musicians must be employed. At least one of these musicians must be paid as a playing musician. If over twenty-five minutes of recorded music is used, six non-playing musicians will be employed. If over twenty-five minutes of live music is used in a dramatic show, at least six playing musicians will be employed. [16]

Electronic Musical Set-Ups

Electronic instruments such as the Moog, RCA Synthesizer, etc., will not be used without the express permission of the Local 802 Executive Board. Permission will be granted if the use of such electronic instruments does not diminish the earning capacity of any musician.

Out-of-Town Break-In

For a week's work during the out-of-town break-in, all musicians will receive the prevailing wage scale plus a separate check for expenses in the amount of $225 per week for the term of the contract.

Work Outside Pit

Orchestra members who are required to play in view of the audience and anywhere outside the pit shall receive in addition to their regular weekly salary the sum of $25 per week. If the musician is in costume, an additional $15 payment will be made.[17]

Week's Work Defined

A week's work shall consist of eight performances or less during six out of seven consecutive days.

Minimum Rates

The minimum salary for any playing musician is $445 per week. The minimum salary for a non-playing musician is $350 per week.[18]

Contractor Paid Extra

The contractor shall receive 50 percent additional, and the conductor shall receive 75 percent additional over and above the appropriate applicable rate set forth.

Librarians Paid Extra

Librarians shall be paid $55.63 per week.

Rehearsal Rates

2½ hours or less up to 6:30 p.m.

For rehearsals terminating not later than 6:30 p.m., the rates shall be as follows for 2½ hours or less:
Per musician: $25

Overtime

Overtime for rehearsals referred to above shall be paid for at the following rates for each thirty minutes or less of such overtime:
Per musician: $5

For One Hour After Night Performance

A one-hour rehearsal may be called immediately after a night performance, for which the following rates shall be paid for one hour or less terminating after midnight. The above one-hour rehearsal after the show may start after a ten-minute break with the usual five-minute intermission during the rehearsal thereafter.
Per musician: $18

For One Hour Before Evening Performance

For a one-hour rehearsal before an evening performance, the following rate shall be paid:
Per musician: $10

For One Hour on a Two-Performance Day or After Matinee

For a one-hour rehearsal on a two-performance day before or after a matinee performance, the following rates shall be paid:
Per musician: $15

After Midnight

Rehearsals starting at or after midnight for one hour or less shall be

paid for at the following rates with overtime in fifteen-minute segments:
Per musician: $18

During Break-In Period

During the break-in period of a show, a 3-hour rehearsal may be substituted in lieu of a performance. When such a rehearsal occurs in the afternoon to be followed by an evening service, it shall terminate no later than 6:30 p.m. The evening service following shall then begin no sooner than 8:00 p.m., allowing 1½ hours for dinner. Such services shall be either rehearsal or performance but not a combination of both.

Rehearsal Pianists

Rehearsal for all shows preparatory to opening and not in conjunction with orchestra shall be paid for at the following rates for a six-day, forty-hour week, exclusive of Sundays:

Per pianist: $445
Overtime prior to midnight: for each fifteen minutes or fraction thereof — $3
Rehearsals on Sunday: for six hours or less shall be paid for at the rate of $72

No more than eight hours' playing shall be permitted within a period of twelve hours in any one day, which must terminate no later than midnight.
Rehearsal pianists employed by the day shall be paid at the following rates:

Day Rate
Two hours or less terminating not later than 7:00 p.m., shall be $37.20.
Overtime on day call for one-half hour or less segments shall be $7.88.
Night Rate
Night rehearsals, three hours or less terminating not later than midnight, shall be $47.25.
Overtime continuing before midnight for one-half hour or less shall be $7.88.
Overtime continuing after midnight for each fifteen-minute segment shall be $5.91.
Audition Pianist
Two hours or less — $26.00.
Overtime (per hour or fraction thereof) — $13.00.[19]

Doubling Rates

No member of an orchestra or stage band can perform on more than one instrument unless he receives additional compensation. If he plays an additional unrelated instrument he must be paid an additional one-eighth basic scale per week, and if he plays two unrelated additional instruments he must receive a further sum of one-sixteenth basic scale per week. Doubling charges need not be paid if he is required to play certain instruments that are set forth in the contract as being very similar. That is, for example, a musician may play more than one member of the saxophone family, or the bassoon and contrabassoon, or the tuba and souzaphone, etc., at no additional charge.[20]

Notice of Closing

Musicians must be given at least one week's notice of the closing of the show unless members of other unions, such as Actors' Equity or Stage Hands, must get more than one week's notice, in which case the musicians must get the same.

Temporary Layoff

The show may be temporarily closed, and the musicians laid off temporarily, only for certain conditions set forth in the contract. If the star's contract permits a vacation, then a layoff for up to two weeks is permitted during any one year, provided that twenty-five weeks have accrued for each week of layoff. If the show is to be closed down temporarily because of poor business, a layoff of up to, but not exceeding, eight weeks may be made during the months of June, July, and August, but only if the consent of the union is obtained, which consent will not be unreasonably withheld. The musicians must be given two weeks' notice of layoff if a show is closed for poor business, and they may leave the engagement. If the show does not reopen after such a layoff, the musicians must be guaranteed at least two weeks' employment.

Dressing Rooms

The musicians must be furnished with convenient dressing rooms, rest rooms, lockers, and sanitary washroom.

Musicians Cannot Invest in Show

The agreement specifically provides that employers who are producers will not engage any musicians who invest in the producer's show.

Pay TV

In the event that there is a closed circuit or pay television production during the period commencing with the tryout period and ending one year after the end of the New York run, the employer must offer employment for said production to the orchestra who played the original show.

Original Cast Album

If an original cast album is made, the musicians that have been employed for the run of the show, and extra performing musicians, must be the ones who record the album.

Schedule Changes

Show schedule changes must be sent to the union as well as notification four weeks in advance of an Actors' Fund performance.

CHAPTER 12

Out-of-Town Pre-Broadway

Purpose—Audience Response

U P UNTIL THE EARLY 1960's, almost every Broadway show would go
out-of-town for a pre-Broadway run prior to the Broadway opening.
The purpose of an out-of-town try-out was to get audience response so that
the show could be fixed before it was subjected to the grueling attention of
the Broadway critics. Since taking a show out-of-town is an expensive
operation, someone eventually came up with the idea that it wasn't really
necessary.

It Depends on the Play

In fact, there are some plays that definitely should be tried out-of-town,
and others where it would make little difference. If a play does not have a
pre-Broadway tryout, it will probably preview on Broadway for a longer
period of time so that the Broadway preview audience response may be
utilized to fix anything that needs fixing, to the extent that it can be fixed, in
the available time.

Dramatic Differs from Musical

A Dramatic show probably should not go out-of-town unless there is a

225

star in the show, a star with out-of-town drawing power. The dramatic show without a star on a pre-Broadway tour is likely to have difficulty finding that audience from which a response is to be measured.

A musical, without a star, likewise should not go out-of-town on a pre-Broadway tour unless there is a subscription audience waiting to see the show when it arrives. If the theatre wants the show, then the theatre will make arrangements for you to take advantage of the subscription patrons which some theatres have. This could mean guaranteed box office receipts of $200,000 more or less each week. An example is the Fisher Theatre in Detroit, or the Mechanic in Baltimore, or the O'Keefe in Toronto, which do have subscription patrons.

A show — dramatic or musical — with a star, or a musical with a subscription ticket sale, should most usually plan on a pre-Broadway tour.[1]

How Long on the Road — And Previews

Most usually a straight dramatic show will stay on the road for from four to six weeks before coming into Broadway, and a musical will generally stay out for between six and ten weeks. After the show comes into New York, it may preview for a few days or a week, or, if it is in trouble and needs a lot of fixing, for several weeks if the money holds out. The very least is a run-through the dress rehearsal prior to the official opening.[2]

If the show does not go out-of-town, it may preview in New York for between one and three weeks. If it does not go out of town, it is likely that there is not an excess amount of money; in most instances, then, it will be difficult to preview the show for more than a week or two, as this costs money. Do not count of making money during the previews. It can happen, but only if you have that big box office drawing star, or if the play is written by a currently "hot" or famous author, or some other such unusual situation.

Sets and Props Moved by Truck or Train

Although the cast and crew may be flown between stops, the sets and props are almost always moved overland. If it is a big hop, it is possible that the sets and props will also be flown, but this is not usual on most moves. It is not usual to risk the chance of bad weather in transporting the sets, for a certain amount of time is required to set up after arrival. Overland means that a certain number of hours will be required from the time the play is out of the theatre; most likely the last truck will leave at about 8:00 a.m. following the last evening performance. There is no assurance if the sets are flown that they will arrive in time to be installed and ready to go for the next scheduled performance.

Where to Go Pre-Broadway

Most knowledgeable producers like to play New Haven because it is the cheapest to get on out-of-town with perhaps one exception — Wilmington, which might in some instances be cheaper, but has many other disadvantages.[3] Even though New Haven is the cheapest to put on, don't count on making money there, for in all probability you won't. The prices that can be charged in New Haven are limited and you will most likely not play there for more than a week or a week and a half. Traveling and setting up is costly, so ideally one would hope to stay in a theatre long enough to pay for the moving, the take-in, and the take-out.

Boston is a very desirable out-of-town tryout city. Boston has major critics (several of whom are well respected in the trade), and most shows can hope for mixed reviews from the Boston critics at the very least, even if the show is less than good. Of course, a good show will come off with unanimous raves. Boston generally means some business even if the show is less than good or just short of a disaster.

Philadelphia was once considered very good for a straight dramatic show. For some reason, not completely known or understood, Philly is now considered less desirable than it used to be.

Desirable Musical Houses

The most desirable musical houses are the very large houses. Weekly operating expenses for a musical are so great that unless the show is in a large theatre there is little chance of making money. The O'Keefe Theatre in Toronto and the Fisher in Detroit are ideal, since they are immense and can easily gross over $250,000 a week if you come in with a hot property.

Moving a Show—Deck Complicates Move

Moving a show is an expensive, complicated procedure. The main complication arises from the fact that the last thing out of the theatre has to be the first thing into the next theatre. The last truck to arrive with the floor (or deck, as it is called) must be the first to go into the new house. What sometimes happens is that some of the other parts of the set can be unloaded and flown while the deck is being put down.

A deck is a platform (usually eight inches deep) which contains all of the turntables and winches. Although some shows do not require a deck, almost all musicals — and many dramatic shows — need one.

Some Shows Own Two Decks

Sometimes a successful road company will own two decks, so that one can be disassembled while, at the next stop, the other is being installed.

Out-of-Town—Union Requirements

The union requirements are different in each theatre out-of-town. One pays more for the cast and there is a per diem expense payment which must be made to the cast and crew.

Out-of-Town Advertising

While it is out-of-town a show advertises in all of the major dailies, as the cost is relatively small. All of the out-of-town advertising for a large musical during a three-week stay in a city, for instance, might amount to a total of $20,000.

New York Advertising

In New York City at the present time, the only really important newspaper for theatre advertising is the *New York Times*. Some small amount is sometimes spent on the *New York Post* because it is an afternoon paper, and because it has an audience which, in some instances, responds to a particular kind of show. [4]

Out-of-Town—When to Fold—When to Get Help—Etc.

A show will never close out-of-town unless the producer runs out of money and has to close, or unless, in that most rare instance, a producer with loads of money decides that the show is so bad that it hasn't a chance and, for his reputation's sake, he must deliver the *coup de grace*.[5] There are countless show biz tales of out-of-town flops going on to become theatre history greats, so producers generally keep their shows alive and bring them in to New York for the opening night reviews if at all possible.

Musicians—On the Road

Usually a musical will carry five or six musicians and pick up enough others on the road to make twenty-five or twenty-six in all. The union does not really care whether the production carries the musicians with them or hires them on the road; however, since some of the out-of-town houses have contracts with the local musicians' union to hire a certain number of musicians, it is wise to leave room for the hiring of that number to fulfill the requirements. Then, too, it is more costly to carry the musicians with the production, and usually unnecessary, especially when very competent musicians may be employed in all of the towns booked into. There are usually between twenty-five to thirty musicians on most musicals.

Out-of-Town Advance Man

The advance man on a show that goes out-of-town is the press agent. If the show is on a road tour, the advance man never sees the company, since he is always a week or two ahead of them. His job is to make sure that as many people as possible learn of the show's coming. To accomplish this, he sets up press interviews for the stars and does whatever else he can to obtain publicity.

On a pre-Broadway tour, the advance man will go out of town two or three weeks ahead of time, but will usually only stay for a day or two in each town. He may come back for any important interviews and will come back for opening night. In his absence the press agent will ask the company manager to act as the clearing house for the local newspaper and radio people. This may be difficult in some instances, for it is not always easy for the company manager to go to a star, who may at the time feel harrassed and overworked, and ask him or her to get up an hour early to see a newspaper reporter that he or she has never heard of and that one cannot know the possible results of.

Out-of-Town License Agreement

The out-of-town license agreement is discussed in detail after the discussion of the Broadway license agreement. If one has an understanding of the Broadway license agreement, it is easier to understand the out-of-town license agreement.

CHAPTER 13

Broadway and Out-of-Town Theatre Licenses

Theatre Arrangement

THE THEATRE should be arranged for as soon as possible after one is certain that the production will proceed. If there is a theatre jam-up, it is possible for a show to wait around for one or two months for a theatre to open up. This could be expensive.[1]

BROADWAY THEATRE LICENSE AGREEMENT

License—Not Lease

The rental agreement for the use of a Broadway theatre is usually a license agreement rather than a lease. (There are some legal differences between a lease and a license agreement, but it will not be necessary to explore these in detail.) The theatre is generally in a strong bargaining position and for this reason the license agreement is usually used.[2]

No Standard License Agreement

There is no standard license agreement; however, there is an agreement

231

that is used by many theatres. Even the theatres not using that particular agreement have an agreement which contains most of the same terms, although sometimes in slightly different language.

Date of Occupancy

The theatre agreement will state that the theatre owner agrees to furnish the theatre from a certain specified date, which is the proposed opening date of the show. It is not unusual for the producer to have the theatre in advance of the opening date for the purpose of running paid previews. Under some circumstances, if a Broadway theatre is dark, it might also be used for rehearsals. This is not usual, however, since it is more economical for the producer to hire a rehearsal studio. In all events, it will be necessary to get into the house at least a few days before the first paid preview for the dress rehearsal.

What Theatre Furnishes

The theatre agreement provides that the theatre will furnish the theatre, house programs, ushers, porters, matrons, doormen, ticket takers, treasurer and assistant treasurer, house manager, and a specified number of stagehands. The stagehands furnished include a head property man, a head carpenter, and a head electrician, but not the company crew or production men working for the producer.

What Producer Furnishes

The producer agrees to present the play and to furnish the scenery, costumes, electrical and sound equipment, literary and musical material, advertising and press, and all other properties, materials, and services not furnished by the theatre.

Star Named and Term of Occupancy

The agreement will sometimes provide that the producer agrees to present the play with a star who is named in the agreement, and hires the theater for not less than twelve months, unless the show closes sooner or the license agreement is terminated, in accordance with the terms of the agreement.

The producer also agrees to display to the theatre owner or operator copies of the agreements with the star, and agrees that he will not alter or modify these contracts without the consent of the theatre.[3]

Percentage Payment for Theatre

The theatre owner is paid a guaranteed payment against a percentage of the box office receipts.

Theatre Guarantee

The guaranteed payment is usually computed as the amount necessary to cover the theatre owner's expenses, so that if the theatre owner is going to make any money it must be because he has a show in his theatre that is selling tickets and earning money at the box office. The range of weekly guarantees on license agreements in the city of New York is from $17,000 to $50,000.

License Fee—Percentage of Gross

The license fee (which would be rental if it were, in fact, a lease rather than a license agreement) is usually 10 percent of the gross weekly box office receipts. Sometimes if the weekly guarantee is larger ($50,000 instead of $17,500) the fee will be 20 percent of the gross weekly box office receipts in excess of the amount required by the theatre to cover expenses. The percentage arrangements will vary, depending largely on how badly the theatre owner or operator wants a particular show in his theatre.

Gross Receipts Defined

Gross receipts are computed as the receipts from the sale of tickets less admissions and other taxes and broker's fees, commissions, and discounts, if any, payable upon such receipts, and less any amounts required to be paid by the theatre or the producer for pension and/or welfare benefits when the source of the payments are funds representing a reduction or elimination of admission's taxes by any governmental entity. This would cover the 5 percent New York City amusement tax which was discontinued, and the proceeds of which were turned over to certain unions to cover payments toward the pension and welfare funds. Losses because of non-payment of checks or non-collection of bank orders reduce the gross receipts to the extent of the loss.

Charge for Air Conditioning

The agreement has a provision that the producer will pay a fixed amount whenever the air-conditioning system is in operation. The additional amount will usually be $100 or $150 per performance.

Stop Clause

Since the theatre owner or operator relies upon the gross box office receipts for the licensing fee, there is also a provision in almost all license agreements to the effect that if the gross box office receipts are less than a specified amount for two weeks (this amount is very often referred to in the license agreement as the "stop clause sum"), then the producer or the theatre may terminate the agreement. The stop clause in some contracts specifies two weeks, and in some contracts two "consecutive" weeks. A stop clause protects both the theatre and the producer in that if the gross receipts of a show fall below the stop clause amount for two consecutive weeks (or non-consecutive, depending upon the contract), then either the theatre or the producer can get out of the obligations of the agreement.[4]

Stop Clause Amount Computation

The stop clause is computed roughly on the basis of what the weekly gross receipts must be for the producer to break even. The amount is sometimes left blank when the license agreement is entered into and later decided upon when the show comes into New York and the parties are in a better position to fix the amount. The stop clause sum usually ranges between $35,000 and $100,000 (although some musicals may finally end up requiring more than $100,000 each week to break even).

Break Even

What a show requires to break even depends upon a lot of factors. If it is a dramatic show, other than a show starring a single performer, then the show may break even at between $60,000 and $75,000 of gross weekly box office receipts. If it is a single performer show, then it might possibly break even for as little as $30,000. If the show is a musical, then it will break even at something between $120,000 and $160,000 of gross box office receipts.

Neither the producer nor the theatre may purchase tickets for the purpose of increasing the gross weekly receipts above the stop clause sum.

Stop Clause Termination Procedure

In order to terminate in accordance with the stop clause, one party must give the other party written notice no later than the Monday night following the two weeks in which the box office receipts were not in the amount of the "stop clause sum." If the notice is given, then the run ends at the close of the evening performance on the next succeeding Saturday.

The agreement may be terminated at the end of any two weeks during which the receipts fall below the stop clause sum, even if the agreement could have been sooner terminated at the end of any prior week, but was not. If the opening performance occurs after the beginning of a week, so that less than eight performances are given before the end of the week, then that part of a week is considered a week for the purposes of the stop clause determination, and the stop clause sum is reduced by one-eighth for every performance less than eight given that week.

Theatre Security Deposit

The producer must make a deposit with the theatre as security for the payments of the minimum weekly guarantee and the other obligations under the agreement. The deposit will generally range roughly between one and two times the weekly guarantee. Thus the deposit will probably be between $30,000 and $50,000. Some theatre agreements also have a provision that the theatre in its discretion may demand an additional deposit from the producer if the theatre estimates that the expenses which will be incurred by the producer, for which the theatre may be responsible, will be in excess of what was originally anticipated. This may seem like a harsh term, and should be deleted from the agreement whenever possible, but one ought not be surprised if it's there.

Increase in Stop Clause Sum and Guarantee

There is another provision in the agreement which is grossly unfair, but is nevertheless often there and should be expected. The agreement may state that the amount fixed as the stop clause sum and the minimum weekly guarantee were based on the potential gross receipts of the theatre at capacity for the play previously presented. If, at any subsequent time, the potential receipts at capacity are increased, then the stop clause sum and the minimum weekly guarantee are to be increased by multiplying each of them by a factor — the denominator consisting of the present gross receipts at capacity, and the numerator consisting of the gross receipts at capacity as so increased.

There is often a further provision to the effect that, regardless of anything else in the agreement to the contrary, the stop clause sum will in no event be less than 50 percent of the potential gross receipts at capacity, and the minimum weekly guarantee will be no less than one-eighth of the potential gross receipts at capacity. This provision is very often deleted from the form agreement, and the specific dollar amount fixed for each of these items is applicable.

Joint Control of Advertising

The agreement also may provide that the advertising is under the joint control of the producer and the theatre; however, the producer's attorney will often succeed in striking this from the agreement so that the producer may control his own advertising.

Must Vacate Theatre Within Fixed Time

If the producer does not remove the production from the theatre within a fixed time (the agreement will say twelve hours, but this may be changed to twenty-four or forty-eight hours) after the closing performance, then the theatre may dispose of the sets and props or store them at the producer's expense.

Producer Pays Extra for Star's Temporary Absence

If a star or featured player is temporarily prevented from appearing in a performance because of illness or otherwise, then the amount of the salary for that person for the period of the non-performance may be deemed a receipt payable by the producer to the box office and divisible according to the provisions under which the gross receipts are divided. Such an amount "may be" deemed a receipt to be treated in this fashion, for the agreement contains such a provision. Sometimes the provision may be stricken from the agreement at the time of the execution, but even if it isn't, this is one of the "owner's provisions" that the owner may enforce, but often does not.

Producer Pays Extra for Star's Termination or Non-Appearance

The agreement further provides that if the employment of the star or featured players, named in the agreement, is terminated, then in addition to any other damagers the theatre may increase its share of the receipts by an additional 5 percent. If a performance is suspended as a result of the star or featured player's non-appearance, then the agreement provides that the producer must pay the theatre an amount equal to the theatre's share of the gross receipts at capacity. These provisions are somewhat harsh and are usually stricken from the agreement before signing. Even if the provisions remain, the theatre may elect not to enforce them. This sometimes does happen.

Theatre May Terminate Agreement If Star Leaves

The theatre may also terminate the agreement upon forty-eight-hours notice to the producer if the star or featured player does terminate. If this part of the agreement cannot be deleted, one should at least attempt to make it applicable solely to a star.

Producer Pays If Opening Delayed

If the producer fails to open the play on the date set forth in the agreement, it is provided that the producer must pay the theatre all of its expenses, including salaries of the theatre personnel during the delay, and must also pay a fixed dollar amount for each week that the opening is

delayed. The payment is prorated for less than an eight-performance week.
It is not unusual that the weekly penalty (the fixed dollar amount added to
the expenses) should be an amount between $2500 and $5000, depending
upon the theatre's bargaining power. In lieu of the expenses and the
additional dollar amount, the theatre may receive the sum which is set forth
as the minimum weekly guarantee, or the pro-rata share if the delay is less
than a week, based on eight performances.

Theatre Sometimes Waives Late Opening Payment

The penalty for a late opening is sometimes waived by the theatre if
there is a good relationship between the producer and the theatre, and if the
opening is delayed only from one to three weeks. Long delays will usually
result in a forfeiture of the weekly guarantee amount for the period of the
delay, especially if the producer wants the theatre to hold the house for him.
Postponements are very difficult for the theatre owner, for the period that
the show is postponed is generally the time that theatre parties are booked,
so that in addition to the loss of revenue, it can mean great inconvenience.

Theatre May Terminate If Opening Is Delayed

If the play is not presented during the two weeks after the scheduled
opening date, the theatre may terminate the agreement by giving written
notice to the producer. If the agreement is thus terminated, the theatre (at its
election) may either receive payment for expenses plus the fixed dollar
amount (the penalty amount previously referred to) for the period from the
opening date until delivery of the notice of cancellation, or in the alternative may receive twice the weekly minimum guarantee.

Guarantee Doubled for Early Closing

If the play closes within two weeks after the opening date, the weekly
guarantee is twice the amount of the minimum weekly guarantee as set
forth in the agreement. This provision is also sometimes stricken from the
contract by mutual agreement at the time that the negotiations take place.

Producer's Insurance

There are specific provisions in the agreement to the effect that a producer must carry certain insurance, and that he agrees to make payment for all social security, unemployment insurance, and disability benefits which he is obligated to pay for his employees.

Concessions are Theatre's

The theatre has the exclusive right to operate or contract with others for the operation of concessions of all kinds. Some license agreements permit the producer to sell souvenir books through the theatre's concessionaire if the producer pays to the concessionaire a commission of not less than 10 percent of the gross sales.

No Radio—TV—or Other Theatre Production

The producer agrees to certain other commitments which he must abide by. He agrees, for example, that he will not permit the play to be done on radio, television, or in any other theatre during the term of the agreement with this theatre, and for a period of eight weeks after the end of the run. There is an exception noted that radio or television broadcasts not exceeding fifteen minutes may be made for publicity purposes. The producer also agrees that if a star or featured player appears on television, the producer will use his best efforts to get credit for the play at the theatre.

Producer Responsible for Theatre Alterations—Compliance with Laws—Etc.

In addition, the producer agrees that he will not make any changes or alterations in the theatre; that he will present the play in accordance with all existing laws; that he will pay for breakage and damage; that he will not violate the copyright laws or infringe upon any literary rights of other persons; that all scenery, costumes, and other props will be fireproofed; that any improvements required by the star or other persons shall be the producer's sole expense, but that any alterations or furnishings placed in the theatre (which can only be done with the theatre's consent) become the property of the theatre; that if the producer receives a payment in consideration of his permitting the star to terminate the contract, then the theatre will receive 50 percent of any such payment, and that the producer will restore the theatre to its original condition if any changes have been made.

Theatre May Terminate If Fire — Act of God — Etc.

If the theatre is rendered unsuitable due to fire, national or local calamity or emergency, act of God, strike, labor dispute or other unforeseen contingency, the theatre is not responsible to the producer and the theatre may terminate the agreement upon twenty-four hours notice to the producer.

Producer Will Not Interfere with Union Agreements

The producer agrees that he will not do anything contrary to or inconsistent with any of the collective bargaining agreements between the theatre and the unions, nor will he interfere with the contract with Playbill, Inc.

Theatre Controls Box Office

Although the sale of tickets is under the joint control of the theatre and the producer, the agreement provides that the theatre has sole and exclusive control of the supervision of the box office and its personnel, and that all gross receipts are under the control of the theatre until a settlement is made. The theatre license issued by the Department of Licenses requires that its employees be in charge of the funds. The tickets are ordered only by the theatre, and the producer agrees that he will not order, distribute, or issue tickets without the theatre's prior consent.

Theatre House Seats and Free Seats

The agreement will provide that the theatre is entitled to purchase a certain number of house seats for opening night and a different number for each performance after opening night. In addition to the house seats which it may purchase, it may also provide that the theatre is entitled to a certain number of free tickets. If the play is a dramatic production, the agreement may provide that the theatre is entitled to purchase between sixty and seventy orchestra tickets for opening night, and if it is a musical, between eighty and ninety. For all other performances, the theatre may be entitled to purchase between thirty and forty house seats, which may be reduced to between ten and fifteen if there is a full theatre party on any specific night. The theatre will try to get between twenty and thirty-five tickets for each performance, including opening night, free of charge. Try to limit or avoid this.

Press Seat Limitation

The number of press seats for opening and second night is under the joint control of the parties and the number is set forth. Opening night and second night will probably have between 160 and 200 free press seats.

Theatre May Terminate If Producer Is Without Funds

The agreement contains two provisions which are eminently unfair to producers and should, if possible, be changed or deleted. One provision is to the effect that the theatre relies upon the representation that the producer has sufficient funds to finance the show and if the theatre, after the agreement is signed, determines *in its sole discretion* that the funds are not available to the producer for this purpose, then the theatre may, upon seven days' notice terminate the agreement and return the security deposit to the producer, less any expenses incurred by the theatre. The theatre ought to decide before it enters into the agreement whether or not it wants a particular production, and ought not be permitted to cancel the agreement if, in its sole discretion, it decides that the producer may not have enough money.

Theatre May Terminate If Producer Breaches Terms or If Law Suit Seems Likely

The other provision which seems unfair is to the effect that the theatre, in addition to its remedies at law or in equity, may terminate the agreement upon forty-eight hours' notice if the producer breaches any of the terms of the agreement, or if the theatre (again in the theatre's sole discretion) determines that the showing of the play will subject the theatre to actions for damages, fines, penalties, revocation of license, copyright infringement, or any other legal action or proceeding. It's perfectly obvious that the way this clause is worded may be an out for the theatre upon any grounds. Any *threatened* action against the theatre, no matter how small, could be used by the theatre as the excuse for terminating the agreement.

Play Must Continue in Theatre

The contract specifically provides that the producer must continue the play in the theatre unless this agreement is terminated, and that even an interim closing of the play for a holiday, star's vacation, or otherwise without the theatre's consent, constitutes a breach of the agreement by the producer.

Physical Limitations

The agreement contains specific provisions with respect to certain physical requirements. The producer agrees that not more than twelve hundred pounds will be placed every twelve inches on the headblock beam, that the spot line cables, platforms, etc. will be constructed and used in a certain manner, etc., and if the producer does not comply with these requirements, the theatre may do so at the producer's expense.

Theatre May Use Injunction

If the producer does not comply with any terms of the agreement, the theatre is entitled to enforce its rights by injunction, and the producer must pay the theatre's reasonable attorney's fees and disbursements.

Changes and Approvals Must Be in Writing

This agreement states that it cannot be changed or terminated orally, and contains the entire agreement between the parties. All approvals required by the theatre are not granted unless they are in writing.

Limitation on Assignment

The producer may not assign or transfer the license agreement except that he may assign it to a corporation controlled by the producer or a limited partnership (of which the producer is a general partner) organized by the producer to produce the play. In the event of such assignment, the producer, of course, continues primarily liable for all his obligations and an executed copy of the assignment must be delivered to the theatre. If the theatre is sold, or if the theatre lease is transferred, the license may be assigned by the theatre and in such event the original theatre owner or operator would be relieved of any further responsibility or liability under the agreement.

Theatre May File Form 1099

The agreement further provides that the producer authorizes the theatre to prepare and file a joint form 1099 information return on behalf of the producer and theatre with respect to all payments by the theatre and the producer to theatre party agents as compensation for services rendered by them.

OUT-OF-TOWN LICENSE AGREEMENT

Sharing of Gross Receipts

The out-of-town first-class Theatre License Agreement is very similar to the Broadway License Agreement. It is most usual that the producer pays $25,000 guaranteed (to cover the theatre expenses) plus 10 percent of the gross weekly box office receipts.

Guarantee and Deposit

The amount of the weekly guarantee and the amount of the security deposit vary with the size of the house, whether or not it is a musical or a non-musical coming into the theatre, and other factors. The weekly guarantee will vary between $7500 and $15,000, and the security deposit is usually the amount of the one-week guarantee.

Stop Clause Not Usual

There is no reason to have a stop clause, since in most instances the play tries out out-of-town only for a very limited engagement.

Equipment Must Comply with Laws

The electrical equipment brought into the theatre by the producer must comply with all local statutes and laws.

P.A. System Furnished but Not Operator

The producer may use the public address system in the theatre at no additional charge; however, it is most usual for the producer to pay for the operator who operates the P.A. system.

Souvenir Book Sales

The license agreement sets forth the maximum that may be charged for souvenir books, and also provides that the theatre must be given either a 10 or 20 percent commission, which is paid to the house concessionaire. All other concessions are reserved for the theatre.

Penalty to Producer if Star Out

In the out-of-town license agreement, there is also a penalty provision in the event that the star or featured player leaves the show or cannot perform.

Theatre Furnishes Treasurer and Assistant

The theatre will furnish a treasurer and assistant treasurer, but if it is necessary to engage a second assistant treasurer in the box office, the salary of the second assistant is shared by the parties in the same percentage that they share the receipts. Any additional box office help required is paid for solely by the producer.

Theatre Use Before Opening

Some out-of-town license agreements will provide that for a stated period prior to opening, a fixed licensing fee is paid. This may be between $1,500 and $2,500 per week. When a fixed sum is paid for the theatre prior to opening, the producer must usually also pay for the cost of electricity during that period. Bear in mind that the theatre must (or ought to at any rate) be used for rehearsals for a few days prior to the opening.

Theatre Designates Newspaper for Advertising—Insurance—Fireproofing Sets—and Miscellaneous

It is not unusual to provide that the theatre may designate the newspapers in which the advertising appears. The theatre maintains jurisdiction of the sale of the tickets at all times. The producer agrees that he will carry liability and compensation insurance during the time that the play is at the theatre. Scenery and paraphernalia must be fireproofed. An out-of-town lease also contains certain limitations on the appearance of the company in clubs, restaurants, or other places patronized by the public. If the show closes for further rehearsals, or due to sickness or inability of the principal performer, there is a provision that the producer must pay a fixed amount each week that it is closed.

CHAPTER 14

Pre-Opening — During Run — After Opening

PRE-OPENING

Star and Director—Raising Money

WITH BUT ONE OR TWO EXCEPTIONS, having a particular star or director helps very little in raising money for a production. The one or two exceptions are those very rare persons whose names have become household words and who cannot possibly do anything that does not make money, even if it is something somewhat less than good.

Record Company Financing

Record companies have in the past invested large sums of money in musicals in exchange for the right to do the original cast album. A record company's investment interest varies from time to time, depending on the recent luck they may or may not have experienced. Very often a producer is in a position to make a pre-production record deal for an original cast album if he wants to, but if it does not include an investment in the show as part of the deal, the producer will usually not accept it, but will wait until after opening to arrange for the cast album. If the play is a smash hit, then the production makes a better deal, and if the production is a flop, the album rights are of little value irrespective of when the deal is made.

Film Company Investing

It has become the current practice of some film companies to make investments and to actually produce some plays. The film company expects a preferred bargaining position on the film rights (such as an option of first negotiation and an option of first refusal). Sometimes a film company will make an outrageous offer for film rights in a play in exchange for the investment and sometimes they don't get it.

Insurance

Most Broadway producers will find it advisable to have the following insurance coverage:

Workman's compensation (this coverage is mandatory).

Disability insurance (mandatory in New York).

A theatrical floater policy. This is an all-risk policy (with some minor exceptions) covering costumes, electrical equipment, sets, and basically all the other personal property of the show except buildings and improvements.

Business interruption coverage. This is coverage for an indirect profit loss caused by loss of the theatre, loss of sets, or some other similar happening.

Personal effects insurance (required by Actors' Equity Association). This is an Inland Marine Form Policy, which covers the actors' and stagehands' jewelry, clothing, furs, and personal property.

Liability insurance insuring injuries to the public and the cast and crew. The coverage includes bodily injury and property damage.

Non-appearance coverage for a star. If the star does not appear for one reason or another, the producer may suffer a large loss. This insurance coverage may range between $200,000 and $500,000.

Of course, there are many other kinds of insurance to cover special things and special events.

The theatres will, in most instances, have the following insurance coverage:

Workmen's compensation for all theatre personnel.

Fire and allied peril coverage on the building.

Fire and allied peril coverage on the contents of the building.

Boiler and machinery insurance covering the heating and air-conditioning equipment.

Business interruption (rental insurance) to compensate for the theatre being dark because of fire or other peril.

Broad form money and securities coverage inside and outside, which would cover box office hold-up and payroll hold-up.

Fidelity bond.

There is a large variety of miscellaneous insurance policies which a theatre owner might carry to cover glass, signs, marquees, and numerous other parts of the theatre.

In most cases, however, there is a very small market for this kind of insurance, and, in some instances, it is not easy to place it.

Bonds Required

Before the show goes into production, the producer will be required to furnish certain bonds and guarantees which have been previously discussed. The following will be required:

Actors' Equity Association — Two weeks' salary.

A.T.P.A.M. — two weeks' salary.

Stagehands, payable to I.A.T.S.E. for Local No. 1 — one week's salary.

American Federation of Musicians — one week's salary.

American Federation of Musicians, Arrangers & Copyists — bond varies in amount, usually between $2,500 and $5,000.

Wardrobe Attendants, Local No. 764 — one week's salary.

United Scenic Artists — payment for the entire set, costume, and lighting design must be made in advance to the union.

The theatre — a deposit usually in the amount of one or two weeks of the guaranteed rental.

The union guarantees are for the minimum salaries provided for in New York City.

Independent Booking Office, Out-of-Town Booking

The Independent Booking Office came into existence as a result of the efforts of the New York theatres to expedite and coordinate out-of-town bookings. It functions as a non-profit corporation and handles the arrangements for all pre-Broadway bookings and all first-class or national tours. It does not handle second-class tours or bus-and-truck tours. In the event that the out-of-town theatre does not have its own license agreement, the Independent Booking Office form is filled in and used.

The fee of the Independent Booking Office is $150.00 per playing week, which is shared equally with the producer paying $75.00 and the theatre owner paying $75.00. For part of a week, the fee is prorated based on a six-day week, so that each party pays $12.50 per day.

Play Doctor

Payment

Rarely does a production call someone in to rewrite a show, as most doctoring comes from directors or persons acting as directors. Generally what is needed is a point of view about the script, and this comes from the director, and not from rewriting. If a top director is called in to doctor a show, it can cost as much as $2,000 per day for his services. Expensive, yes, but if it means saving the show, it is money well spent. Usually the doctor–director will be paid $5,000, or $10,000 as a fee, plus 1 or 2 percent of the gross receipts. Directors have also done doctoring for different considerations. On one occasion the doctor was given a well-known European sports car for the job. (It happens to have been a used car at that!) Other gifts are sometimes settled on.

Billing

The billing credits are often a hassle when there is a director replacement. Often the new director does not want his name on the billing, and often the original director agrees with him. If the new director wants billing and the original director will not permit the removal of his name, the producer has just one more problem to deal with and to settle. But then this is a producer's role.

Advertising

Most usually the first big ad for a show is run during the second or third week of rehearsal; however, it the show has a big star, the first big ad might be as early as four or five months before the scheduled opening.

Advance Sale

The treasurer handles the money and is personally responsible if there is a shortage or if the show closes and there are insufficient funds to make refunds for the advance sale. Although tickets are printed as far in advance as needed, on a dramatic show it is unlikely that they would be printed farther in advance than ten weeks (sometimes six weeks, or something between six and ten) unless the show has a lot of theatre parties signed. A musical show would most likely start with tickets for twelve weeks in advance, unless there is indication of a huge advance sale and a long run.

A large advance sale by itself is not enough to provide a producer with a great feeling of security. What is important is how far the advance sale is spread out. Even a million dollar advance on a big musical might not by itself spell success. In a theatre grossing $250,000, that would mean that the equivalent of four weeks' tickets are sold in advance. If the equivalent of four weeks' tickets is spread over thirty weeks or more and there is little sale at the window, the show would be in big trouble — million dollar advance sale notwithstanding.

Ticket Sale Deductions

There are no amusement or other taxes on the sale of theatre tickets. The only deduction is the 5 percent that used to be for the New York City amusement tax, which is now used for the union pension and welfare plans and shared by the unions in accordance with the arbitration award of Burton Turkus, dated April 23, 1963.

Ticket Brokers

The box office personnel deal with the ticket brokers. By and large, ticket brokers can do very little to make or break a show, since they more or less cater to the demand for tickets rather than being a very moving force in creating the demand.

Theatre Parties

In a Shubert House, the theatre takes care of the theatre party arrangements. In other houses, the general manager or the producer arranges an audition for the theatre party agents. It is then necessary to find out what dates each may want and shuffle things around so that everyone is happy.

A theatre party contract will specify the name of the star and if that star does not appear in the show, then the party may be cancelled and the money must be refunded.

DURING RUN

Range of Production Costs

The range of cost of a dramatic show is between $250,000 and $350,000, and a musical between $1,000,000 and $1,500,000.

Potential Weekly Gross and Weekly Net

One can plan on a dramatic show grossing between $100,000 and $150,000 at capacity, depending upon the size of the theatre, and a musical at capacity grossing between $150,000 and $250,000. A dramatic production will likely break even when it grosses between $40,000 and $65,000, and a musical between $125,000 and $175,000.

Time Necessary to Recoup

If a dramatic show is doing sold out business, it is not unusual for it to break even and recoup the total investment in six or seven weeks. A show grossing $125,000 per week could have a $60,000 profit each week and recoup a $350,000 investment in six weeks. These are not unusual amounts.

A movie sale can, of course, speed the recoupment considerably since, as has been noted, the production will share 40 percent of such receipts.

A musical will take longer to recoup since it will cost much more to mount. However, the amounts of money that may be made from a musical are commensurate with the risk. They can make a lot of money.

AFTER OPENING

Reviews—What to Do

The morning after the opening there is customarily a meeting in the office of the advertising agency to plan the expenditure of money for advertising. The producer, the press agent, the general or company manager, and sometimes the attorney are present. If the show gets raves the job is an easy one. If the show gets unanimous pans, although painful, the job is once again an easy one. The difficult area is when a play gets mixed reviews and there is a chance that it could make it, but it's hard to tell how good that chance is and therefore difficult to know how much money to spend to try to keep it alive.

When to Close

It is not an easy decision to close a show if there is the possibility of business developing at a later date. One has to weigh the amount of the advance sale and the number and size of the theatre parties against the current box office sales and try to come up with some kind of divination of what the future holds. It isn't always easy. Usually when a show starts downhill there is very little chance that it will make it, and often ego, or what have you, motivates keeping it open.

National Company

If a show is a big hit in New York, then there is no problem at all with a national company since the show will probably get guarantees of a certain amount everywhere it goes.

Generally the production must be simplified technically — that is, the scenery and props — so that it may be moved in and out of towns with some degree of speed. The staging is most generally a duplication of the Broadway production. Usually the stage manager puts the show together and then the original director comes in for the last week of rehearsals and takes it out of town through the opening night.

Most often the show will have a dress rehearsal with the Broadway set before it leaves New York, with an invited audience, for the first performance out of town is generally with a paid audience.

As with the pre-Broadway tour, the independent booking office sets up the bookings and is paid, as with the pre-Broadway bookings, $75 each week by the producer and another $75 by the theatre.

Producer

A producer ought to do what the name implies, "produce." Strangely enough, show biz happens to appeal to a wide assortment of people. Sometimes people go into the business for the wrong reasons. Playboys should restrict their activities to other than theatre. Sharpies who want to cash-in-quick should stick to the racetrack. One ought not practice being a dilettante while producing. Producing means making a lot of difficult decisions and carrying them out. Painful as it may be, it sometimes means firing your favorite star, or even your favorite person, if he happens to be the director and is not right for the show.

A producer has to be in a position to select wisely, raise money, hire, fire, influence people, convince people that they should or should not do something, mediate disputes, encourage and assist people to work together and to get along together, buy wisely, sell sharply, hold hands and soothe heads, comfort the sick, assist the needy, and to be all things to all people. In a word, to "produce."

Appendices

APPENDIX A

Dear   :

This letter will confirm our agreement in connection with your
furnishing part of the front money for a proposed
             presently entitled   ,
by   .

In consideration of your investing the sum of $10,000 to be used
for pre-production expenses in connection with the proposed
production of   , it is agreed that you will receive
the percentage that amount will purchase as a limited partner in
the limited partnership which will be formed to produce the
           and, in addition, there will be assigned to you a
percentage from the general partner's share of the profits equal
to the percentage the $10,000 purchases for you as a limited
partner. For means of illustration only, in the event that the
production is budgeted for   , then you will receive
  % of the profits of the production company as a limited partner
and   % of the net profits of the company from the general
partner's share of such profits.

All payments to you from the general partner's share assigned to
you will be paid to you at the same time and under the same terms
and conditions that the general partner's profits are paid to
           as general partner.

The budget for the   has not as yet been completed and
the figures as above set forth are only for the purposes of
illustration.

Money that you have turned over to me (or us) as front money will
be used for the proposed production of   . However, you
do understand that as front money it is risk capital and that
my (or our) only obligation will be to spend the money for proper
pre-production expenses in connection with the proposed
production. If for any reason the   is abandoned by me
(or us), the only obligation will be to account to you for the
funds spent and to return to you and the other front-money
investors any unused balance of such funds on deposit, which
funds will be returned to the front-money investors pari passu.

With the hope that this turns out to be a profitable investment
for all of us.

Sincerely,

_____

ACCEPTED AND AGREED TO:

_____

APPENDIX B

AGREEMENT made as of this   day of   , 19 ,
by and between   , residing at
(hereinafter sometimes referred to as the "Purchaser") and
          , residing at   (hereinafter
sometimes referred to as the "Owner"), with respect to the
original literary work entitled   .

In consideration of the covenants and conditions
herein contained and other good and valuable consideration,
it is agreed:

FIRST: The Owner does hereby warrant and represent
that:

(a)   is the sole author of an
original literary (type of work) entitled
(hereinafter sometimes referred to as the "Work"); that
the Work was registered for copyright in the Copyright
Office on the   day of   , 19 , under Entry
No.   , in the name of   .

(b) The aforesaid copyright was renewed in the
Copyright Office in the name of   on the
day of   , 19 , under Entry No.   .

(c) Motion picture and television rights in the
Work have been conveyed to   .

(d) The Owner has full right and authority and
is free to enter into this Agreement and to grant, upon
the terms and conditions hereof, the rights herein
granted and no right, title, and interest now valid or
outstanding for or to the Work or the rights herein
granted by which such rights or the full enjoyment and
exercise thereof might be encumbered or impaired
heretofore has been conveyed or granted to any other
person, firm or corporation by the Owner or his
predecessor in interest.

(e) No adverse claim has been made on him with
respect to the rights herein granted in the Work, and
he knows of no claim that has been made that the Work
infringes upon the copyright in any other work or
violates any other rights of any person, firm or
corporation, and the Work was not copied in whole or
in part from any other work.

(f) The Owner has the sole unencumbered,
unrestricted and lawful right to enter into this
Agreement and to make the grant hereinafter provided
for and has the full right, power and authority to
make, enter into and to fully perform this Agreement
in each and every respect; no consent or permission
of any authors' society, performing rights society,
firm or corporation whatsoever is required in
connection with the grant in this Agreement made, or
in connection with any of the subject matter of this
Agreement.

(g) At the present time there are outstanding no
rights to present a stage adaptation or radio
production and the only rights (other than the
publishing rights) which are still in effect are the
motion picture and television rights heretofore
referred to.

(h) There is no claim or litigation concerning
or purporting to affect the Owner's right or title in
or to the Work as herein presented or conveyed.

SECOND: The Owner does hereby convey, grant and assign
to the Purchaser the sole and exclusive rights to use, adapt,
translate, subtract from, add to and change the Work and the
title thereof in the production of a legitimate musical stage
presentation, and to use the Work or any part or parts thereof
and the title and any similar title and any or all of the
characters and characterizations of the Work in connection with
such legitimate musical stage presentation (hereinafter sometimes
referred to as the "Play") based upon the Work; together with the
further sole and exclusive rights, by mechanical or electrical
means, to record, reproduce and transmit sound, including the
spoken words, dialogue, music and songs, whether extracted from
the Work or otherwise, and to change such spoken words, dialogue,
music and songs in or in connection with or as part of the
production, performance and presentation of such Play; the sole
and exclusive right to make, use, license and vend any and all
records required and desired for such purpose; to produce or
cause the musical Play to be produced upon the regular speaking
stage throughout the world, and to use, sell, lease or otherwise
dispose of the musical Play and all rights of every kind and
nature therein now or hereafter ascertained and to authorize
others so to do for any and all purposes and by any and all means

throughout the world subject, further however, to the rights in
the Work previously granted as hereinabove set forth; and,
subject to the reservations of rights or reverter to the Owner
hereunder, the exclusive right to copyright the Play in the name
of the Purchaser or his nominee, and to obtain extensions and
renewals of such copyright. The right to use the title
is granted exclusively only for and in connection
with the Play, based in whole or in part upon the Work, and the
Owner makes no warranty with respect to the rights of the
Purchaser so to use such title, except insofar as same is
affected by Owner's acts or omissions.

THIRD: The Purchaser will cause a completed musical
play to be written and composed and upon completion of the Play,
any and all rights therein, whether presently known or hereafter
ascertained, of any kind, nature and description, including but
not limited to television, radio, motion picture, foreign,
commercial, second-class touring, stock, amateur, tabloid, sequel,
remake, shall become the sole and exclusive property of the
Purchaser.

FOURTH: The Purchaser has paid to the Owner, upon the
execution hereof, the sum of
as a non-returnable advance payment on account of the following
royalties, also to be paid the Owner:

(a)   percent of the gross box
office receipts from all first-class stage
presentations of the musical in the United States of
America, the Dominion of Canada and Great Britain,
authorized or licensed hereunder as provided in the
Dramatists Guild, Inc. Minimum Basic Production
Contract for a musical, and in addition
percent (making a total of   percent of the gross
box office receipts from the production of the Play,
after the total production costs of the Broadway Play
have been recouped.

(b) That proportion of the Authors' share of all
proceeds, emoluments and other things of value received
from the sale, lease and disposition of any and all
other rights in the musical, including, but not limited
to, motion picture, publication of libretto, radio,
television, stock, amateur, foreign, commercial,
operetta, grand opera, second-class touring, "remake,"
"sequel" and condensed tabloid versions and all other

rights now known or hereinafter to be known in the
proportion that   percent shall bear to
the total percentage of gross box office receipts
payable as royalties to the Author, Composer, Lyricist
and Owner, however, in no event less than an amount
equal to   percent of the total of such net
proceeds received by Author, Composer, Lyricist and
Owner.

FIFTH: The rights herein granted shall cease and
terminate and shall automatically revert to the Owner without any
obligation of any kind to the Purchaser:

(a) Unless the Purchaser shall have written or
cause to have written a completed play based on the
Work.

(b) Unless the Play is presented on the stage,
before a paying audience, on or before the
day of   , 19 .

Nothing herein contained shall be deemed to obligate the
Purchaser to produce the Play. The time period herein provided
may be extended as hereinafter provided for in Paragraph "SIXTH"
of this Agreement.

SIXTH: The Purchaser shall have the option of
extending the time within which to cause the completed Play to
be produced, as hereinabove provided, for an additional year,
that is, until   , upon serving written notice upon the
Owner of the exercise of such option on or before   ,
and by paying to the Owner the additional sum of
                         as a further non-returnable
advance against royalties.

SEVENTH: It is mutually agreed that:

(a) The Author shall be deemed to be the sole
Author of the musical for all purposes hereof and
shall have full and exclusive rights and privileges
as Author with respect to all matters relating to the
production of the musical (such as, but not limited to,
choice of cast, director and sale of motion picture
[if not in conflict with any existing contracts
concerning the motion picture rights] and other
subsidiary rights, etc.). No signatures of the Owner
shall be necessary in connection with any of the
foregoing, provided, however, that the Author will
furnish to the Owner fully conformed copies of each

Agreement made regarding any sale or other disposition upon the execution of any such Agreement.

(b) Commencing with the date hereof and continuing until the termination of all the Purchaser's rights hereunder, the Owner will not grant the right to adapt or redramatize the Work or any part thereof in any form and will not sell, lease, license, assign or otherwise dispose of any performing rights in or to said story.

(c) Upon presentation of the musical for a first-class performance for twenty-one (21) professional paid performances, the musical and the Work shall be deemed merged forever and in perpetuity in the sense that the Owner shall not convey or dispose of any rights in or to the Work, including the copyrights therein and thereto, without the prior written consent of the Purchaser. Under no circumstances shall the sale of the Work be limited anywhere. Notwithstanding any such merger, however, the Owner and their assignees and licensees may continue exclusively to exercise their respective rights of publishing and selling copies of the Work (as distinguished from the musical) in any and all territories of the world and to derive and retain for their account all royalties and proceeds therefrom, and, in this connection, the Owner's rights in the copyrights of the Work or any part thereof shall continue to be vested in the Owner, subject, however, in all respects, to the terms and conditions of this Agreement. If the Work shall merge in the Play as herein provided, then the Purchaser shall have the sole right to sell, lease, license or otherwise dispose of the motion picture and subsidiary rights therein (subject, of course, to any previous grant by the Owner). In extension and not in limitation of the foregoing, it is specifically understood and agreed that the Purchaser's rights in motion picture, subsidiary rights, British Isle production rights and other related rights shall be effective upon a merger of the Work and Play as herein provided. If the original run of the musical shall terminate prior to the aforementioned minimum period, the Owner shall thenceforth be completely free to exploit any and all

of his respective rights in such story for the sole
and exclusive benefit of himself, his successors,
licensees and assigns.

(d)   All leases, licenses or other dispositions
of any right or interest in or in connection with the
musical and/or the subsidiary and/or the motion picture
rights thereof shall be in writing and made in good
faith on the basis of the best efforts and interests
of all concerned.

(e)   All contracts executed by the Purchaser and
Author of the musical in connection with any of the
rights in the musical or pertaining thereto, which are
the subject of this Agreement, or the rights of the
Owner therein or herein, shall acknowledge the interest
of the Owner pursuant to the terms of this Agreement.
In instances where the Owner is entitled to any of the
proceeds, Purchaser will exercise his best efforts to
provide in any contract that express provision shall
be made for payments directly to the Owner through his
agent as hereinafter provided and copies of all such
contracts relating to the rights herein, confirming,
affecting or relating to any of the Owner's rights
hereunder shall be furnished to the Owner through his
agent, as hereinafter provided, promptly upon the
execution thereof.

(f)   The Owner shall not be entitled to receive
any share from, nor to receive any accounting for, any
and all royalties and other compensation from
publication of the original lyrics and music in and of
the musical, mechanical reproductions and original cast
album and other recordings including statutory and
copyright royalties, and so-called small rights arising
out of the music publication and recording contracts by
the Purchaser or anyone else for his original music and
lyrics, and all royalties and dividends, etc. that may
be derived by the Purchaser or anyone else, as
lyricist(s) and composer(s), from such organizations as
the American Society of Composers, Authors and
Publishers, Broadcast Music, Incorporated, and other
similar organizations. It is understood, however, that
any sale or disposition of synchronization rights for
use in connection with the making of a motion picture

and/or of a television program shall be deemed a disposition of motion picture and/or television rights, as the case may be, and the Owner shall share in the proceeds therefrom in accordance with his rights to share in the disposition of motion picture and television rights as herein provided for.

EIGHTH: If the musical shall not be produced on the legitimate speaking stage, pursuant to the terms hereof, on or before the date herein provided for, as the same may be extended pursuant hereto, or if the rights do not merge as herein provided, then,

(a) All rights in the Work granted to or acquired by the Purchaser hereunder shall forthwith revert to the Owner with the same force and effect as if this Agreement had never been entered into.

(b) All rights in such portion of the musical as shall not be contained in or taken from or incidental to the Work shall forthwith revert to the Purchaser.

(c) The Purchaser shall be free to make such use and disposition of his original music and lyrics of the musical as he sees fit, but it is expressly understood and agreed that the Purchaser or his assignee shall not have any right to retain or use the name of the Play (or any title of which such name or title is part) as the title of any works or rights which may revert to them hereunder, or in any way have the right to capitalize on the fact that such right and/or music and/or lyrics were once a part of the musical and/or associated with any version of such play.

NINTH: The Purchaser agrees that the name of shall appear in all advertising and publicity issued by or with the consent or under the control of the Purchaser wherever the Author's name shall appear, with the same size and prominence as Author's name. If the title   is not used as the title of the Play, then that title will appear in the credits as the story on which the Play is based.

TENTH: The Purchaser agrees to hold in the name of the Owner two (2) pairs of house seats for each performance of the Play in New York City (except theatre parties and benefit performances), which seats shall be held until noon of the day preceding the performance with respect to a matinee performance and until 6:00 P.M. of the day preceding with respect to evening performances, which seats shall be paid for at the regularly established box office prices therefor. The Owner shall also have the right to purchase four (4) pairs of house seats for the New York opening.

ELEVENTH: Subject to the terms and conditions hereof, the terms of this Agreement shall be for the period of the original copyright of the musical and the renewal thereof.

TWELFTH: Purchaser will advise or cause the Owner to be advised in writing, in full and complete detail, of all offers for the purchase of the motion picture and/or television rights to the musical as soon as possible after the receipt of such offers but not later than forty-eight (48) hours prior to the acceptance of any such offer.

THIRTEENTH: Purchaser will keep and maintain, or by contract cause to be kept and maintained, full and correct books and records relating to the presentation of the musical hereunder and all transactions in which the Owner may have an interest hereunder and the proceeds derived therefrom. Such books and records will be kept in New York, New York. The Owner and/or his agent and/or representatives shall have access to such books and records during all regular business hours and may take or cause to be taken excerpts and/or extracts therefrom. Payments herein required to be made to the Owner shall be made at the same time and in the same manner as payment to Author and pursuant to the terms and conditions of the Option Agreement. Payments to the Owner shall be accompanied by copies of all such statements as are required to be furnished to Authors by the Dramatists Guild, Inc. Minimum Basic Production Contract and such rules and regulations.

FOURTEENTH: The addresses of the parties herein shall be for all purposes as follows:

Copies of all notices shall be mailed to Donald C. Farber, Esq., Conboy, Hewitt, O'Brien, & Boardman, 600 Madison Avenue, New York, New York 10022. All notices required to be given hereunder shall be in writing and sent by certified mail addressed as above provided, except as may, from time to time, be otherwise directed in writing by the respective parties.

FIFTEENTH: Any claim, dispute, misunderstanding or controversy or charge of unfair dealing arising under, or in connection with, or out of this Agreement, or the breach thereof, shall be submitted to arbitration to be held under the rules and regulations of the American Arbitration Association. Failure by the Producer to pay any amount claimed to be due by the Owner is evidence of a dispute entitling the claimant to an arbitration. Judgment upon the award rendered may be entered in the highest court of the forum, State or Federal, having jurisdiction. The arbitrators are empowered to award damages against any party to the controversy in such sums as they shall deem fair and reasonable under the circumstances. The arbitrators are also empowered to require specific performance of a contract, or in the alternative money damages, and have power to grant any other remedy or relief, injunctive or otherwise, which they deem just and equitable.

The arbitrators are also empowered to render a partial award before making a final award and grant such relief, injunctive or otherwise, in such partial award as they deem just and equitable. The artibrators may determine and indicate in their written award by whom and in what proportion the cost of arbitration shall be borne.

SIXTEENTH: The Owner hereby acknowledges that (name of agent or attorney) (hereinafter referred to as ("the Agent" or "the Attorney")) has acted for the Owner in the negotiation and consummation of this Agreement, and the Owner therefore agrees that so long as the Owner or their assignees shall have any rights under this Agreement or any extensions of renewals hereof or under any agreements amendatory hereof or in substitution hereof or under any first-class dramatic production agreement which may proceed from this Agreement,   shall be the sole exclusive and irrevocable agent of the Owner with respect to the Owner's interest in this Agreement and in the rights and privileges granted herein, with the sole and exclusive right and power to deal therewith for the Owner and, further, that as such agent, shall be entitled to receive any and all monies due the Owner pursuant hereof and to deduct and retain for itself ten percent (10%) thereof, except where such monies are applicable to an exercise of the amateur rights of the musical, in which case it may deduct and retain for itself twenty percent (20%) of such monies. This designation of   as sole and exclusive agent for the Owner shall be irrevocable and Purchaser hereby is directed by the Owner to make payment to
        of any and all sums payable to the Owner hereunder. The Owner acknowledges that all such payments by the Purchaser to

, when made, shall be deemed to be payments by the
Purchaser to the Owner hereunder.

SEVENTEENTH: This Agreement, irrespective of its place
of execution, shall be construed and interpreted in accordance
with the Laws of the State of New York as though, and with the
same effect, as if it had been actually executed and delivered
within such State.

EIGHTEENTH: This Agreement shall be binding upon and
shall inure to the benefit of the parties hereto and their
respective heirs, executors, administrators, personal
representatives, successors and assigns.

NINETEENTH: Purchaser shall have the right to assign
this Agreement, provided, however, that the assignee shall in all
respects be subject to, and assume in writing directly to the
Owner each and every term, provision, condition and obligation
herein contained.

TWENTIETH: This Agreement constitutes the entire
understanding between the parties hereto and no warranty,
representation, inducement or agreement not contained herein
shall be binding on the parties. This Agreement can be modified
only by a written instrument duly authorized by the parties
hereto or the authorized representatives of each of the parties.

IN WITNESS WHEREOF, the parties hereto have executed
this Agreement as of the day and year first above written.

_____

OWNER

_____

PURCHASER

APPENDIX C

CO-PRODUCTION AGREEMENT

AGREEMENT made as of this   day of   , 19 ,
by and between John Jones (hereinafter sometimes referred to
as "Jones") and Henry Smith (hereinafter sometimes referred to
as "Smith").

FIRST: The parties hereto do hereby form a Joint
Venture to be conducted under the firm name of
(hereinafter sometimes referred to as the "Joint Venture"), for
the purpose of producing and presenting in New York City the
        play "   ," written by
(hereinafter sometimes referred to as the "Play").

SECOND: The parties agree, as soon as possible, to
form a Limited Partnership under the laws of the State of New
York (hereinafter sometimes referred to as the "Limited
Partnership") to produce the said Play. The said Limited
Partnership will be known as   .

(a) The parties hereto will be the General
Partners of the Limited Partnership, and the parties
contributing to the capital thereof will be the Limited
Partners of the Partnership.

(b) The capital of the Limited Partnership will
be in an amount not more than
($) and not less than
($), or such other amount as may mutually be
agreed upon between the parties to this Agreement. The
parties contemplate producing the Play in an (Off-
Broadway, middle, Broadway) theatre.

(c) The Limited Partnership Agreement shall be
based on a theatrical limited partnership agreement as
prepared by Donald C. Farber, of Conboy, Hewitt,
O'Brien, & Boardman, 600 Madison Avenue, New York, New
York 10022, the Attorney for the Joint Venture and the
Limited Partnership.

(d) Each party agrees to use his best efforts to
raise as much of the capital of the Limited Partnership
as possible. In the event that the parties hereto
cannot raise the complete capital necessary for the
Limited Partnership and it is necessary to pay someone
any money or share of the General Partners' profits,
for the raising of any part of said capital, if the
parties hereto are in agreement with respect to such an

arrangement, then the amount so paid to said party(s) shall be contributed equally by the parties hereto.

(e) The Limited Partners shall receive Fifty Percent (50%) of the net profits of the Limited Partnership, and the General Partners shall receive the remaining Fifty Percent (50%) of the net profits. The net profits shall first be used to repay the Limited Partners to the extent of their investment in the Limited Partnership before the profits are shared with the General Partners.

If any star(s) or other person(s) are entitled to receive any part of the gross receipts or net profits, the same shall be deemed to be an expense and deducted before computing the net profits to be divided between the General and Limited Partners.

(f) Regardless of the amount of capital raised or contributed by each party to this Agreement, the producers' share of any net profits shall be divided equally between them, that is   percent (%) to   and   percent (%) to

(g) Any net losses of the Limited Partnership over and above the capital thereof shall be borne by the parties hereto in the same proportion as they share in the General Partners' share of the profits; that is, equally.

(h) The parties agree to assign to the Limited Partnership, at their original cost, all rights in and to the option to produce the play which they have heretofore acquired and any other agreement entered into for the purpose of producing the Play.

(i) The producers' fee payable by the Limited Partnership shall be in the amount of   Percent of the gross weekly box office receipts until the production budget is recouped and will, thereafter, be in the amount of   Percent of the gross weekly box office receipts. The cash office charge shall be   ($) each week for each company and shall commence three weeks prior to rehearsals and shall terminate one week after the close of each production. Both the producers' fee and the cash office charge will be shared by the parties equally.

THIRD: Any and all obligations of any kind or nature for the Joint Venture and for the Limited Partnership shall be incurred only upon the consent of both parties to this Agreement.

FOURTH: All contracts and all checks on behalf of the Joint Venture and on behalf of the Limited Partnership may be signed by either party to this Agreement, or someone delegated to so sign by both parties to this Agreement.

FIFTH: Wherever producers' credits are given, the credits shall be as mutually agreed to by the parties to this Agreement.

SIXTH: Each party shall devote as much time as is reasonably necessary for the production and presentation of the Play, it being recognized and agreed that each party may be engaged in other activities, whether or not of a competing nature, so long as he devotes sufficient time to the Joint Venture and to the Limited Partnership, and to the proper running of the business of producing and presenting the Play.

SEVENTH: The Joint Venture shall terminate upon the happening of the first of the following:

(a) The formation of the Limited Partnership;

(b) Such date as the parties hereto may mutually agree upon;

(c) The withdrawal of any of the parties hereto.

EIGHTH: It is agreed that the pre-production money, that is the front money, shall be furnished equally by the parties to this Agreement, and in the event that it is necessary to assign any share of the producers' profits to someone else in exchange for front money, then the assignment shall be made equally by the parties to this Agreement.

All front monies so advanced, by the parties to this Agreement, as well as other expenditures on behalf of the Joint Venture, by either party, approved by the other party, shall be repaid to the party expending such sum immediately upon full capitalization of the Limited Partnership.

NINTH: It is agreed that the following parties will be engaged by the Joint Venture and the Limited Partnership in the following capacities:

(a) Donald C. Farber, Esq., as the Attorney;

(b)

TENTH: It is agreed that all decisions, artistic and business, will be made by the parties jointly. In the event that

there is a dispute of an artistic nature which cannot be
resolved, then the final decision will be made by   ,
and his decision shall be final and binding. In the event of a
dispute of a business nature which cannot be resolved, then the
final decision will be made by   , and his
decision shall become final and binding.

    ELEVENTH: Other than those decisions specifically
covered in Paragraph TENTH of this Agreement, any and all
disputes or differences in connection with this Agreement, or
the breach or alleged breach thereof, shall be submitted to
arbitration to be held in New York City, by one arbitrator, under
the rules and regulations of the American Arbitration Association
then obtaining, and each of the parties hereto agrees to be bound
by the determination of the arbitrator. Judgment on the award
rendered may be entered in the highest court of the forum having
jurisdiction.

    TWELFTH: If any party(s) wish to terminate the run of
the Play and the other party(s) wish to continue it, the party(s)
wishing to continue (the "continuing party(s)") shall assume
complete control of the production and presentation of the Play
commencing immediately upon giving written notice to such effect
after the party(s) seeking to terminate the run (the "retiring
party(s)") shall have given notice thereof, and the continuing
party(s) shall thereafter bear all the expenses and liabilities
of the production of the Play and be entitled to receive all of
the net profits in connection therewith as well as the management
fee and office charge. The continuing party(s) shall indemnify
the retiring party(s) from any liability incurred after the
takeover and shall evidence such indemnity by appropriate
instruments. The retiring party(s) shall forfeit all rights,
title and interest in and to the production of the Play and the
proceeds therefrom commencing with such takeover, but this shall
not affect proceeds accrued prior thereto but not received,
including proceeds from subsidiary rights in the Play.

    THIRTEENTH: The provisions of this Agreement shall
survive the termination of the Joint Venture and shall continue
to bind the parties hereto. This Agreement shall be binding and
shall inure to the benefit of the parties, their respective
successors and assigns. This Agreement sets forth the entire
Agreement of the parties and may not be changed except by an
instrument in writing signed by each of the parties. The
validity, construction, interpretation and effect of this

Agreement shall be determined by and in accordance with the laws of the State of New York.

IN WITNESS WHEREOF, the parties hereto have set their hands and seals to this Agreement as of the day and year first above written.

_____

_____

APPENDIX D

<u>MINIMUM BASIC PRODUCTION CONTRACT</u>

(The terms contained in this Contract and
the accompanying Schedule are the Minimum Terms to
which the Author is entitled. While the Author may
obtain terms more favorable, no provision of the
Contract or Schedule may be waived by the Author in
consideration of a greater interest or more
favorable terms under any other provision thereof.)

THIS CONTRACT, made and entered into as
of the   day of
by and between

whose address is

hereinafter collectively referred to as the
"Producer,"* and

whose address is

hereinafter collectively referred to as the
"Author."

W I T N E S S E T H :
- - - - - - - - -

WHEREAS, the Author, a member of the
Dramatists Guild, Inc. (hereinafter called the
"Guild"), has been preparing the book, music and/
or lyrics** of a certain play or other literary

_____

*Where the Producer is a partnership the
agreement shall be with the partnership and each
individual general partner.
**Strike out what is not appropriate.

property, now entitled

(hereinafter referred to as the "Play"); and

WHEREAS, the Producer is in the business of producing plays and desires to produce the Play in the United States and Canada and to acquire the Author's services in connection therewith;

NOW, THEREFORE, in consideration of the premises and the mutual promises and covenants herein contained, and other good and valuable consideration, it is agreed:

FIRST: The Author hereby:

(a) Warrants that he is the Author of the book, music and/or lyrics* of said Play and has the right to enter into this agreement;

(b) Agrees that on compliance with this Contract, the Producer shall have the exclusive right to produce the Play on the speaking stage in the United States and Canada and acquire the Author's services in connection therewith;

(c) Agrees that he will perform such services as may be reasonably necessary in making revisions;

(d) Agrees that he will assist in the selection of the cast and consult with, assist and advise the Producer, director, dance director, conductor and scenic and costume designers in the problems arising out of the production;

(e) Agrees that he will attend rehearsals of the Play as well as out-of-town performances prior to the New York opening of the play, provided, however, that he may be excused from such attendance on showing reasonable cause.

SECOND: Although nothing herein shall be deemed to obligate the Producer to produce the Play, nevertheless, unless the Producer produces and presents the Play on the speaking stage under his

---

*Strike out what is not appropriate.

own management in a regular evening bill (other
than a tryout performance) in a first-class
theatre in a first-class manner, with a first-
class cast and a first-class director, on or before
the   day of   , 19   or one
year from the date hereof (whichever date occurs
first), his right to produce the Play and to the
services of the Author shall then automatically
and without notice terminate.

   THIRD: In consideration of the foregoing SEE
and of the Author's services in writing the Play PARAGRAPH
and the Author's agreement to perform services in TENTH
connection with its production as hereinabove
provided, the Producer agrees to pay:

   (a) Until the production of the Play,
and so long as he desires to maintain his right
to produce, a fixed monthly compensation (no part
of which shall in any event be returnable to the
Producer) of $ or $200 (whichever amount
shall be greater), each to the Bookwriter,
Composer and Lyricist*, commencing with the
signing of this Contract, and monthly thereafter,
until the production of the Play or the
termination of this Contract under SECOND above,
whichever event shall occur first; provided
however, that if subdivision (b) is not selected,
or that, if selected, it does not become operative,
then (i) if the Producer pays $ or $500
(whichever amount be greater) on the signing of
this Contract, such payment shall be in lieu of
payments for the first three months and (ii) the
monthly payment for the next three months shall
be $ or $100 (whichever amount be greater)
and (iii) the monthly payment for the next six
months shall be $ or $200 (whichever
amount be greater).

   Where the Contract provides that the
musical has not been completed, or is in the
process of being written, at the time this
Contract is being signed, the payments specified

---

  *Strike out what is not appropriate.

in this subdivision shall commence only when a
"completed musical work" is submitted to the
Producer. The production date in paragraph
SECOND shall be one year from the date such
"completed musical work" is submitted. Solely
for the purpose of determining when such payments
shall commence and when the said period shall
begin to run, a "completed" musical shall be
deemed to mean a book of at least 80 pages,
single-spaced, plus a score consisting of music
and lyrics for at least 12 songs.

(Check and
initial al-
ternative
desired)
The following subdivision (b)
☐ shall
☐ shall not
be included in this Contract as
part of the parties' agreement.

(But subdivision (b) shall not apply if the
parties select alternative (d) (i) below.)

(b) (1) Provided that the Producer
has made, or shall make, comparable arrangements
with the director, choreographer, actors, and with
respect to the fees of the Producer himself, and
subject to the conditions hereinafter set forth,
and the Author agrees to accept, compensation for
not more than 30 consecutive weeks of performances
(including all out-of-town performances prior to
the New York opening, New York preview performances,
New York performances, and road performances after
the New York run) commencing with the first
performance of the Play out-of-town, and if there
are no out-of-town performances, then commencing
with the first New York performance as follows:

(i) One-half of the compensation
provided for each said week in
subparagraphs (c), (d) (ii), or
(e) below, as the case may be,
or   % of the gross weekly box
office receipts for each of such
weeks, whichever is greater,
provided that

(ii) when compensation has been paid
for an aggregate of thirty weeks

under (i) above, full compensation
shall thereafter be paid to the
Author, pursuant to provisions of
(e) below.

(2) If the "Production Expenses"
(as hereinafter defined in Paragraph TWELFTH) shall
have been recouped prior to the end of the thirtieth
week in which reduced compensation may be paid under
Clause (1) above, said Clause (1) shall become
inoperative at the end of the week in which such
recoupment shall take place, and full compensation
shall thereafter be paid to the Author pursuant to
the provisions of subdivisions (c), (c) (ii) and
(e) below, as the case may be. It is understood
that "Production Expenses" as defined in Paragraph
TWELFTH, do not include the principal amount of any
bond or any security or collateral deposited
therefor, but for the purposes of this Paragraph
THIRD (b), "Production Expenses" shall include
management fees and office charges, subject to the
limitations of THIRD (b) (5) (iv) paid during the
period commencing two weeks prior to the opening
of rehearsals and terminating with the official
New York opening.

(3) In determining whether
"Production Expenses" have been recouped, there
shall be taken into account as income to the
Producer, applicable to the recoupment of such
expenses, all income to the Producer derived
directly or indirectly from the production of the
Play, including not only income from the first-
class performances and other activities controlled
by the Producer (such as the sale of souvenir
programs, payments from music publishers and the
like) but also, and without limiting the generality
of the foregoing: (i) the share of net receipts
paid to the Producer pursuant to Paragraph SEVENTH
hereof, during any week in which compensation is
paid under (1) above, and (ii) the share of net
receipts to which the Producer shall thereafter
become entitled (pursuant to Paragraph SEVENTH)
with respect to any disposition of rights

specified therein, made during or prior to any such week, although such share of net receipts is not actually paid, or does not become payable to the Producer, until after the termination of such week.

(4) If "comparable arrangements" are not made with each and every one of the following:

Director, choreographer, actors and Producer (including any general partner, "persons in control" of a corporate Producer as herein defined, or person(s) otherwise participating in the production with, or in association with, the Producer),

with respect to the period in which compensation shall be paid to the Author under Clause (1) above, then this entire subdivision (b) shall become inoperative and full compensation shall be paid to the Author pursuant to subdivision (c), (d) (ii) or (e) below, as the case may be.

(5) "Comparable arrangements" (as used in this subdivision (b)) shall mean arrangements contained in written contracts executed prior to the first rehearsal by the Producer:

(i) With the director — Whereby the director shall receive as compensation, during the period in which Clause (1) is in effect, one-half of the percentage of weekly box office receipts which he is to receive during the New York run, but such compensation during said period shall not be required to be reduced below % of the gross weekly box office receipts.

(ii) With the choreographer — Whereby the choreographer shall receive as compensation, during the period in which Clause (1) is in effect, one-half of the percentage of

weekly box office receipts which
he shall receive during the New
York run, but such compensation
during said period shall not be
required to be reduced below one-
half of 1% of the gross weekly
box office receipts.

(iii)   With actors — Whereby the actor
shall receive as compensation,
during the period in which Clause
(1) above is in effect, one-half
of the guaranteed salary and/or
one-half of the percentage of
weekly box office receipts (or
other compensation measured
thereby) which he shall receive
during the New York run, but such
compensation during said period
shall not be required to be
reduced below $2,000 per week;
further provided that no such
arrangement need be made with
any actor who is to receive less
than $2,000 during the New York
run and is not to receive any
percentage of the box office
receipts (or compensation
measured thereby).

(iv)   With respect to Producers' Fees —
That during the period in which
Clause (1) above is in effect, any
management fee and/or percentage
of gross weekly box office
receipts payable to the Producer
(or any general partner, "persons
in control" of a corporate
Producer as herein defined, or
person(s) otherwise participating
in the production with or in
association with, the Producer)
shall be one-half the amount of
the management fee or percentage

of box office receipts, payable
during the New York run, except
that in no event shall such
management fee and/or percentage
of gross weekly box office
receipts during the period in
which Clause (1) is in effect
exceed one-half of one percent
of the gross weekly box office
receipts. In addition, during
the period in which Clause (1)
is in effect, the Producer shall
not pay or make any charge for
office expenses in excess of $350
per week.

Provided further that in no
event shall the compensation of any of the persons
named in (i), (ii), (iii) and (iv) above, during
the period in which Clause (1) is in effect, be
required to be reduced below such percentage or
amount which bears the same proportion to the
compensation which such person shall receive during
the remainder of the New York run, as the
compensation to be paid to the Author under THIRD
(b) (1) (i) bears to the compensation paid to him
under THIRD (c), (d) (ii) and (e).

(6) Nothing herein contained shall
be deemed to require the Producer to make the
foregoing arrangements or any other arrangements
with the director, choreographer, actors, or with
respect to Producer's fees in connection with the
production, and the Author shall have no right to
compel the Producer to make such "comparable
arrangements"; it being understood that the
foregoing provisions are set forth as a condition
upon the happening of which this subdivision (b)
shall become operative and if "comparable
arrangements" referred to in Clause (5) above are
not made, the only consequence shall be that this
subdivision (b) shall be deemed inoperative and
full compensation shall be paid to the Author
pursuant to subparagraphs (c), (d) and/or (e)

below, as the case may be.

        (7)   It is understood that the
Author has elected this subdivision (b) on the
Producer's representation and agreement that
the "comparable arrangements" with the other
persons referred to above will be arrived at,
and carried out, by the Producer in good faith,
and will be bona fide arrangements in order to
permit the recoupment of "Production Expenses"
as promptly as possible; it being understood that
if "comparable arrangements" are made, or carried
out, in such manner, that any of said other
persons shall, in fact, receive more during said
period than they would have by a good faith
compliance herewith, then the Author would suffer
damages to the extent of the one-half of the full
compensation he will have foregone during said
period by reason of his acceptance of this
subdivision (b).

        (8)   The Producer agrees to furnish
to the Author and to the Guild within ten days
after the execution thereof and no later than two
weeks before the commencement of rehearsals,
copies of all contracts (and amendments thereto)
with the director, choreographer and actors
(referred to in (5) above) respecting arrangements
for their compensation, and any contracts
concerning production or management fees (referred
to in (5) above); he shall also furnish to them at
the same time a schedule listing all members of
the cast and the director and the amount and terms
of compensation to be paid to each during the New
York run; the Producer shall also submit to the
Guild, prior to the New York opening, a statement
or budget of the "Production Expenses" of the Play
and shall submit promptly to the Author and to the
Guild weekly statements of operating expenses for
each week during the run of the Play; the Producer
shall also submit to the Guild copies of all
financial statements or reports issued by the
Producer to stockholders, limited partners, joint
venturers or other backers, including a copy of

the final financial statement with respect to the production.

Upon written request of the Author or the Guild the Producer agrees that either of them may examine, or cause to be examined by independent public accountants, the books of the Producer during and/or after the run of the Play insofar as they relate to the production of the Play, provided that not more than one such examination shall be made in any six-month period and that no examination may be made more than eighteen months after the close of the last performance of the first-class run; it being understood that the purpose of such examination shall be to determine whether the foregoing provisions of this subdivision (b) have been performed.

(c) For each week of out-of-town performances prior to the New York opening and for preview performances in New York prior to the official opening, 6% or   % (whichever is greater) of the gross weekly box office receipts. Such payments shall not exceed $1,500 in any one of the first four weeks of such out-of-town performances prior to the New York opening, provided that if any of said weeks is not a full calendar week then the maximum for such shorter week shall be prorated, except that said $1,500 limitation shall not apply in the event subdivision (b) hereof is elected and operative.

(d) For the first three consecutive weeks beginning with the official New York opening, the amounts fixed in that one of the following alternatives which has been checked in the box in the margin and initialed by the parties:
(N.B. If this alternative (d) (i) is selected, subdivision (b) of this Paragraph THIRD shall be deemed deleted from this Contract.)

(i) The sum of $6000 to be paid to the order of the Guild, in escrow for the benefit of the Author, at lease one week prior to the first

rehearsal. The Producer shall
send to the Author and the Guild
at least ten days prior thereto
written notice of the date of the
first rehearsal. The Guild shall
pay said sum to the Author
immediately after the New York
opening.

   If the Producer has not paid
the $6000 as herein provided,
compensation at the rates
specified in the first sentence
of subdivision (c) hereof except
that the Author shall have the
option to terminate the contract
by written notice sent to the
Producer and the Guild within
three days after the default.

   The Guild shall repay said   SEE
$6000 whenever the Producer has   PARAGRAPH
notified the Guild in writing that   TENTH
he has abandoned any intention to
produce the play in New York, and
in such event the Producer shall
have no right later to produce the
play in New York unless the
Producer shall have given 64 out-
of-town performances within a
period of 80 days. If the play is
then produced in New York the
Author shall be entitled to
compensation at the rates
specified in the first sentence
of subdivision (c) hereof.

(ii)   6% or   % (whichever is greater)
       of the gross weekly box office
       receipts.

   (e) For each week of New York performances   SEE
commencing with the fourth successive consecutive PARAGRAPH
full calendar weeks after the New York opening, 6% TENTH
or   % (whichever is greater) of the gross weekly
box office receipts.

(f) For each week of road performances, after the New York run, the compensation at the rates specified in the first sentence of subdivision (c) hereof, provided that, if such payment would result in there being no operating profits (as hereinafter defined) for a particular week, then the Author shall receive only such compensation for that week as shall not result in an operating loss, except that in no week shall the Author receive less than $500.

(g) The payments required to be made pursuant to subdivision (a) may be deducted from the percentage compensation payable pursuant to any of the foregoing subdivisions, but can in no event be deducted from the fixed payment provided for in subdivision (d) (i).

FOURTH: (a) If the Producer has produced the Play for one of the periods specified in Section 2 of the annexed Schedule and has otherwise complied with this Contract, he shall have the exclusive right to produce the Play on the speaking stage in the United Kingdom of Great Britain and in Ireland (hereinafter called "British Isles") for a consecutive run as theatrically understood, in a regular evening bill, upon all the terms and conditions which apply to a New York production, at any time up to and including six months after the close of the first-class production in New York, upon sending the Author, in care of the Guild, written notice within one month after said closing performance, accompanied by a payment of $500, of his intention so to produce the play, except that such payment need not be made if the Producer has produced the play in the United States for at least 208 performances and all other provisions of the contract have been complied with.

(b) The Producer shall pay to the Guild for the account of the Author 6% or   % (whichever is greater) of the gross weekly box office receipts.

(c) The payments made in accordance with subdivision (a) hereof may be deducted from the compensation to be paid under subdivision (b).

(d) Provided the Producer has complied
with the provisions of subdivision (a) hereof, he
may produce the Play in association with or under
lease to a British producer subject to the Author's
written consent. In such case the Producer's
obligation to make the payments herein provided
shall remain unimpaired. Such contract between the
Producer and the British producer shall require the
Play to be produced in the manner and on the terms
provided in subdivisions (a) and (b) hereof.

(e) If the Producer has not produced
the Play in the British Isles within the period
hereinabove provided, then the Author shall
thereafter have the sole right to produce or
authorize the production of the Play, provided,
however, that if the Producer has otherwise complied
with this Contract the Author shall pay the Producer
25% of the net proceeds received by him as the
result of any contract for the production of such
Play made within five years after the New York
opening, including any proceeds from subsidiary
rights.

FIFTH: (a) The portion of any gross
receipts or net profits due to the Author shall
belong to the Author and shall be held in trust by
the Producer as the Author's property until
payment. The trust nature of such fund shall not
be questioned, whether the monies are physically
segregated or not. In the event of breach of
trust hereunder, the Author may, at his option,
pursue his remedies at law or in equity in lieu
of the arbitration procedure established by this
Contract.

(b) Within 7 days after the end of each
calendar week the Producer agrees to forward to
the Guild for the Author's account the amount due
as compensation for such week and also, within such
time, to furnish to the Guild daily box office
statements for each Author, of each performance of
the Play during such week, signed by the Treasurer
or Treasurers of the theatre in which performances
are given, and countersigned by the Producer or

his duly authorized representative. Box office
statements and payments due for plays presented
more than 500 miles from New York City may be so
furnished and paid within 14 days after the end of
each week; for plays presented in the British Isles,
within 21 days. In cases where the Author's
compensation depends on operating profits or losses,
weekly operating statements shall be sent to the
Guild for each Author with his check.

      (c) All checks shall be sent to the
Guild. Checks for payments due under Paragraphs
THIRD (a) and (d)(i) and FOURTH (a) shall be drawn
to the order of the Guild. All other checks shall
be drawn to the order of the Author or, where he
indicates in writing to the Producer and the Guild
that he is represented by an agent, to the agent,
provided the agent is a member in good standing of
the Society of Authors' Representatives, Inc.

      SIXTH: (a) The Producer, recognizing
that the Play is the artistic creation of the Author
and that as such the Author is entitled to protect
the type and nature of the production of his
creation, hereby agrees:

        (i) Under his own management to
            rehearse, present and continue
            to present the Play, including
            road companies thereof, with a
            cast, director, conductor and
            dance director mutually agreeable
            to him and to the Author, and to
            announce the name of the Author
            as sole Author of the book,
            music and/or lyrics* of the Play
            upon all programs and in all
            advertising matter in which the
            name of the Producer appears.
            After the opening of the Play any
            change in the cast or any
            replacement of a director,
            conductor or dance director shall

_____

    *Strike out what is not appropriate.

likewise be subject to the mutual
consent of the parties. The Author
may designate another person to act
on his behalf with respect to such
approvals and appointments. If the
Author is not available for
consultation in the United States,
the provisions of this subdivision
shall not apply unless he shall
have designated another person to
act on his behalf who is available
for consultation in the United
States.

(ii) To rehearse, produce, present and
continue to present the Play,
including road companies, thereof,
with only such additions,
omissions or alterations as may be
specifically authorized by the
Author. The Author shall make no
additions, omissions or
alterations in the manuscript of
the Play as contracted for
production without the consent of
the Producer. Any change of any
kind whatsoever in the manuscript,
stage business or performance of a
play made by anyone shall be
deemed to be a part of the Play
and shall belong to the Author of
the book, music or lyrics, as the
case may be. The Author shall not
be obligated to make payment to
any person suggesting or making
any such changes unless he has
entered into a bona fide written
collaboration agreement to do so.
The Author shall without any
obligation to the Producer be
entitled to use any parts of the
play omitted.

(b) Where the approval or consent of the

Author is required, Composers, Lyricists and Book
Writers, respectively, shall vote as separate units,
with one vote to each unit.

(c) In any case where, after the play
has run in New York for at least three weeks, the
Producer, because of some emergency, requests the
approval of the Author to make changes or
replacements as provided in subdivision (a)(i),
and the Producer is unable to obtain any Composer's,
Lyricist's or Book Writer's response to such request
72 hours after having sent him and the Guild
telegrams requesting the same, then such Composer's,
Lyricist's or Book Writer's right to vote shall be
forfeit and the votes of the others shall control.

(d) The Producer may complain to the
Guild that the Author is unreasonable in refusing
to make changes or additions. In such event the
Guild shall appoint a representative or
representatives and, if they so advise, shall lend
its best efforts to prevail upon the Author to
make the suggested changes, it being understood,
however, that the Guild shall have no power to
compel the Author to agree to such changes.

SEVENTH: Although the Producer is
acquiring the Author's services solely in
connection with the production of the Play, the
Author recognizes that by a successful production
the Producer makes a contribution to the value of
uses of the Play in other media. Therefore,
although the relationship between the parties is
limited to play production as herein provided, and
the Author alone owns and controls the Play with
respect to all other uses, nevertheless, if the
Producer has produced the Play as provided in
Section 2 of the annexed Schedule, the Author
agrees:

(a) That he will not authorize or permit
any outright sale of the right to use said Play for
any of the purposes described in subdivisions (c),
(d) and (e) hereof and during the period therein
specified without the Producer's prior consent. In
no event shall there be any outright sale of any

such rights prior to the first-class production of the Play, except that an outright sale of motion picture rights prior to such first-class production may be permitted if made subject to the provisions of Section 61 of the annexed Schedule.

(b) That he will use his best efforts to exploit the Play for any of the purposes described in subdivisions (c), (d) and (e) hereof.

(c) That the Producer shall receive the percentage of net receipts (regardless of when paid) specified hereinbelow if during any of the periods there set forth any of the following rights are disposed of: motion picture; or with respect to the continental United States and Canada any of the following: radio; television; second-class touring performances; foreign language performances; condensed and tabloid versions; so-called concert tour versions; commercial uses; grand opera; and, if Paragraph THIRD (b) is not selected or, if selected, does not become operative, stock performances and amateur performances:

If before the expiration of 10 years
after the last performance
hereunder of the last first-class
run of the Play: 40%

SEE
PARAGRAPH
TENTH

If within the next succeeding 2
years: 35%

If within the next succeeding 2
years: 30%

If within the next succeeding 2
years: 25%

If within the next succeeding 2
years: 20%

(d) That, if Paragraph THIRD (b) is selected and becomes operative, subdivision (c) above shall not apply to stock and amateur performances and the Producer shall receive the percentage of net receipts (regardless of when paid) specified hereinbelow if, during the period there set forth, any of the following rights are disposed of with respect to the continental United States and Canada: stock performances; amateur

performances; Off-Broadway performances:
>   If before the expiration of 5 years
>   after the last performance
>   hereunder of the last first-class
>   run of the Play: 40%

(e)   That if the Producer has produced
the Play in the British Isles in accordance with
the provisions of Paragraph FOURTH hereof and
Section 14 of the annexed Schedule and has otherwise
complied with all the terms and conditions of this
Contract, then he will have the same financial
interest in the right to use said Play for any of
the purposes specified in subdivisions (c) and (d)
hereof (other than motion picture rights) when they
are exploited in the British Isles as therein
provided with respect to the United States.

EIGHTH: The Author shall have the
exclusive right without limitation to negotiate and
contract for all performances or for any of the
other purposes specified in subdivisions (c) and
(d) of Paragraph SEVENTH, outside the Continental
United States, Canada or the British Isles, and
shall pay to the Producer   % of the net proceeds
he receives from such contracts so executed within
7 years after the New York opening.

NINTH: All compensation from whatever
source derived shall, where there is more than one
Author, be shared as follows:

>   Name   Share

TENTH: Additional Clauses
To the extent that any provision of the
Additional Clauses contained in this Paragraph
"TENTH" conflicts with any other portion of this
Contract (which includes the Schedule of Additional
Production Terms), such provision of these
Additional Clauses shall prevail.

A.   The Authors shall receive billing in
all advertising and publicity issued by, authorized
by, or under the control of Producer, excluding so-

called "ABC" and "teaser" ads, where only the title
of the Play, the name of the theatre, and the names
of the stars or a director of prominence appears.
The Authors' billing shall be on a separate line
beneath the title of the Play and the name of the
Authors shall be at least   Percent of the size
of the type used for the title of the Play. No
persons other than the star(s) whose name(s)
appear(s) above the title shall receive billing
larger or more prominent than that accorded Authors.
Wherever the name of any Author appears, all names
will appear. No casual or inadvertent failure to
comply with the provision of this Paragraph shall
be deemed a breach unless same shall not be
rectified promptly upon notice.

        B. For each performance of the Play under
the management of the Producer, Producer shall cause
four (4) adjoining house seats within the first
seven (7) rows of the center section of the
Orchestra to be held at the box office for each
Author or his designee to purchase at the regular
box office price, provided, however, that in
connection with benefit and theatre party
performances the Authors shall be entitled to two
(2) house seats only if such house seats are
available to the Producer. The tickets will be
held until forty-eight (48) hours prior to the
performance, unless the Producer's office or the
box office of the theatre is informed prior to that
time that the tickets will be picked up later and
that the Authors guarantee payment thereof, in
which case they will continue to be held for
purchase by the Authors or their designee up to
the time of performance. In addition, each Author
shall have four (4) pairs of such house seats
reserved in the orchestra section for the official
New York City opening of the Play. Authors agree
to comply with all Laws of the State of New York
and rules and regulations including those
promulgated by the Attorney General of the State
of New York, with respect to such house seats.

        C. The Producer agrees to deliver to

the Authors' agents, as the Authors' property,
within thirty (30) days after the New York City
opening, or prior to the closing of the Play,
whichever first occurs, a neat and legible copy of
the Play as produced on the New York opening
containing lighting, costume and property plots
and scene diagrams, as well as other details and
information customarily contained in a "Stage
Manager's Script."

      D. The Authors approve of
as Director of the Play and approve of
as Producer or Co-Producer.

      E. The Producer shall have the right to
assign this Contract to any Partnership or other
entity in which the Producer or the individuals
who are officers of the Corporate Producers are
General Partners or have the controlling interest
in said entity subject to Section 49 of the Schedule
of Additional Production Terms.

      F. Gross Weekly Box Office Receipts shall
be computed in the manner set forth in Article 3,
Section 9, of the Schedule of Additional Production
Terms annexed hereto provided, however, that in
making such computation there shall be deducted
(i) any Federal Admissions taxes or any similar
taxes which may or hereafter be imposed on
admissions; (ii) any commissions paid in connection
with Theatre Parties or Benefits or credit card
plans, automated ticket distribution or remote box
offices, e.g., Macy's and Ticketron but not ticket
brokers; (iii) those sums equivalent to the former
five percent (5%) New York Amusement Tax, the net
proceeds of which are now set aside in Pension and
Welfare funds of the Theatrical Unions and ultimately
paid to said funds, provided the Dramatists Guild,
Inc. agrees and (iv) fees paid or discounts allowed
in connection with subscriptions and group sales.

      G. The Producer shall be entitled to
proceeds under Paragraph "EIGHTH" hereof only if
the Producer is entitled to proceeds under Paragraph
"SEVENTH".

      H. If the Play is produced in the British

Isles hereunder, all of the approvals accorded to
Authors with respect to production in the United
States and Canada shall apply also to such British
production.

I.   The initial performance referred to
in Paragraph "SECOND" hereof shall be the first
paid first-class public performance of the Play
hereunder.

J.   Simultaneously herewith Producer is
paying the Authors the sum of Two Thousand Five
Hundred Dollars ($2,500.00), non-returnable, in
lieu of the payments specified in Paragraph
"THIRD (a)" hereof.   Such Two Thousand Five
Hundred Dollar ($2,500.00) payment shall entitle
the Producer to maintain his right to produce the
Play for a period of one (1) year from the date
hereof.   In the event Producer requires additional
time to produce the Play due to the unavailability
of a star, director, theatre, or no more than one-
half (1/2) of the financing needed to form the
partnership, Producer may extend the option to
produce the Play for not in excess of six (6)
months by making payment of an additional $200 each
month prior to the end of the month preceding the
month for which the $200 constitutes payment.

K.   If the Play is produced in Great
Britain by the Producer in association with a
British manager or on lease from the Producer to
British manager, by reason of which association or
lease the Producer receives an advance against
royalties or profits, or a lump sum as royalties
or in lieu of a portion of royalties, the Author
shall receive fifty percent (50%) of such advance
or lump sum, as an advance against the Authors'
percentage compensation with respect to such
British production.   Such advance to the Author,
if greater than the payments to which the Author
may be entitled under Paragraph "FOURTH (a)"
hereof, shall be inclusive thereof.

L.   In addition to the box office and
any other statements sent to the Dramatists Guild
pursuant to this Contract, the Producer shall at

the same time send three (3) duplicate copies of
such statements to:

      M. The Schedule of Additional Production
Terms is part of this Contract whether or not a
copy of same is attached.

      N. The Authors agree to use their best
efforts to require that the Producer receive visual
billing with respect to all motion pictures, or
live or filmed television productions based on the
Play.

      The Authors agree that Producer may also
produce or authorize first-class "bus and truck"
tours of the Play and Las Vegas, Lake Tahoe and
Reno productions. In connection with any such
"bus and truck" tour engagements or Las Vegas,
Lake Tahoe, Reno and similar types of productions,
the Authors' royalties shall be computed on the
basis of the Producer's receipts (including but
not limited to, fixed fees, guarantees and any
Producer's share of box office receipts), plus any
sums paid directly to a star(s) and/or director by
the theatre at which the Play is presented, less
booking fees, wardrobe and loaders, but only if
the following conditions exist in connection with
such engagements or productions:

      (i) That the Producer's gross
compensation whether direct or
indirect, for presenting the
production is a fixed fee or a
combination of a guarantee and
a share of the box office receipts,
payable to the Producer by a so-
called "local promoter" or a
"local sponsor" or other third
party acting in a similar
capacity;

      (ii) That all other creative royalty
participants' royalties and the

Producer's management fee be
computed on the same basis; and

(iii)   The royalty computation in this
paragraph shall be applicable
only to performances given in
other than first-class theatres.

If the foregoing conditions in subdivision (i),
(ii) and (iii) are not met, the Authors' royalties
shall be computed on the gross box office receipts
of any such engagements and productions.

O. Pursuant to the Rules and Regulations
of the United Scenic Artists, Scenic Designing
Artists and Theatrical Costumes Designers Contracts,
the Authors undertake and agree that they will not
sell, lease, license or authorize the use of any of
the original designs of scenery and costumes created
by the designers under the standard Scenic Designing
Artists and Theatrical Costume Designers Contracts
for the production without the designer's consent
and the Producer's consent.

P. The Authors do hereby warrant and
represent that they are the sole owners of the Play
and the owners of the said copyright and have the
right to deal with all the rights herein granted.
Authors further warrant and represent except for
material in the public domain that the Play does not
infringe upon the copyright of any other work or
violate any other rights of any other person, firm,
corporation or other entity, and that no claim has
been made against them adversely affecting the Play
or the copyright or any of the rights herein granted,
and they have full power to enter into this Agreement
and hereby agree to indemnify and hold the Producer
harmless against any claims, demands, suits, losses,
costs, expenses or damages actually sustained by
reason of any material breach of the above
warranties. Producer similarly agrees to indemnify
Authors as their interest appears with respect to
any material which the Producer or anyone under
Producer's control may incorporate into the Play.
Anything to the contrary in this paragraph
notwithstanding, nothing contained herein shall be

deemed to alter the rights and obligations of the
parties under Section 41 of the Schedule of
Additional Production Terms.

      Q. Anything to the contrary herein
notwithstanding, the Authors will be jointly paid
for each company presenting the Play, a royalty of
      Percent of the gross weekly box office
receipts (or the Producer's receipts as defined in
Paragraph "TENTH N") until the production budget
is recouped and   Percent
thereafter for each such company which has recouped
its production budget.

      R. A copy of all notices shall be sent
to Donald C. Farber, Esq., Conboy, Hewitt, O'Brien,
& Boardman, 600 Madison Avenue, New York, New York
10022.

      S. The reasonable "hotel" and "traveling"
expenses to be paid by the Producer to each Author
while away from their home in
pursuant to Article III, Section 13 of the Schedule
of Additional Production Terms shall be (i)
      Dollars a day for hotel and/or other
living expenses during the rehearsal period and
(ii) economy rail or jet transportation expenses to
and from New York City and from place to place out-
of-town. In the event of any first-class production
of the Play in the British Isles by the Producer,
each Author shall receive (i) the equivalent sum
of   Dollars in English Pounds for each
day they are in England for the rehearsal period
and (ii) economy-class jet transportation to and
from England and economy rail transportation from
place to place outside of London when such travel
is required to attend rehearsals and tryouts.

      T. The Producer with the approval of the
Composer and Lyricists which approval shall not be
unreasonably withheld, shall have control over the
disposition of the rights to make a phonograph
record, "cast album" or "show album" of the music
and lyrics of the Play (including, but not limited
to, dialogue from the Play for introductory or
bridging purposes). The net proceeds received from

the disposition of such cast album or show album
rights shall be divided forty percent (40%) to
the Producer and sixty percent (60%) to the
"Author," such "Author's" share to be divided
between the Composer and Lyricists/Bookwriters.

Author represents that his contract with
the Publisher of the music and lyrics of the Play
does contain or will contain a provision to the
following effect:

"The Music Publisher agrees that
it will make no contract that will
interfere with the disposition of the
motion picture and related rights in the
Play, and that it will execute, without
additional compensation, such instruments
and agreements as the Author, or the
motion picture company acquiring such
rights, may reasonably request, consistent
with the contract or proposed contract
which the Author shall make or desire to
make, with said motion picture company.

The music publisher further agrees
that it will grant to any Cast Album
record company contracted with by the
Producer of the Play, and record
companies contracted with by the Author
with regard to other authorized Cast or
Sound Track Albums, such recording license
as is usual, and standard terms and
conditions for such record license."

After a period of five (5) years from the close of
the first-class production, Composer may license
any of the songs written for the Play without the
approval or participation of the Producer provided,
however, that no more than one such song shall be
licensed in connection with any single production
and provided further that there has been no sale of
any motion picture rights in the Play. There shall
be no restriction on the licensing of musical
compositions after 10 years from the close of the
first-class production except as provided in a
contract, if any, for the sale of motion picture

rights.

U.   Composer shall have the right of
approval of the orchestrator, vocal arranger,
dance music arranger and conductor, which approvals
shall not be unreasonably withheld.

V.   Author shall have the right of approval
of the scenic, lighting and costume designer which
approvals shall not be unreasonably withheld.

W.   Whenever the Composer is living away
from home during the pre-Broadway rehearsal period
pursuant to Paragraph "TENTH" herein and under
Article III, Section 13 of the Schedule of
Additional Production Terms, the Producer will, at
the request of the Composer, provide an upright
piano in the Composer's hotel room.

X.   Producer agrees to satisfy Equity
obligations concerning payment of three (3) weeks'
salary to each actor used in the showcase production
at the   Theatre and not used in the
first-class production.

Y.   The Authors shall jointly have the
right to examine the books and records of the
Producer pertaining to the production of the Play
during regular business hours no more than twice
yearly.

[An agency clause(s) is usually included
here detailing the role and payment of the respective
agent(s) of the bookwriter(s), composer(s), and
lyricist(s).]

ELEVENTH: Any claim, dispute or
controversy arising between the Producer and the
Author under, or in connection with, or out of the
Contract or the breach thereof, shall be submitted
to arbitration as specified in Article XIII of the
annexed Schedule unless the Author selects other
remedies as permitted by Paragraph FIFTH (a) hereof.
The Guild shall receive notice of such arbitration
and shall have the right to be a party to the same.

TWELFTH: The following words and phrases
when used in this Contract or the annexed Schedule
shall mean and include as follows:

Author: Each Dramatist, Collaborator or

Adaptor of the Play and each Composer, Lyricist,
Novelist or Author of any other literary or musical
material used in the Play but not including a person
whose service is only that of a literal translator.

Commercial Uses: Toys, games, figures,
dolls, novelties or any physical property
representing a character in the Play or using the
name of a character or the title of the Play or
otherwise connected with the Play or its title,
provided the Author has consented to such use.

Contract: This contract and the Schedule
of Additional Production Terms annexed thereto.

End of First-class Run: Whenever the
Producer has lost his right to reopen the play or
has in writing declared that he will not reopen it.

New York: The theatrical district of the
Borough of Manhattan of the City of New York.

Off-Broadway Performances: Performances
in theatres located in the City of New York which
are classified pursuant to the terms of the minimum
basic contract of Actors Equity as "Off-Broadway."

Continental United States: Shall be
deemed to include the States of Hawaii and Alaska,
geographical inconsistencies notwithstanding.

Production Expenses: Fees of designers
and directors; cost of sets; curtains, drapes and
costumes; cost or payments on account of properties,
furnishings and electrical equipment; premiums for
bonds and insurance; unrecouped advances to authors;
rehearsal charges, transportation charges, reasonable
legal and auditing expenses, advance publicity and
other expenses actually incurred in connection with
the production and presentation preliminary to the
opening of the Play in New York, including any out-
of-town losses, but there shall not be included any
compensation to the Producer or to any person
rendering the services of a producer other than a
charge for office expenses not to exceed $250 per
week commencing two weeks before the opening of
rehearsals and continuing until the New York
opening. No items charged as production expenses
shall be charged against operating profits, or vice

versa.

Weekly Operating Profits: The difference
between the Producer's share of the box office
receipts (after meeting any theatre minimum guaranty)
and the total weekly expenses determined as follows:
$500 for Author's minimum compensation, salaries of
the cast, business manager, press agent, orchestra,
and miscellaneous stage help, compensation payable
to the directors, transportation charges, office
charge not to exceed $450, advertising, rentals,
miscellaneous supplies, and all other reasonable
expenses of whatever kind actually incurred in
connection with the weekly operation of the Play as
distinguished from production costs, but not
including any compensation to the Producer or a
person rendering the services of a producer, nor
any monies paid by way of percentage of the receipts
or otherwise for the making of any loan or the
posting of any bond.

THIRTEENTH: This Contract shall be
binding upon and inure to the benefit of the
respective parties hereto and their respective
successors in interest (except as herein otherwise
limited), but shall be effective only when
countersigned by the Guild. No change or
modification of this Contract shall be effective
unless reduced to writing, signed by the parties
hereto, and countersigned by the Guild. If the
Producing Managers Contract is assigned by the
Guild pursuant to Paragraph XXI thereof, (i) this
Contract shall be deemed to have been amended as
of the date of such assignment so that the name of
the assignee shall be substituted in place of the
words "Guild," "Dramatists Guild" or "The Dramatists
Guild of the Authors League of America, Inc."
wherever such words shall appear; (ii) the name of
the Council or governing body of said assignee shall
be deemed to have been substituted in place of the
name of the Council of the Guild wherever it shall
appear; and (iii) such assignee and its governing
body shall succeed to and assume all rights,
privileges, duties and obligations of the Dramatists

Guild of the Authors League of America, Inc. and its
Council under this Contract.

      FOURTEENTH: Should any part, term or
provision of this agreement be decided by the courts
to be in conflict with any law of the state where
made or of the United States, the validity of the
remaining portions or provisions shall not be
affected thereby.

      FIFTEENTH: In making proof of the
execution of this Contract or of any of the terms
thereof, for any purpose, the use of a copy of this
Contract filed with the Dramatists Guild shall be
sufficient provided (a) that the copy produced from
the files of the Guild need not have attached to it
the particular printed copy of the Schedule of
Production Terms annexed thereto at the time of
deposit with the Guild but may be produced with
any identical printed copy of said Schedule, and
(b) that at any time after two years from the date
of execution hereof there may be produced from the
files of the Guild, in lieu of the copy of this
Contract originally deposited therein, a microfilm
of said copy.

      IN WITNESS WHEREOF, the parties hereto
have hereunto set their hands and seals the day and
year first above written.

                                   _____

                                   Author of the Book

                                   _____

                                   Lyricist

                                   _____

                                   Composer

                                   _____

                                   Producer*

_____

     *Where this contract is signed by a corporate
Producer, the officer signing should state his office
and the corporate seal should be affixed. Where the

officer signing for the corporation is other than the
President, a certified copy of a resolution should be
furnished showing the authority of said person so to
sign.

Where this contract is signed by a partnership,
all the general partners must sign and the
partnership name should also be stated.

(If Producer is a corporation, the following
must be signed by the person or persons in control
thereof, i.e., the person or persons (a) owning or
controlling a majority of its stock or a majority of
its voting stock; or (b) using their name as part of
the corporate title; or (c) rendering services in
connection with the play as Producer; or (d) whose
name is included in publicity, advertising or
programs as Producer or co-Producer of the play.)

In consideration of the execution of this
Contract by the Author, the undersigned (if more
than one, then the undersigned jointly and severally)
hereby agrees to be jointly liable with the Producer
for the full performance of each and every covenant
and provision of this Contract on the Producer's
part to be performed, including but not limited to
the payment of all monies due the Author hereunder.

_____

COUNTERSIGNED:
THE DRAMATISTS GUILD, INC.

By_____

APPENDIX E

COLLABORATION AGREEMENT

AGREEMENT made as of this   day of   , 19
by and between   (sometimes hereinafter referred to as
"   " or the "Bookwriter-Lyricist" and   (sometimes
referred to as "   " or the "Composer").

W I T N E S S E T H :

WHEREAS, the parties to this Agreement are collaborating
on a Musical Play for which   will write the book and the
lyrics and   will compose the music, which Play is at
this time entitled   .

NOW, THEREFORE, the parties do agree as follows:

1. The parties agree that Bookwriter-Lyricist will
write the book and lyrics and that Composer will write the music
for the Play. The parties agree that they will jointly register
and own the copyright in the music and lyrics. It is agreed that
all receipts from all sources in connection with the Play shall
be shared by the parties as follows: two-thirds (2/3) to
          and one-third (1/3) to   . All rights in
the individual musical compositions for the Play shall be held
by   and   jointly and they (and their publishing
companies) shall participate equally in the so-called "small
performing rights" in the musical compositions contained in the
Play as well as the publishing and recording contracts.

2. Each of the parties represents and warrants that
the material written and/or hereafter written by such party for
the Play shall be original with such party and shall not violate
or infringe the copyright, common law copyright, right of privacy,
or any other personal or property right whatsoever of any person
or entity or constitute a libel or slander, and that such party
fully owns and controls such material and all rights therein and
has full right to enter into this Agreement and all production
contracts and other contracts and consents to be entered into
hereunder.

3. No contract for the production, presentation or
publication of the Play, the music and lyrics, or any part
thereof, or the disposition of any right therewith connected,
shall be valid without the signature thereto of both of the
parties to the Agreement. Both parties shall have approval of
the Director of the Play. Bookwriter-Lyricist shall have all

authors' approvals, except that Composer shall have approval of
the Musical Director and Arranger thereof. Powers of Attorney
may, however, be granted by one party to the other, by written
instrument, setting forth specific conditions under which said
Power of Attorney shall be valid. For services rendered under
this Power of Attorney, whether in conducting negotiations or
consummating a contract, no agency fee or extra compensation will
be demanded.

      4. Any contracts concerning the use of the Play for a
first-class production shall be based on the Minimum Basic
Production Contract of the Dramatists Guild, Inc., which is
current and in use at that time, with any changes approved by
Donald C. Farber, Esq.

      5. Duplicate contracts concerning the Play, the music
and the publishing and recording rights therein, including but not
limited to the production thereof or the disposition of any rights
in the Play, shall be given to each of the parties to this
Agreement. Payments to each of the parties shall be made in
accordance with the specific instructions from each such party.

      6. In any contract for the production or presentation
of the Play or for the disposition of any rights therein, the
parties shall use their best efforts to secure the insertion in
said contracts of clauses providing that on programs, billings,
posters, advertisements or other printed matter used in connection
with any production thereof or other use thereof in any manner,
the names   as Bookwriter-Lyricist and   as Composer
shall be in all billing credits, in that order, in equal size and
prominence of type. It is further agreed that in no event shall
either name appear as an author without the other name.

      7. No change or alteration shall be made in the book
or lyrics of the Play by either of the parties without the written
consent of   . No change or alteration shall be made in
the music of the Play without the written consent of   .
Such consent will not be unreasonably withheld.

      8. In the event that either of the parties to this
Agreement wishes to sell, pledge, lease or assign, or otherwise
dispose of or encumber his share of royalty interests, stock, or
subsidiary interest, motion picture interests, foreign interest
or the like, or any part or portion thereof (other than the small
performing rights and publishing rights reserved to each), it is
agreed that such party (called the "selling party") shall give
to the other (called the "buying party") in a written notice with

full particulars, sent by registered mail, an option for a period
of fourteen (14) days during which the buying party may purchase
such rights in said Play as may be offered, at a price and upon
such terms as stated in said written notice. Should the buying
party fail, within the said fourteen (14) days, to exercise said
option in writing, or if the option is exercised, fail to complete
the purchase upon the terms and conditions stated in the said
notice, then the selling party may sell such rights to any other
person, subject to the conditions set forth in the following
paragraph.

Before the consummation of the sale to any other
person the selling party must give the other party to this
Agreement written notice containing the name and all conditions
of the proposed sale to said third party and must give the other
party to this Agreement ten (10) business days within which to
match the said offer in all respects exclusive of any specific
terms which would not be expedient for the other party to this
Agreement to match such as the procuring of a particular star,
director, etc. If said offer is not matched within the said ten
(10) business days, then the selling party may complete said sale
to said third party upon such terms and conditions, and a copy of
the contract for the sale of such rights shall be sent to the
other party hereto forthwith.

9. All expenses which may reasonably be incurred under
this Agreement shall be mutually agreed upon in advance and shall
be shared one-half (1/2) by   and one-half (1/2) by
         . This also applies to any tax or assessment made by
the Dramatists Guild, Inc. on the Play.

10. It is expressly understood that the parties hereto
do not form, nor shall this Agreement be construed to constitute,
a partnership between them.

11. Anything to the contrary hereinabove
notwithstanding, the contributions of the respective parties
hereto shall be owned by the contributor thereof, and the written
consent of both parties shall be required for any sale, license
or other disposition of the Play, provided, however, that in the
event of an official opening of an authorized production of the
Play within a period of   years from the completion thereof
the respective contributions of the parties hereunder to the Play
shall be deemed merged for all purposes in the sense that no party
may deal with the Play or any parts thereof except as herein
provided, and the term of this Agreement shall be co-extensive

with the life of the copyright in and to the Play. In the event
that an official opening of an authorized production does not
take place within a period of   years from the completion
of the Play, this Agreement shall be deemed terminated and of no
further effect and each of the parties hereto shall continue to
own their respective contributions to the Play free and clear of
any interest therein of the other party thereto. In the event of
death of either of the parties hereto during the existence of
this Agreement, then the survivor of the parties shall have the
sole right to change the Play, negotiate and contract with regard
to the disposition thereof, and act generally with regard thereto
as though he were the sole author thereof, except, however, that
the name of the decedent shall always appear as provided in
Paragraph 6 of this Agreement, and the said survivor further shall
cause to be paid to the heirs or legal representatives of the
deceased party the agreed upon per centum of the net receipts of
the said Play, and furnish true copies of all agreements to the
personal representatives of the deceased.

      12. Any controversy or claim arising out of or relating
to this contract, or the breach thereof, shall be settled by
arbitration by one arbitrator in accordance with the rules of the
American Arbitration Association and judgment upon the award
rendered by the arbitrator may be entered in any court having
jurisdiction thereof.

      13. The terms and conditions of this Agreement shall be
binding upon and shall inure to the benefit of the executors,
administrators and assigns of the parties hereto.

      IN WITNESS WHEREOF, the parties hereto have hereunto set
their hands and seals as of the day and year first above written.

_____

_____

APPENDIX F

AGREEMENT made as of the   day of   , 19
between   (hereinafter sometimes referred to as
the "Owner" or "Author") and   (hereinafter sometimes
referred to as the "Producer") with respect to the option to
perform the   play presently entitled
        (hereinafter sometimes referred to as the "Play"),
written by   .

1. The Owner does hereby warrant and represent that
        is the sole owner of the Play which was originally
copyrighted under the name   dated
and the Owner is the owner of the said copyright and has the right
to deal with all the rights herein granted. The Owner further
warrants and represents that the Play does not infringe upon the
copyright of any other work or violate any other rights of any
other person, firm, corporation or other entity, and that no claim
has been made against the Owner adversely affecting the Play or
the copyright, or any of the rights herein granted, and the Owner
has full power to enter into this Agreement and hereby agrees to
indemnify and hold the Producer harmless against any claims,
demands, suits, losses, costs, expenses, damages actually
sustained by reason of any material breach of the above
warranties. Producer similarly agrees to indemnify Owner as his
interest appears with respect to any material which the Producer
or anyone under Producer's control may incorporate into the Play.

2. The Owner does hereby grant to the Producer the sole
and exclusive right and license to produce the Play and to present
it as a professional   production in the City of New York.
In addition, Producer is also given the right to produce the Play
and present it for a pre-off-Broadway tour. In consideration of
the sum of   , payable upon the
execution of this Agreement, the Owner does hereby grant to the
Producer the option to produce the Play to open on or before
        . The Producer may extend this option to produce
the Play to open on or before   upon payment to the
Owner of an additional   on or before   .
The payments made pursuant to this Paragraph 2 of this Agreement
shall be deemed to be non-returnable advances against the royalty
payments provided for in Paragraph 4 of this Agreement.

3. The rights granted to the Producer are the sole and exclusive rights to produce the Play (the Producer may acquire an option pursuant to the terms of this Agreement as hereinafter set forth to produce the Play in the British Isles and in the U.S. and Canada and on tour, and the Owner agrees that will not grant the rights to permit anyone to perform the said Play in any media (exclusive of movies) within the United States of America, Canada or the British Isles, during the term of the option herein granted and the run of the Play, or during the period that the Producer retains any rights or option to produce the Play anywhere in the United States, Canada or the British Isles, and further agrees that will not grant the right to anyone to do a movie version of the Play which would be released during the term of the option or the run of the Play, or during the period that the Producer retains any right or option to produce the Play in the United States, Canada or the British Isles, without the written consent of the Producer, which consent will not be unreasonably withheld.

4. The Author shall be paid of the gross weekly box office receipts as a royalty payment during each week. The Author agrees to waive so much of the royalty each week which, if paid, would cause the Play to operate at a net operating loss, on condition that the Producer likewise waive so much of his Producer's fee in each such week. Such waiver, to the extent that the royalties and Producer's fee are reduced, will be pari passu amongst the party(s) constituting the "Author" and the Producer. The term "Gross Weekly Box Office Receipts" as used herein shall mean all receipts at the box office from the sale of tickets, less: theatre party commissions, discount and cut-rate sales, all admission taxes presently or to be levied, Ticketron charges or the cost of any other automated ticket distributor, those sums equivalent to the former 5% New York amusement tax, the net proceeds of which are now set aside in pension and welfare funds of the theatrical unions and ultimately paid to said funds, any subscription fees and actors' fund benefits. The Producer agrees to keep accurate books and records and will furnish the Owner with a signed box office statement together with each royalty payment which will be made on or before each Wednesday for the previous week's performances, and the Owner or his representative shall have the right to examine the books and records of the Producer pertaining to the Play upon giving the Producer reasonable notice.

5. Although the Producer is acquiring the rights and

services of the Owner solely in connection with the production of
the Play, the Owner recognizes that by a successful production
the Producer makes a contribution to the value of the uses of the
Play in other media. Therefore, although the relationship
between the parties is limited to play production as herein
provided, and the Owner owns and controls the Play with respect
to all other uses, nevertheless, if the Producer has produced the
Play as provided herein, the Owner agrees that the Producer shall
receive the percentage of net receipts (regardless of when paid)
specified hereinbelow, if the Play has been produced for the
number of consecutive performances specified below and if, before
the expiration of ten (10) years, subsequent to the date of the
last public performance of the Play in New York City, any of the
following rights are disposed of anywhere throughout the world:
motion picture, or with respect to the Continental United States
and Canada, any of the following rights: radio, television,
touring performances, stock performances; Broadway performances;
off-Broadway performances; amateur performances; foreign language
performances; condensed tabloid versions; so-called concert tour
versions; commercial uses; original cast albums, tapes, cassettes
and records made therefrom and video cassettes or discs:
Percent if the Play shall run for at least twenty-one (21)
consecutive paid performances;   Percent if the Play shall
run for at least forty-two (42) consecutive paid performances;
          Percent if the Play shall run for at least fifty-six (56)
consecutive paid performances;   Percent if the Play shall
run for sixty-five (65) consecutive paid performances or more.
For the purposes of computing the number of performances, provided
the Play officially opens in New York City, the first paid
performance shall be deemed to be the first performance, however,
no more than ten (10) paid preview performances shall be counted
in making this computation.

          6. For all public performances of the Play, the
Producer shall make available for purchase by the Owner, at
regular box office prices, four (4) pairs of orchestra tickets in
the first eight (8) rows of the theatre. Such tickets shall be
held at the box office until 6:00 P.M. of the day before each
evening performance and until 12:00 noon of the day before each
matinee performance. The Producer also agrees to make available
for purchase by the Owner ten (10) pairs of seats in a desirable
location in the orchestra section for the official opening of the
Play in New York City. The Owner acknowledges that he will keep

and maintain complete and accurate records in accordance with
the rules and regulations of the Attorney General of the State
of New York.

7. The Producer agrees that the Author will receive
billing credits in all advertisements, programs, billboards and
houseboards wherever the name of the Play appears. The name will
appear in all paid advertising except ABC ads, shallow double ads
and teasers.

8. In the event that the Play opens in New York City
and runs for twenty-one (21) performances commencing with the
first paid preview (for the purposes of this computation only
          paid previews shall be counted), then the Producer is
granted the right up to   months after the official opening
of the New York City production of the Play to give notice that
the Producer wishes to contract for the touring rights to the
Play in the United States and Canada upon the following terms and
conditions:

If the tour is to be a first-class tour, then upon
the minimum terms and conditions as set forth in the Dramatists
Guild, Inc. Minimum Basic Production Contract for such a tour,
which the parties agree to expeditiously enter into.

If the tour is to be a second-class tour, the
royalty to be paid shall be   Percent of the gross weekly box
office receipts or of the contracted fee. Upon receipt by the
Owner of written notice from the Producer up to   months
after the official opening of the New York City production, the
parties agree to expeditiously thereafter enter into a contract
containing the above terms, which contract shall provide for a
payment to the Owner of a non-returnable advance against
royalties in the amount of   , and
shall further provide that said tour may commence at any time up
to   months after the giving of said notice.

9. The Producer shall have the exclusive right during
the term of this option or any extensions thereof, to originally
produce the Play on Broadway in New York City or to transfer the
production of the Play to a Broadway theatre up to sixty (60)
days after the close of the middle theatre or off-Broadway run
of the Play and in the event that the Producer exercises this
right, the parties agree to enter into a Dramatists Guild, Inc.
Minimum Basic Production Contract upon the minimum terms of such
contract within seven (7) days after receipt by the Owner of the
Producer's written notice of his intention to exercise this said

right.   In the event that the parties do enter into a Dramatists
Guild, Inc. Minimum Basic Production Contract, then the Producer
shall be entitled to the financial interest in subsidiary rights
and production rights which are most favorable to the Producer
under either this Agreement or the Dramatists Guild, Inc. Minimum
Basic Production Contract but shall not be entitled to such
interest in both agreements collectively.

　　　　10.   In the event that the Play opens in New York City
and runs for twenty-one (21) performances (for the purpose of this
computation, only　　　　paid previews shall be counted), then
the Producer is granted the right up to　　　　months after the
official opening of the New York City production of the Play to
give notice that the Producer wishes to contract for the right to
produce the Play in the British Isles.   The parties agree after
notice is given to expeditiously enter into a contract containing
the terms hereinafter set forth, which contract shall provide that
the English production may open at any time up to twelve (12)
months after the receipt of such notice.

　　　　Said contract shall further provide that the royalty
payments due to the Owner for the British production rights shall
be a sum equal to　　　　Percent of all gross weekly box office
receipts.   In the event of a West End production, the Producer
shall acquire the same interest in the British subsidiary rights
depending upon the length of the West End run as hereinabove
provided in Paragraph 5 of this Agreement for the New York City
production.

　　　　Said British contract shall also provide for payment
to the Owner of an advance against royalties in the amount of
$　　　　for a West End production, and $　　　　for a production
outside of the West End.

　　　　11.   In the event that the Play opens in New York City
and runs for twenty-one (21) performances (for the purpose of this
computation, only　　　　preview performances shall be counted),
then the Producer shall have the right to produce the Play in any
city in the United States and Canada (in addition to, and
independent of, a first- or second-class tour) upon giving written
notice to the Author up to　　　　months after the official
opening of the New York City production.

　　　　In the event that the Producer wishes to do a first-
class production of the Play, then the parties will, within seven
(7) days of receipt of the Producer's written notice of such
intention, enter into a Dramatists Guild, Inc. Minimum Basic

Production Contract, upon the minimum terms.

      If the Producer wishes to do other than a first-class production, he will, together with the notice, forward an option payment in the amount of \$ for each city in which he wishes to produce the Play, which will grant the Producer the right to produce the Play in each such other city. Said option payments shall be deemed to be non-returnable advance payments against a royalty payment of   Percent of the gross weekly box office receipts. Each proposed production must open before a paid audience within   months after mailing of the notice and \$ check for each city.

      12. The Owner shall have approval of the director and star(s) which approval will not be unreasonably withheld. In the event that the Owner does not approve or disapprove within three (3) days of the request for (his, her, or their) approval, it shall be deemed to be an approval.

      13. If the Play is produced within the option period herein granted, the right to produce the Play in New York City shall continue during its continuous run. The Play shall be deemed closed (that is, the continuous run shall have terminated) if no paid performances have been given in New York City for a period of one (1) month. After the Play has closed and after all options to produce the Play have expired, then the rights herein granted to produce the Play shall revert to the Owner, subject to any other terms specifically herein set forth.

      If the Play is produced outside the City of New York on tour or otherwise, the rights to produce the Play after the one-year option period herein stated shall continue during its continuous run. Continuous run as herein defined shall mean that there shall not be a lapse of more than five (5) weeks that there is not a presentation of the Play before a paying audience. If the one-year option period has expired and if more than five (5) weeks elapse between any paid production, then all rights shall revert to the Author except those that may have been specifically herein vested.

      14. The Producer may assign this Agreement and may license or assign any of the rights granted hereunder, providing, however, that the assignment of the right to produce the Play in New York may be made only to a Limited Partnership, corporation or other entity in which the Producer is one of the major principals. Any assignment shall be subject to all of the terms and conditions of this Agreement and any assignee agrees to be

bound by such terms.

15. Any controversy or claim arising out of, or relating to this Agreement, or the breach thereof, shall be settled by arbitration in New York City by one arbitrator in accordance with the rules then obtaining of the American Arbitration Association, and judgment upon the award rendered may be entered in any court of the forum having jurisdiction hereof.

16. This Agreement shall be binding upon, and inure to the benefit of the parties, their respective heirs, next of kin, executors, administrators, assigns and legal representatives.

17. This Agreement represents the entire understanding of the parties and cannot be changed or amended unless by a document in writing duly signed by the parties hereto.

18. All rights not specifically herein granted to the Producer are reserved for the Owner.

19. The Producer shall make no script changes without the Owner's approval.

20. All notices herein provided for shall be sent by registered mail or by telegram to the parties as follows:

A copy of all notices will be sent to:

Donald C. Farber, Esq.

Conboy, Hewitt, O'Brien, & Boardman

600 Madison Avenue

New York, New York 10022

21. All rights herein granted shall be automatically extended for the duration of any period occasioned by a strike, lockout, or any act of God that makes the presentation of the Play impossible.

IN WITNESS WHEREOF, the parties hereto have hereunto set their hands and seals as of the day and year first above written.

_____   _____

APPENDIX G

NOTIFICATION UNDER

REGULATION "A"

SECURITIES AND EXCHANGE COMMISSION

Washington, D. C.

Form 1-A

The following information is given with respect to an offering of securities to be made pursuant to Regulation A of the General Rules and Regulations under the Securities Act of 1933. The offering circular required by Rule 256 is filed with and is deemed to be a part of this Notification.

ITEM 1. THE ISSUER

A. The Issuer is (General Partner's name) and the Issuer will be (name of producing company) , a Limited Partnership (hereinafter sometimes referred to as the "Partnership") when formed.

B. The Partnership will be formed pursuant to the Laws of the State of New York when the aggregate Limited Contributions (as such term is used in the Limited Partnership Agreement of the Issuer   , filed herewith as an Exhibit under Item 11 A and hereinafter called the "Partnership Agreement") have been raised as a result of the offering of the Limited Partnership interests by   on behalf of the Partnership.

C. The Issuer proposes to conduct its principal business operation in the State of New York.

D. The Issuer is not subject to Rule 253 (b) of Regulation A, and it does not hold or propose to hold any properties in any country other than the United States.

ITEM 2. PREDECESSORS, AFFILIATES AND PRINCIPAL
        SECURITY HOLDER OF ISSUER

A. The Issuer does not have, and has not had, a predecessor.

B.   is an affiliate of the Partnership and will be the General Partner thereof.

C. No person owns of record, or is known to own beneficially Ten Percent (10%) or more of the outstanding securities of any class of the Issuer, but upon the organization of said Limited Partnership, it is contemplated that as General Partner of the Partnership, will be entitled to receive Fifty Percent (50%) of the net profits of the Partnership as defined in the Partnership Agreement.

ITEM 3. DIRECTORS, OFFICERS AND PROMOTERS

A.   The Issuer has no directors.

B.   The Issuer has no officers.

C.   The Partnership will be organized as set forth in
ITEMS 1 and 2 hereinabove and   , the Promoter of the
Partnership, will be the General Partner thereof.

ITEM 4.   <u>COUNSEL FOR ISSUER AND UNDERWRITERS</u>

Donald C. Farber, Esq., of Conboy, Hewitt, O'Brien, &
Boardman, 600 Madison Avenue, New York, New York 10022, will be
counsel for the Issuer in connection with the proposed offering.
No underwriter is involved in connection with the proposed
offering.

ITEM 5.   <u>ACTIONS AGAINST THE ISSUER OR ITS</u>
<u>PREDECESSORS OR AFFILIATED ISSUERS</u>

Neither the Issuer, its predecessors nor any affiliated
Issuer:

(i)   has been convicted of any crime or offense
involving the purchase or sale of securities;

(ii)   is subject to any order, judgment or decree of any
court temporarily or permanently restraining or enjoining such
person from engaging in or continuing any conduct or practice in
connection with the purchase or sale of securities; or

(iii)   is subject to a United States Post Office fraud
order.

ITEM 6.   <u>ACTIONS AGAINST DIRECTORS,</u>
<u>OFFICERS OR OTHERS</u>

No promoter, general partner or principal security
holder of the Issuer (there being no underwriters, directors or
officers):

(i)   has been convicted of any crime or offense
involving the purchase or sale of any security or arising out of
any such person's conduct as an underwriter, broker, dealer or
investment advisor;

(ii)   is subject to any order, judgment or decree of any
court enjoining or restraining such person from engaging in or
continuing any conduct or practice in connection with the purchase
or sale of any security, or arising out of such person's conduct
as an investment advisor, underwriter, broker or dealer;

(iii)   has been or is suspended or expelled from
membership in any national or professional security dealers'
association or national security exchange or Canadian securities
exchange; or

(iv)   is subject to a United States Post Office fraud

order.

ITEM 7.   CONNECTION OF UNDERWRITERS
          WITH OTHER OFFERINGS

No underwriter is involved in connection with the
proposed offering.

ITEM 8.   JURISDICTIONS IN WHICH
          SECURITIES ARE TO BE OFFERED

A.   The Issuer does not conduct or propose to conduct
its principal business operations in Canada and therefore is not
subject to Rule 253(b) of Regulation A.

B.   The Issuer does not propose to offer the securities
covered by this Notification through underwriters, dealers or
salesmen.

C.   The Issuer proposes to offer the Limited Partnership
interests covered by this Notification by means of the mails,
telephone and personal communication. While it is contemplated
that the securities covered by this Notification will be offered
principally in the State of New York, they may also be offered
in the states of

D.   No part of the offering is to be made by use of the
facilities of any securities exchange.

ITEM 9.   UNREGISTERED SECURITIES ISSUED
          OR SOLD WITHIN ONE YEAR

A.   The Issuer, its predecessors and affiliates have not
issued any unregistered securities of the Issuer or any of its
predecessors or affiliates which were sold within one (1) year
prior to the date of the filing of this Notification.

B.   No unregistered securities of the Issuer or any of
its predecessors or affiliates were sold within one (1) year prior
to the date of the filing of this Notification by or for the
account of any person who at the time was a director, officer,
promoter or principal security holder of the Issuer of such
securities, or was an underwriter of any securities of such Issuer.

C.   No unregistered securities of the Issuer or any of
its predecessors or affiliates were sold within one (1) year prior
to the date of the filing of this Notification. Reference to any
section of the Act or rule or regulation of the Commission under
which exemption for registration was claimed with respect to the
sale of unregistered securities is inapplicable.

ITEM 10. OTHER PRESENT OR PROPOSED OFFERINGS

Neither the Issuer nor any of its affiliates is
presently offering or presently contemplating the offering or

sale of any securities in addition to those covered by this
Notification.

ITEM 11.   EXHIBITS

A.   Four (4) copies of the Limited Partnership Agreement
of (name of Producing Company) , describing the rights of the
General and Limited Partners of the Partnership, are filed with
the Commission concurrently herewith and are incorporated hereat
as an exhibit hereto.

B.   No underwriting contracts exist relating to the
securities to be offered hereunder.

C.   No underwriters are, or have consented to be, named
in this Notification or Offering Circular as underwriters of the
securities offered hereunder.

D.   None of the securities proposed to be offered
hereunder are to be offered for the account of any person other
than the Issuer.

E.   and   are residents of the United
States.

F.   Four (4) copies of an Offering Circular, required
pursuant to Rule 256 of Regulation A, are filed concurrently
herewith and constitute a part hereof.

G.   No accountant, engineer, geologist, appraiser or
other professional person is named as having prepared or certified
any part of this Notification or the Offering Circular; no
statement is embodied pursuant to Rule 257 of Regulation A; and
no person is named as having prepared or certified a report or
validation.   Four (4) copies of the Consent and Certification by
the Attorney named herein are filed herewith.

H.   No escrow or other similar arrangements are relied
upon to meet the requirement of Rule 253(c) of Regulation A
because in computing the amount of securities which may be offered
hereunder, there have been included, in addition to the securities
specified in Rule 254 of Regulation A, any security specified in
Rule 253(c) of Regulation A.

This Notification has been signed in the City of New
York, State of New York, on the   day of   , 19 , by

_____

CONSENT AND CERTIFICATION BY ATTORNEY

    The undersigned hereby consents to being named as attorney in a Notification and Offering Circular filed with the Securities and Exchange Commission by   and   , a Limited Partnership when formed, pursuant to Regulation A in connection with a proposed offering of Limited Partnership interests in   (name of Producing Company)   to the public.

                                 _____

                                      DONALD C. FARBER

Dated:

APPENDIX H

LIMITED PARTNERSHIP AGREEMENT

   Limited Partnership Agreement between   ,
residing at
(sometimes hereinafter referred to as the "General Partner" or
"Producer") and the parties who shall execute this agreement as
hereinafter provided (each of whom is sometimes hereinafter
referred to as a "Limited Partner").

   1. PURPOSE.

   The parties hereby form a Limited Partnership
(hereinafter referred to as the "Partnership") pursuant to the
provisions of Article Eight of the Partnership Law of the State
of New York, to produce and present the musical play
   (sometimes hereinafter referred to as the "Play") as a
professional production in a Broadway theatre in New York City,
to open on or before   in accordance with the
Option Agreement entered into as of the day of
  and assigned to Producer by a separate agreement, as amended,
copies of which are on file and may be examined at the offices of
Donald C. Farber, of Conboy, Hewitt, O'Brien, & Boardman, 600
Madison Avenue, New York, New York 10022, the attorney for the
production. The Partnership is being formed for the purpose of
producing and presenting the Play and for the purpose of exploiting
and turning to account the rights at any time held by the
Partnership in connection with the production and presentation of
the Play, and for no other purposes.

   2. FORMATION.

   The Partnership shall commence on the day on which,
pursuant to the New York Partnership Law, the Certificate of
Limited Partnership is duly filed in the Office of the Clerk of
New York County, which Certificate shall be filed after the
execution of this Agreement by the first Limited Partner. The
Partnership will terminate upon the death, insanity or retirement
of a General Partner, or a date fixed by the General Partners
after abandonment of all further partnership activities. A
notice containing the substance of the Certificate of Limited
Partnership shall be published as required by the New York
Partnership Law. When the aggregate Limited Contributions have
been raised an amended Certificate of Limited Partnership will be
filed expeditiously with the Office of the Clerk of New York
County reflecting the additional limited partners and their
contributions as well as any other changes.

3. <u>CAPITALIZATION</u>.

A. The estimated production requirements shall be in the sum of   . Each Limited Partner shall contribute to the capital of the Partnership the sum set forth as his or her contribution opposite his or her signature hereto. The contribution of each Limited Partner shall be payable at the time of execution of this Agreement. Such sums may be used for payment of all expenses incurred in connection with the production and presentation of the Play.

B. Each Limited Partner will not be required to contribute any additional amounts to the Partnership above his initial contributions.

C. In the event that the expenses incurred shall exceed the estimated production requirements, the General Partner may advance or cause to be advanced, or may borrow on behalf of the Partnership such sums as shall equal the excess. Such additional contributions or loans shall not have the effect of reducing the share of net profits payable to the original Limited Partners. In the event that loans are made to the Partnership, they shall be entitled to be repaid in full without interest, prior to the return of any contributions to the Limited Partners.

4. <u>ASSIGNMENT OF RIGHTS TO THE PARTNERSHIP</u>.

Subject to the provisions of Paragraphs "23," "27" and "28" of this Agreement, the General Partner will, upon the organization of the Limited Partnership, assign to the Partnership all right, title and interest in all assets acquired by him for the presentation of the Play, for which he will be reimbursed by the Partnership funds for the actual expenditures by the General Partner to acquire such assets.

5. <u>DEFINITIONS</u>.

A. The term "net profits" as used herein shall be deemed to mean the excess of "gross receipts" over all "production expenses," "running expenses" and "other expenses," as such terms are defined in this Paragraph of this Agreement. The General Partner heretofore incurred or paid out, and prior to the inception of the Partnership, will incur or pay certain production expenses and the General Partner shall be reimbursed therefor, including but not limited to advances to the Author.

B. The term "gross receipts" shall be deemed to mean all sums derived by the Partnership from any source whatsoever from the exploitation or turning to account of its rights in the Play, including all proceeds derived by the Partnership from the

liquidation of the physical production of the Play at the
conclusion of the run thereof, and from return of bonds and
other recoverable items included in "production expenses."

C. The term "production expenses" shall include fees
of the Director, Designers, cost of sets, curtains, drapes,
costumes, properties, furnishing, electrical equipment, premiums
for bonds and insurance, cash deposits with Actors' Equity,
Association or other similar organizations by which, according
to customs or usual practices of theatrical business, such
deposits may be required to be made, advances to authors, rehearsal
charges and expenses, transportation charges, cash office charge,
reasonable legal and auditing expense, advance publicity, theatre
costs and expenses, and all other expenses and losses of whatever
kind (other than expenditures precluded hereunder) actually
incurred in connection with the production of the Play preliminary
to the official opening of the Play. The General Partner has
heretofore incurred or paid, and prior to the inception of the
Partnership, will incur or pay, certain production expenses as
herein set forth, and the amount thereof, and no more, shall be
included in the production expenses of the Partnership, and (but
only if the aggregate limited contributions in full shall have
been paid in) the General Partner shall be reimbursed for the
expenses so paid by him.

D. The term "running expenses" shall be deemed to mean
all expenses, charges and disbursements of whatsoever kind
actually incurred as running expenses of the Play, including
without limitation of the generality of the foregoing, royalties
and/or other compensation to or for authors, business and general
managers, director, orchestra, cast, stage help, transportation,
cash office charge, reasonable legal and auditing expenses,
theatre operating expenses, and all other expenses and losses of
whatever kind actually incurred in connection with the operation
of the Play and taxes of whatsoever kind and nature other than
taxes on the income of the respective Limited and General Partner.
Said running expenses shall include payments made in the form of
percentages of gross receipts as well as participations in profits
to or for any of the aforementioned persons, services, or rights.

E. The term "other expenses" shall be deemed to mean
all expenses of whatsoever kind or nature other than those
referred to in the two preceding paragraphs hereof actually and
reasonably incurred in connection with the operation of the
business of the Partnership, including, but without limiting the

foregoing, commissions paid to agents, monies paid or payable in connection with claims for plagiarism, libel, negligence, etc.

    F. The term "expenses" shall be deemed to include contingent expenses and liabilities, as well as unmatured expenses and liabilities and until the final determination thereof, the General Partner shall have the absolute right to fix, as the amount thereof, such sums as the Producer in Producer's sole discretion, deems advisable.

    6. ALLOCATION OF NET PROFITS AND LOSSES.

    The net profits and losses that may accrue from the business of the Partnership shall be distributed and divided among the General Partner and Limited Partners in the following proportions.

    A. The Limited Partners shall each receive that proportion of Fifty Percent (50%) of the net profits which his contribution bears to the aggregate limited contributions, excluding, however, from such Limited Partners all persons who, pursuant to Paragraph "3" hereof, may be entitled to compensation only from the share of the General Partner in such net profits and excluding from such aggregate limited contributions the contributions as Limited Partners so made by such persons. The General Partner shall receive

    B. Until net profits shall have been earned, losses suffered and incurred by the Partnership, up to but not exceeding the aggregate limited contributions and additional contributions referred to in Paragraph "3" hereof, shall be borne entirely by the Limited Partners in proportion to their respective contributions. After net profits shall have been earned, then, to the extent of such net profits, the General Partner and Limited Partners shall share such losses pro-rata in the same percentage as they are entitled to share in net profits pursuant to the provisions of this Paragraph "6."

    7. DISTRIBUTIONS.

    After payment or reasonable provision for payment of all debts, liabilities, taxes and contingent liabilities of the Partnership, and after provision for a reserve in the amount as

set forth in Paragraph "26" of this Agreement, all cash in
excess of said contingent liabilities, expenses, debts,
liabilities, etc. shall be distributed at least semi-annually
to the Limited Partners together with the unaudited statement of
operation herein provided for, pro-rata, until their contributions
to the Limited Partnership shall have been repaid and thereafter
all cash in excess of said contingent liabilities, etc. shall be
paid to the General Partner and Limited Partners in the proportion
in which they share in the net profits of the Limited Partnership.

    8.   <u>LIMITED PARTNER'S LIABILITY</u>.

No Limited Partner shall be personally liable for any
debts, obligations or losses of the Partnership beyond the amount
of his contribution to the capital of the Partnership, except, a
Limited Partner who agrees to the use of his funds prior to
formation of the partnership acknowledges that the funds may be
used for the purpose of paying for production or pre-production
expenses involved with the presentation of the Play on Broadway
or elsewhere as a pre-Broadway tryout and that such Limited
Partner may under certain circumstances be personally liable as
a General Partner for debts incurred prior to the formation of the
Partnership. If any sum by way of repayment of contribution or
distribution of net profits shall have been paid prior or
subsequent to the termination date of the Partnership, and at any
time subsequent to such repayment there shall be any unpaid debts,
taxes, liabilities or obligations of the Partnership, and the
Partnership shall not have sufficient assets to meet them, then
each Limited and General Partner shall be obligated to repay to
the Partnership up to the amount of capital so returned to him,
and net profits so distributed to him, as the General Partner may
need for such purpose and demand. In such event the Limited
Partners and General Partner shall first repay any profits
theretofore distributed to them, respectively, and if such
distributed profits shall be insufficient, the Limited Partners
shall return contributions of capital which may have been repaid
to them, such return by the Limited Partners, respectively, to be
made in proportion to the amounts of contributions of capital
which may have been so repaid to them, respectively. All such
repayments by Limited Partners shall be repaid promptly after
receipt by each Limited Partner from the General Partner of a
written notice requesting such repayment.

    9.   <u>DISTRIBUTION OF ASSETS UPON TERMINATION</u>.

Upon the termination of the Partnership, the assets of

the Partnership shall be liquidated as promptly as possible and the cash proceeds shall be applied as follows in the following order of priority:

(i) To the payment of debts, taxes, obligations and liabilities of the Partnership and the necessary expenses of liquidation. Where there is a contingent debt, obligation or liability, a reserve shall be set up to meet it, and if and when such contingency shall cease to exist, the monies, if any, in said reserve shall be distributed as provided for in this paragraph.

(ii) To the repayment of capital contributed by the Limited Partners, said Partners sharing such repayment proportionately to their respective contributions.

(iii) The surplus, if any, of said assets then remaining shall be divided among all the Partners in the proporation that they share in the net profits.

10. DEATH OR INSANITY OF LIMITED PARTNER.

If a Limited Partner shall die, his executors, administrations, or if he shall become insane, his committee or other representative shall have the same rights that the Partner would have had if he had not died or become insane, and the share of such Limited Partner in the assets of the Partnership shall, until the termination of the Partnership, be subject to all of the terms, provisions and conditions of this Agreement as if such Limited Partner had not died or become insane.

11. BOOKS, RECORDS AND FINANCIAL STATEMENTS.

The General Partner agrees that:

A. At all times from the inception of financial transactions during the continuance of the Partnership, the General Partner shall keep or cause to be kept full and faithful books of account in which shall be entered fully and accurately each transaction of the Partnership. All of said books of account shall be at all times open to the inspection and examination of the Limited Partners, or their representatives. The General Partner shall likewise have available for examination and inspection of the Limited Partners or their representatives, at any time, box office statements received from the theatre (or theatres, as the case may be) at which the Play is presented by the Partnership. The General Partner agrees to deliver to the Limited Partners:

(i) not later than ninety (90) days after the opening of the Play a complete statement of production expenses prepared by independent certified public accountants;

(ii) an annual statement which may or may not be audited;

(iii) an unaudited statement of operation at least semi-annually together with the payments, if any, provided for in Paragraph "7" of this Agreement; and

(iv) such other financial statements as may be required by the New York Theatrical Syndication and Financing Act and the Regulations promulgated thereunder.

B. The General Partner will deliver to the Limited Partners all information necessary to enable the Limited Partners to prepare their Federal and State Income Tax Returns.

C. The General Partner will render in connection with the theatrical productions such services which are customarily and usually rendered by producers, and to devote as much time thereto as may be necessary. The General Partner shall have the complete control over all business decisions with respect to the productions.

12. SERVICES OF THIRD PARTIES
PERFORMED BY GENERAL PARTNER.

In the event that a General Partner finds it necessary and is able to perform any services of a third person, the General Partner may, if he so desires, receive the compensation for said services that the third person would have received for said services.

13. NO RIGHT TO DEMAND PROPERTY
NO PRIORITY IN REPAYMENT.

The Limited Partners shall have no right to demand and receive property other than cash in return for their contributions. Except as provided in Paragraph "14" herein, no Limited Partner shall have priority over any other Limited Partner in the repayment of capital contributions, the dividing of profits or otherwise.

14. BONDS AND GUARANTEES.

The General Partner may arrange for the deposit of bonds required by the Actors' Equity Association or any other union or organization or theatre guarantees, without, however, reducing the percentage of net profits payable to the Limited Partners. Such arrangements may provide for obtaining such bonds or guarantees from persons who may or may not be Limited Partners upon terms which require that prior to the return of Limited Partners' contributions, or the payment of any net profits, all funds

otherwise available for such purposes shall be set aside and paid
over to the Actors' Equity Association or other such union,
organization or theatre, in substitution for and in discharge of
the bonds and guarantees furnished by such others. In the event
that such arrangements reduce the estimated production
requirements, the General Partner shall have the right to assign
from the percentage of net profits allocable to the limited
partners, a percentage up to the amount that would otherwise have
been allocable to the capital required for the respective bonds,
to the person contributing such guarantee or security, provided,
however, that in no event shall the shares of net profits payable
to each Limited Partner hereunder be less than the percentage
that would otherwise have been payable to said Limited Partner
had the amount of the respective bonds been contributed by the
Limited Partners as part of the estimated production cost.

     15.   USE OF CONTRIBUTIONS.

     The aggregate limited contributions in the discretion
of the General Partner may be used to pay running expenses and
other expenses as well as production expenses.

     16.   POWER OF ATTORNEY.

     Each of the Limited Partners and each of the additional
Limited Partners does hereby make, constitute and appoint the
General Partner(s) his true and lawful attorney and in his name,
place and stead, to make, execute, sign, acknowledge and file
(1) the Certificate of Limited Partnership of the Partnership, and
to include therein all information required by the Laws of the
State of New York; (2) such amended Certificate of Limited
Partnership as may be required pursuant to this Agreement; and
(3) all papers which may be required to effectuate the dissolution
of the Partnership after its termination.

     17.   COUNTERPARTS.

     This Agreement may be executed in counterparts, all of
which taken together shall be deemed one original.

     18.   ARBITRATION.

     Any dispute arising under, out of, in connection with,
or in relation to, this Agreement, or the making or validity
thereof, or its interpretation, or any breach thereof, shall be
determined and settled by arbitration in New York City pursuant
to the rules then obtaining of the American Arbitration
Association. Any award rendered thereon may be entered in the
highest court of the forum, state or federal, having jurisdiction.
The provisions of this paragraph, or any other provisions of this

Agreement, shall not operate to deprive the investors of any
rights afforded to them under the Federal Securities Laws.

    19. COPIES OF PARTNERSHIP AGREEMENT.

    Each of the Partners agrees that one original of this
Agreement (or set of original counterparts) shall be held at the
office of the Partnership, that a Certificate of Limited
Partnership and such amendments thereto as are required shall be
filed in the Office of the County Clerk in the County of New York
and that a duplicate original (or set of duplicate original
counterparts) or each shall be held at the offices of the attorney
for the Partnership and that there shall be distributed to each
Limited Partner a conformed copy hereof.

    20. ADDITIONAL LIMITED PARTNERS AND
        ASSIGNMENT OF PARTNERSHIP INTERESTS.

    The General Partner shall have the right to admit
additional Limited Partners and/or permit Limited Partners to
increase their interests in the Partnership without obtaining
the consent of any Limited Partner until the Partnership has
received contributions of $. A Limited Partner may not
assign his interest without the consent of the General Partner.
No Assignee of a Limited Partner shall have the right to become
a substitute Limited Partner in the place of his assignor.

    All references herein to "Limited Partners" or "original
Limited Partners" shall refer as well to "Additional Limited
Partners" thus all terms and conditions governing Limited Partners
or original Limited Partners would also govern Additional Limited
Partners.

    21. RIGHT TO CO-PRODUCE.

    The General Partner shall have the unrestricted right,
in his sole discretion, to co-produce the Play with any other
entity and to enter into any agreement, including partnership
agreements or joint venture agreements; provided, however, that
no such co-production or similar arrangement shall decrease or
dilute the respective interests of the Limited Partners.

    22. ABANDONMENT OF PRODUCTION.

    In the event that the General Partner at any time shall
determine in good faith that continuation of the production of the
Play is not in the best interests of the Partnership and should be
abandoned, they shall have the right to make arrangements with any
person to continue the run of the Play on such terms as they may
feel is to the best interests of the Partnership, or abandon the
same.

23. ADDITIONAL COMPANIES AND OTHER PRODUCTIONS.

A. In the event the General Partner shall desire the Partnership to organize a company or companies in addition to the original one, to present the Play in the British Isles, the United States and Canada, or any other part of the world (if the right to produce the Play in such areas accrues to the Partnership), then the General Partner shall have the right so to do without notice and in such event no net profits shall be distributed until there is further accumulated in the bank account, in addition to the reserve referred to in Paragraph "7" of this Agreement, in the amount as set forth in Paragraph "26" of this Agreement, a sum which, in the opinion of the General Partner, will be sufficient to pay the production expenses of each such additional company. In the event there is more than one company being presented at the same time, the reserve fund provided for in Paragraphs "7" and "26" shall be maintained for each separate company before repayment of contributions or distribution of net profits.

B. The Partnership may also enter into an Agreement with respect to the disposition of British Production and subsidiary rights in the Play, with any Partnership, Corporation, or other firm in which the General Partner may be in any way interested, provided that such Agreement shall be on fair and reasonable terms. The General Partner shall also have the unrestricted right to employ an English producer or manager, to pay him an amount they deem appropriate and to give him production billing either as a co-producer or associate producer.

C. In addition, the General Partner alone or associated in any way with any person, firm or corporation, may produce or co-produce other productions of the Play in other places and in other media, and may receive compensation therefor without any obligation whatever to account to the Partnership or the Partners hereof; provided, however, that the Partnership shall receive from any such producing entity, the customary fees and royalties payable to it, if any, as Producer of the original Play in connection with such second Play.

D. The General Partner shall have the right, in his sole discretion, to make arrangements to license any rights in the Play to any other party or parties they may designate, provided the Partnership receives reasonable royalties or other reasonable compensation therefor, and provided, further, that the Partnership shall not be involved in any loss or expenses by reason thereof. In the event of any such license of rights, none

of the Limited Partners or the General Partner shall be
disqualified from participating in such proposed action by
investment of their funds or otherwise as a separate enterprise.
In the event of any such license of rights the General Partner
may render services to the licensee in connection with
exploitation by the licensee of the rights so licensed.

24. PURCHASE OF PRODUCTION RIGHTS
BY GENERAL PARTNER AFTER
TERMINATION OF PARTNERSHIP.

If, upon the termination of the Partnership, the first-
or second-class production rights of the Play for the United States
and Canada, with or without the physical production of the Play
and with or without the Partnership's interest in the proceeds of
the subsidiary rights of the Play, are purchased by the General
Partner (as distinguished from a Limited Partner or Partners),
then, and in the event, the amount paid by said party shall be
the fair and reasonable market value thereof, or an amount equal
to the best offer obtainable, whichever is the higher.

25. PRODUCER'S FEE AND CASH-OFFICE CHARGE.

The General Partner shall be paid a producer's fee of
 % of the gross weekly box office receipts until recoupment
of the production budget and   % thereafter for each production
that so recoups and shall be paid the sum of $ weekly for
each production for the cash-office charge, which shall be paid
commencing three (3) weeks before rehearsals and ending one (1)
week after the close of each production of the Play.

26. CASH RESERVE.

The cash reserve referred to in Paragraphs "7" and
"23" of this Agreement shall be in the amount of $.

27. PRODUCTION RIGHTS ACQUIRED.

A. Anything to the contrary herein notwithstanding,
the option to produce the Play acquired by the Producer is
pursuant to a Dramatists Guild, Inc. Minimum Basic Production
Contract which provides that the Producer has an option to
produce the Play to open on or before   , all in
accordance with such Dramatists Guild, Inc. Minimum Basic
Production Contract entered into between   , the
director of the Play, and the Authors dated   ,
as amended by agreement between the Producer and the Authors
copies of which (hereinafter the "Contract") are filed in the
office of Donald C. Farber, Esq., 600 Madison Avenue, New York,
New York 10022, the Attorney for the production. The Contract

dated   was assigned in its entirety to the
Producer by means of a separate agreement also on file in the
office of Donald C. Farber. If the Producer has produced the
Play and it is presented in New York City for twenty-one (21)
consecutive performances computed as set forth in Subparagraph
"27A. (iv)" or for sixty-four (64) consecutive performances
outside of New York within eighty (80) days of the first
performance, the Author agrees that the Producer shall receive
the percentage of net receipts (regardless of when paid) specified
herein below in Subparagraph "27A. (iii)," if, during any of the
periods therein set forth any of the following rights set forth in
Subparagraphs "27A. (i) and (ii)" are disposed of:

     (i)   worldwide motion pictures;

     (ii)   with respect to the United States and Canada,
radio; television; second-class touring performances; stock
performances; amateur performances; condensed tabloid
performances; foreign language performances; so-called
concert tour versions; commercial uses; grand opera; play
albums; tapes; records; or cassettes.

     (iii)   If before the expiration of ten (10) years after
the last performance of the last first-class run of the
Play   %; if within the next succeeding two years   %; if
within the next succeeding two years   %; if within the
next succeeding two years   %; if within the next succeeding
two years   %.

     (iv)   For the purposes of computing the number of
performances, provided the Play officially opens in New York
City, each preview performance given in New York within ten
days of the official New York opening shall be counted in
computing twenty-one performances provided the box office
prices for the previews are at least   percent of
the announced box office prices for the New York run and that
such performances are advertised in the "ABC" ads of the New
York Times.

     B.   The Producer has acquired the exclusive rights to
present the Play as a first-class production in the United States
and Canada on tour or otherwise and if the Play is produced as
set forth in Subparagraph "27 A." herein, the Producer shall also
acquire additional rights to present the Play in the United
Kingdom of Great Britain and Ireland, all as specifically provided
in detail in the aforesaid Contract on file in the Office of
Donald C. Farber.

C. The General Partner will assign to the Limited
Partnership when formed all the rights granted to it, including all
interests in subsidiary rights and production rights, by the
Author, pursuant to the Contract.

28. PAYMENTS OF GROSS WEEKLY BOX OFFICE RECEIPTS.

Partners' share in net profits will be computed after
payment of the following percentages of gross weekly box office
receipts: Authors will be jointly paid   % until recoupment of the
production budget and   % thereafter; the Director will be paid
  % until recoupment of the production budget, and   % thereafter;
it is anticipated that the choreographer will be paid no more than
  %; it is anticipated that the scenic designer and costume
designer may jointly be paid   % of the gross weekly box office
receipts; it is anticipated that the Theatre will be paid   % of
the gross weekly box office receipts. The Producer will be paid   %
until recoupment of the production bugdet and   % thereafter.

29. INVESTMENTS HELD IN TRUST.

All monies raised shall be held in trust by the General
Partners in a special bank account at   and may not be
used (except to the extent consented to by the individual
subscribers) until aggregate limited contributions in the amount of
$ have been raised and then only for production and
pre-production purposes. If the aggregate limited contributions
have not been contributed on or before   , all contributions
shall immediately be returned to the investors, except for those
who waive their right to reimbursement.

30. REIMBURSEMENT OF INVESTMENT
IF PARTNERSHIP NOT FORMED.

Any Limited Partner who shall sign this Agreement as
"Limited Partners Authorizing Immediate Use of Funds Waiving
Refund" shall not be entitled to reimbursement of his investment in
the event the Play is abandoned and especially authorizes the
General Partner to utilize the money invested by such Limited
Partner for production and pre-production expenses incurred prior to
the $ having been raised. All those signing as Limited Partners
in any category other than "Limited Partners Authorizing Immediate
Use of Funds Waiving Refund" do not waive the return of their
contribution in the event the Play is not produced.

IN WITNESS WHEREOF, the parties hereto have hereunto set
their hands and seals to the Limited Partnership Agreement as of
the   day of   .

AS GENERAL PARTNER

_____

AS LIMITED PARTNERS

Name, Social Security No. and Residence Address	Cash Amount Agreed to be Contributed	Percentage of Profits to be Received
_____	_____	_____
_____	_____	_____
_____	_____	_____

LIMITED PARTNERS AUTHORIZING IMMEDIATE USE OF FUNDS
BUT NOT WAIVING REFUND

The following sign the foregoing Agreement as Limited Partners and agree that their contribution may be used forthwith by the General Partner for the business of the Partnership. Persons so signing do not waive refund in the event of insufficiency of funds or abandonment prior to production of the Play.

_____ _____ _____

_____

_____

LIMITED PARTNERS AUTHORIZING IMMEDIATE USE OF FUNDS
WAIVING REFUND

The following sign the foregoing Agreement as Limited Partners and agree that their contribution may be used forthwith by the General Partner for the business of the Partnership. Persons so signing do waive refund in the event of insufficiency of funds or abandonment prior to production of the Play.

_____ _____ _____

_____

_____

LIMITED PARTNERS CONTRIBUTING OTHER THAN CASH

The following sign the foregoing Agreement as Limited Partners,

but in lieu of a cash contribution agree to make their
contribution by giving, or causing to be given, the following
described obligation of the following face amount:

_____   _____   _____

_____   _____   _____

_____   _____   _____

APPENDIX I

THESE SECURITIES ARE OFFERED PURSUANT TO AN EXEMPTION FROM REGISTRATION WITH
THE UNITED STATES SECURITIES AND EXCHANGE COMMISSION. THE COMMISSION DOES
NOT PASS UPON THE MERITS OF ANY SECURITIES NOR DOES IT PASS UPON THE ACCURACY
OR COMPLETENESS OF ANY OFFERING CIRCULAR OR OTHER SELLING LITERATURE.

THE OFFERING

, residing at
intends to produce the musical play
tentatively entitled   . He offers Limited
Partnership interests in a Partnership to be formed for that
purpose and he will make no financial contribution but will
receive fifty percent (50%) of any net profits. If there are
no net profits, Limited Partners will bear the entire risk of
loss to the extent of their respective contributions. Any
losses in excess of that amount will be borne by the General
Partner. Partner's share in net profits, if any, will be
computed after payment to others of as much as an estimated
forty-one percent (41%) of the gross weekly box office receipts
and after recoupment of the total production budget as much as
an estimated forty-four percent (44%) of the gross weekly box
office receipts and deductions of all other expenses from the
balance of the gross receipts.

There is no minimum fixed amount that each individual
Limited Partner must contribute. An initial contribution of
$ entitles a Limited Partner to a one percent (1%) share
of any net profits. The sum of $ will be raised, with
which the Producer believes he can present the Play.

The rights and obligations of the General and Limited
Partners are set forth in the Limited Partnership Agreement.
This must be signed by all subscribers to Limited Partnership
interests and may be obtained from the Producer or from Donald
C. Farber, the Attorney for the Partnership, at 600 Madison
Avenue, New York, New York 10022; telephone number: PL8-8000.

(A Table of Contents follows here.)

THE RISK TO INVESTORS

1.   While no accurate industry statistics are available, it has been claimed that of the plays produced for the New York stage in the   season, a vast majority resulted in loss to investors.

2.   On the basis of estimated expenses, the Play would have to run for a minimum of approximately   weeks (performances) to a full-capacity house, even to return to Limited Partners their initial contribution. A vast majority of the plays produced for the New York stage in the   season failed to run this long. Of those that did, a mere handful played to capacity audiences.

3.   Even if the show is successful, the investors may not have their investment returned to them because the Partnership Agreement provides that the Producer may withhold Partners' profits for investments in other productions of the Play.   To this end, the General Partner also has the right to recall any initial contributions or profits returned.   In such event no net profits shall be distributed until there is further accumulated in the bank account in addition to a $ reserve, a sum that in the opinion of the General Partner will be sufficient to pay the production expenses of each additional company.   In addition, in the event that there is more than one company being presented at the same time, the $ reserve fund shall be maintained for each separate company before repayment of contributions or distribution of net profits.

4.   A subscriber who agrees to use of his funds prior to the raising of $ may, under certain circumstances, be personally liable as a General Partner for the Production debts incurred prior to the formation of the Partnership and amendment of the Certificate of Limited Partnership, if required.   Investors should note that there is a distinct disadvantage in entering into such an agreement since persons who do so risk the loss of their entire investment even if the Partnership is never formed or the Play is abandoned prior to production.

5.   The sole business of the Partnership will be the production of the Play   . In such a venture the risk of a loss is especially high in contrast with the prospects for any profits. These securities should not be purchased unless the investor is prepared for the possibilities of total loss.

6.   The limited partnership agreement provides that if

the General Partner believes that the funds raised through his offering are insufficient to produce the Play, he may advance or cause to be advanced, or may borrow on behalf of the Partnership, whatever additional funds he deems to be necessary, and that such advances or loans are to be repaid prior to the repayment of the contribution of any limited partner. Investors should note that even if the Play is successful, such loans or advances, if made, might result in a considerable delay in the repayment of limited partner's contributions, or in a complete loss to investors since such loans or advances may equal or exceed the revenues from the production.

   7. The Producer may abandon the production at any time, for any reason whatever, if he decides that the continuation is not in the best interests of the Partnership.

   8. Pursuant to the Limited Partnership Agreement, the General Partner, Limited Partners and other parties may contribute in lieu of cash to the Limited Partnership guarantees or bonds as may be required by Actors' Equity Association, theatres and other unions or organizations and receive as Limited Partners the limited partnership interest allocable to the amount of bonds or guarantees contributed, and furthermore they shall have the right to be reimbursed in full prior to the return of capital to other Limited Partners.

   9. (Name of Producer) has never produced a Broadway show.

SUBSCRIPTIONS

   Offers to subscribe to Limited Partnership interests are subject to acceptance by the Producer. Contributions must be paid in cash at the time of signing the Limited Partnership Agreement and will be held in trust by the Producer in a special bank account at   located at , New York, New York and may not be used (except to the extent consented to by the individual subscribers) until $ has been raised and then only for production or pre-production expenses. All contributions will be returned in full if $ has not been received by   , on which date production rights expire, except to the extent that contributions have been expended by consent of individual subscribers who have also waived their right to refund.

   The Partnership shall commence on the day on which,

pursuant to the New York Partnership Law, the Certificate of
Limited Partnership is duly filed in the Office of the Clerk of
New York County which Certificate shall be filed after the
execution of this Agreement by the first Limited Partner. The
Partnership will terminate upon the death, insanity or retirement
of a General Partner, or a date fixed by the General Partner
after abandonment of all further partnership activities. A
notice containing the substance of the Certificate of Limited
Partnership shall be published as required by the New York
Partnership Law. When the aggregate Limited Contributions in the
amount of $ has been raised an amended Certificate of
Limited Partnership will be filed expeditiously with the Office
of the Clerk of New York County reflecting the additional limited
partners and their contributions as well as any other changes.

   Any one of the following may apply:

   (1) An individual subscriber may agree in writing
to the use of his contribution prior to the raising of $
without waiving his absolute right of full refund on abandonment
prior to production of the Play due to an insufficiency of funds;
the Producer will be liable to the subscriber, who agrees to
immediate use but does not waive full refund of his contribution.

   (2) The individual subscriber may contribute by
waiving his right to such refund.

   (3) The Producer may accept as an investment in
lieu of cash, a cash deposit for Actors' Equity, or other union
bonds, or the theatre deposit.

   (4) A subscriber may also invest by purchasing a
non-assignable assignment from a Limited Partner. Any such
assignment must first be approved by the General Partner.

   A subscriber who agrees to earlier use may, under
certain circumstances, be personally liable as a General Partner
for production and pre-production debts incurred prior to the date
of the formation of the Partnership and amendment of the
Certificate of Limited Partnership, if required. Investors should
note that there is no advantage to entering into these agreements.
In fact, if they waive refund there is a distinct disadvantage
since such persons risk loss of their entire investment even if
the Play is not produced.

   The Producer reserves the right to give to any
individual investor an additional participation in net profits
for any reason whatever provided such participation is solely
from the Producer's share and does not affect the percentage of
net profits payable to the subscribers.

OVERCALL

There is no overcall provided for in the proposed Limited Partnership Agreement, and if additional money is needed above the amount raised, the General Partner must make funds available (unless the need is due to invasion, strikes, or acts of God) in a manner that will not reduce the percentage interest of the original Limited Partners in the net profits of the Limited Partnership. Any additional funds advanced or loaned to the company may be repaid prior to the return of contributions of Limited Partners.

THE PRODUCER

(A biography follows:)

The Producer will receive   percent of the gross weekly box office receipts until recoupment of the production budget and   percent thereafter.

THE PLAY

(A description follows:)

THE BOOKWRITER AND LYRICIST

(A biography follows:)

The Bookwriter and Lyricist will jointly receive percent of the gross weekly box office receipts until recoupment of the production budget and   percent thereafter.

THE COMPOSER

(A biography follows:)

The Composer will receive   percent of the gross weekly box office receipts until recoupment of the production budget and   percent thereafter.

THE DIRECTOR

(A biography follows:)

will receive a fee of $ to direct the Play plus
       percent of the gross weekly box office receipts of the
production until recoupment of the production budget and
percent thereafter.

THE CAST

To date none of the cast has been selected. It is not
contemplated that the compensation of any member of the cast will
include a percentage of the gross receipts or net profits.

THE THEATRE

No contract has yet been entered into for a theatre.
However, it is estimated that the New York theatre in which the
Play will be booked will have a box office capacity of
approximately $ per week. It is anticipated that the
theatre will be paid   percent of the gross weekly
box office receipts.

THE SCENIC DESIGNER AND THE COSTUME DESIGNER

To date the Scenic Designer and the Costume Designer
have not been selected. It is anticipated that the Designers may
be jointly paid up to   percent of the gross weekly box office
receipts.

CHOREOGRAPHER

To date the Choreographer has not been selected. It
is anticipated that the Choreographer may be paid   percent
of the gross weekly box office receipts until recoupment of the
production budget and   percent thereafter.

COMPENSATION OF GENERAL PARTNER

In addition to his 50% share of any net profits,
            , will receive the following compensation and
advantages whether or not the Partnership returns a net profit.
As a Producer's management fee,   % of the gross
weekly box office receipts, until the total production budget is
recouped, and   % thereafter.

For furnishing the office space and secretarial services, the General Partner will receive $500 per week for each company presenting the Play. The office charge shall commence three weeks before the commencement of rehearsals and end one week after the close of each company presenting the Play. The offices will be tentatively located at
                                                    and will not be used exclusively for the Partnership. To the extent that charges received from the Partnership by the General Partner for office space and other items furnished by him exceed his own cost, he will receive additional compensation.

In the event that the General Partner finds it necessary to perform any services of a third person, the said General Partner may, if he so desires, receive the compensation for said services. In the event that the Producer deems it advisable, he may lease theatre space from a partnership, corporate or other entity in which he has an interest, providing that the rental terms are reasonable and no less favorable than the terms would be if it were rented from a third person.

The General Partner will receive no compensation, other than stated above, for any services, equipment or facilities customarily rendered or furnished by a General Partner, Producer or Author of a theatrical venture; nor will he receive concessions of cash, property or anything of value from persons rendering services or supplying goods to the Production.

The Producer or a company controlled by him may purchase British production and subsidiary rights for his own behalf. If this right is exercised, the Partnership would still receive its share of the proceeds; however, individual Limited Partners would have no legal standing to assert that the price or terms of sale were not the best available. The Producer has undertaken that such a sale will only be on fair and reasonable terms.

As of the date of this offering, the Producer has advanced approximately $ as pre-production expenses for which he will be reimbursed by the Partnership prior to the production of the Play.

USE OF PROCEEDS

[Sample figures]

SCENERY
Design	$ 10,000	
Painting & Building	120,000	
Misc. Purchases & Expenses	10,000	
Props, Purchases & Rentals	25,000	
		$ 165,000

COSTUMES & HAIR
Costume Design	7,500	
Hair Design	2,500	
Execution	125,000	
		135,000

ELECTRICAL & SOUND EQUIPMENT
Lighting & Sound Design	7,500	
Purchases & Rentals	50,000	
		57,500

FEES
Stage	6,500	
Choreographer	6,500	
Vocal Coach & Arranging	10,000	
Music Orchestration & Copying	75,000	
		98,000

REHEARSAL EXPENSE
Salaries:
Principals - Company (22 x 355 x 5)	40,000	
Company Crew & Stagehands	15,000	
Production Assistant	2,000	
Wardrobe & Dressers	5,000	
Pianist	2,500	
Conductor & Musicians	25,000	
Company Manager	3,600	
Stage Managers	10,000	
Theatre Expenses & Rent	12,000	
Scripts & Parts	2,000	
Casting & Auditions	3,500	
Miscellaneous	1,500	
		122,100

ADVERTISING & PUBLICITY

Press Agent Salary & Expense	7,500	
Newspaper, Radio, TV Ads	100,000	
Photos & Signs	8,000	
Printing & Promotion	16,500	
		132,000

GENERAL & ADMINISTRATIVE

General Manager	10,000	
Office Expense	4,000	
Legal Fees & Disbursements	15,000	
Accounting Fee	4,000	
Transportation	5,000	
Union Welfare	3,500	
Payroll Taxes	12,000	
Carting	7,500	
Per Diem & Living Expenses	7,500	
Insurance	5,000	
Preliminary Box Office	2,000	
Take In - Stagehands	35,000	
Miscellaneous	2,400	
		112,900

PRODUCTION COST	822,500

ADVANCES & BONDS & DEPOSITS

Authors	2,500	
Theatre	25,000	
AEA	40,000	
Local 802	–	
I.A.T.S.E.	5,000	
A.T.P.A.M.	3,000	
T.W.A.U.	2,000	
		77,500

RESERVE	100,000
CAPITAL	$1,000,000

ESTIMATED WEEKLY BUDGET

The weekly budget for the Play, once it opens in New York, is estimated at approximately $ at capacity. Based on a theatre capacity of $ (and taking into consideration royalty payments and theatre rental aggregating
percent of the gross weekly box office receipts before recoupment

of the total production budget and thereafter   percent
to Author, General Partner, Director, Theatre and others, based
on a percentage of gross weekly box office receipts, the Play
would have to run a minimum of approximately   weeks (
performances) at full capacity merely to return to Limited
Partners their original investment. Of course, there can be no
assurance that the Play will run for that length of time or that
it will have audiences of any specified size for any length of
time. Furthermore, additional running or other expenses may be
incurred which would increase the budget, and consequently the
period of time required to recover invested capital.

NET PROFITS

"Net profits" consist of the excess of gross receipts
over all "productions," "running" and "other" expenses, as those
terms are defined in the Limited Partnership Agreement.

As of the date of this Offering Circular, running
expenses may be expected to include payment to the owner of the
rights in the original Play, Adaptors and other persons, amounting
to   percent of the gross weekly box office receipts,
until the production budget is recouped and thereafter
percent of the gross weekly box office receipts. The effect of
this is to reduce the Limited Partners' share to   percent of
the net profits, attributable to roughly   percent of
gross box office receipts, until the production budget is recouped
and thereafter attributable to roughly   percent of the
gross weekly box office receipts. It is not anticipated that
anyone else will be engaged at a percentage of gross receipts or
net profits.

RETURN OF CONTRIBUTIONS - SHARE OF PROFITS

The Limited Partners as a group will receive fifty
percent (50%) of any net profits, each in the proportion his
or her contribution bears to the total Limited Contributions.
Any net profits will be distributed only after the Broadway
opening and after all the contributions have been paid and when
such distributions will still leave the Partnership with a
$ reserve (plus any amounts that the Producers wish to
accumulate for the formulation of additional companies to present
the Play).

Before net profits are earned, all losses will be borne
by the Limited Partners to the extent of their respective
contributions. After the net profits are earned, the General and
Limited Partners will bear losses to the extent of the net profits
in proportion to their respective interests. If the Partnership
liabilities exceed its assets, all partners will be required to
return pro rata any net profits distributed to them, and if a
shortage remains, any repaid contributions as well. Even if the
show is successful, the Investors may not have their investment
returned to them because the Partnership Agreement provides that
the Producer may withhold Partners' profits for investment in
other productions of the Play without notice.

PRODUCTION RIGHTS ACQUIRED

Anything to the contrary herein notwithstanding, the
option to produce the Play acquired by the Producer is pursuant
to a Dramatists Guild, Inc. Minimum Basic Production Contract
which provides that the Producer has an option to produce the
Play to open on or before   , all in accordance
with such Dramatists Guild, Inc. Minimum Basic Production Contract
entered into between   , the director of the Play and
the Authors dated   , as amended by agreement
between the Producer and the Author, copies of which (hereinafter
the "Contract") are filed in the office of Donald C. Farber, Esq.,
of Conboy, Hewitt, O'Brien, & Boardman, 600 Madison Avenue, New
York, New York 10022, the Attorney for the production. The
Contract dated   was assigned in its entirety to
the Producer by means of a separate agreement also on file in the
office of Donald C. Farber. If the Producer has produced the
Play and it is presented in New York City for twenty-one (21)
consecutive performances computed as set forth in Subparagraph
"27 A. (iv)" or for sixty-four (64) consecutive performances
outside of New York within eighty (80) days of the first
performance, the Author agrees that the Producer shall receive
the percentage of net receipts (regardless of when paid) specified
hereinbelow in Subparagraph "27 A. (iii)," if, during any of the
periods therein set forth any of the following rights set forth
in Subparagraphs (i) and (ii) are disposed of:

(i) worldwide motion pictures;

(ii) with respect to the United States and Canada,
radio; television; second-class touring performances; stock

performances; condensed tabloid performances; foreign
language performances; so-called concert tour versions;
commercial uses; grand opera; play albums; tapes; records;
or cassettes.

(iii) If before the expiration of ten (10) years after
the last performance of the last first-class run of the
Play 40%; if within the next succeeding two years 35%; if
within the next succeeding two years 30%; if within the
next succeeding two years 25%; if within the next succeeding
two years 20%.

(iv) For the purposes of computing the number of
performances, provided the Play officially opens in New
York City, each preview performance given in New York within
ten days of the official New York opening shall be counted
in computing twenty-one performances provided the box office
prices for the previews are at least sixty-five percent
(65%) of the announced box office prices for the New York
run and that such performances are advertised in the "ABC"
ads of the New York Times.

The Producer has acquired the exclusive rights to
present the Play as a first-class production in the United States
and Canada on tour or otherwise and if the Play is produced as
set forth hereinabove, the Producer shall also acquire additional
rights to present the Play in the United Kingdom of Great Britain
and Ireland, all as specifically provided in detail in the
aforesaid Contract on file in the office of Donald C. Farber.

The General Partner will assign to the Limited
Partnership when formed all the rights granted to it, including
all interests in subsidiary rights and production rights, by the
Author, pursuant to the Contract.

OTHER FINANCING

Except as described above, no person has advanced
anything of value toward the production of the Play.

FINANCIAL STATEMENTS

The ultimate issuer of these securities will be the
Partnership to be formed. Accordingly, no financial statements
are available. Limited Partners will be furnished with all
financial statements required by the New York Theatrical

Financial Act and Regulations in accordance with New York law, and will include, after formation of the Partnership, quarter-annual unaudited statements of operations. In cases where a long-enough period elapses after the initial expenditure of investors' funds, financial statements may have to be furnished even before formation of the Partnership. If the Producers furnish an unaudited annual statement, Limited Partners will not have the benefit of a certified public accountant and will rely wholly upon the Producers' figures for the determination of their share in any net profits.

PRODUCTION PERSONNEL

Donald C. Farber, whose offices are located at 600 Madison Avenue, c/o Conboy, Hewitt, O'Brien, & Boardman, New York, New York 10022, is the Attorney for the Production.
, whose offices are located at
is the General Manager for the Production.

APPENDIX J

<u>CERTIFICATE OF LIMITED PARTNERSHIP</u>

WE, THE UNDERSIGNED, being desirous of forming a Limited Partnership pursuant to the laws of the State of New York, do hereby certify as follows:

<u>FIRST</u>: The name of the Partnership is

.

<u>SECOND</u>: The business of the Partnership shall be to act as theatrical producer of, and turn to account all rights held in the musical play entitled .

<u>THIRD</u>: The Partnership's principal place of business shall be located at

.

<u>FOURTH</u>: The Partnership shall commence upon the date on which, pursuant to the New York Partnership Law, this Certificate of Limited Partnership is filed in the office of the Clerk of New York County, and shall terminate upon the death or insanity of the General Partner or a date fixed by the General Partner after abandonment of all further Partnership activities.

<u>FIFTH</u>: The time when the contributions of each Limited Partner is to be returned is as follows: After (a) the opening of the Play in New York, and (b) the establishment and maintenance of a cash reserve of $ by the Limited Partnership and (c) the payment or provision for payment of all debts, liabilities, taxes and contingent liabilities in connection with the production of the Play by the Limited Partnership, all cash receipts shall be paid at least semiannually to the Limited Partners until their total contribution shall have been fully repaid. If the General Partner desires, he may organize additional company(s) and accumulate net profits for production expenses of additional company(s) prior to return of contributions or distribution of net profits.

If the company presenting the Play shall close before the contributions shall have been repaid, and if further intention to produce the Play has been abandoned, the assets of the Partnership shall be liquidated and the cash proceeds applied to payment of all debts, taxes, obligations, liabilities and liquidation expenses of the Partnership and if there is a contingent debt, obligation or liability, a reserve shall be set up to meet it, which reserve shall be distributed if and when the contingency ceases to exist. Any balance then remaining shall be applied in repayment of the contributions of the Limited Partners, each of such repayments to be in the same proportion as his respective cash contribution.

    SIXTH: Any sums paid to the Limited Partners or to the General Partner (whether as repayment of contribution or distribution of profits) shall be returnable to the Partnership in such manner and at such times as are more specifically set forth in the Limited Partnership Agreement, if and to the extent that the Partnership shall have insufficient assets to meet its liabilities.

    SEVENTH: The General Partner may admit additional Limited Partners upon the terms and conditions set forth in the Partnership Agreement.

    EIGHTH: The General Partner shall have the right to arrange for bonds and guarantees of third parties without, however, reducing the percentage of net profits payable to the Limited Partners, on such terms as they may deem appropriate, to cover Actors Equity, the theatre and other such bonds and guarantees on the basis of the first proceeds being applied to payment of the amount guaranteed and the establishment of a special reserve for the purpose of eliminating the responsibility for the guarantees as aforesaid.

    NINTH: The General Partner shall have the right to admit additional Limited Partners and/or to permit Limited Partners to increase their interests in the Partnership, without the consent of any Limited Partners, until the Partnership has received contributions of $. A Limited Partner may not assign his interest without the consent of the General Partner. No assignee of a Limited Partner shall have the right to become a substitute Limited Partner in the place of his assignor.

    TENTH: The name and place of residence of General Partner and of the Limited Partner, the amount of cash contribution of the Limited Partner, and the percentage of net profits to be received by the Limited Partner is:

GENERAL PARTNER

LIMITED PARTNER

Name and Address	Contributed	Percentage to be Received

IN WITNESS WHEREOF, the parties hereto have set their hand and seal this   day of   .

GENERAL PARTNER

_____

LIMITED PARTNER

_____

STATE OF NEW YORK   )
                       : ss.:
COUNTY OF NEW YORK   )

        On the   day of   , before me came
            , to me known to be the individual described
in, and who executed, the foregoing instrument, and acknowledged
that he executed the same.

_____
            NOTARY PUBLIC

STATE OF NEW YORK   )
                       : ss.:
COUNTY OF NEW YORK   )

        On the   day of   , before me came
            , to me known to be the individual described
in, and who executed, the foregoing instrument, and acknowledged
that he executed the same.

_____
            NOTARY PUBLIC

APPENDIX K

<u>DIGEST OF CERTIFICATE</u>
<u>OF LIMITED PARTNERSHIP</u>

Substance of Cert. of Limited Partnership filed N.Y. City Clerk's
Office on   . Name: , Address:

Principal business: Theatrical production of play,
Gen Partner (G.P.):
Limited Partner (L.P.).   Investment and % of Profits:
                                   . Partnership commences
on filing and ends on abandonment of all partnership activities,
or death, retirement or insanity of the G.P. After opening and
establishment of cash reserve of $ and payment or
provision for payment of all liabilities, capital contributions
will be repaid. Net profits may be retained for additional
company(s) at discretion of G.P. Capital contribution and
profits distributed is returnable as provided in agreement if
partnership has insufficient assets to meet liabilities. L.P.'s
interest assignable only with consent of G.P. Assignee of L.P.
has no right to become substitute L.P. Additional L.P.'s may be
admitted as set forth in agreement. G.P. may arrange bonds or
guarantees with first monies received being used to release bond
or guarantees provided it does not reduce the % of profits payable
to L.P.'s.

APPENDIX L

County Clerk
New York County

Dear Sir:

Would you please designate the
        as the newspaper, together with the New York Law
Journal, in which the digest of the Certificate of Limited
Partnership of (name of Producing Company) will advertise.

Sincerely yours,

DONALD C. FARBER

Notes

CHAPTER 1

1. The copyright law was enacted in various stages beginning in 1790, when the subjects of protection were maps, charts, and books. In 1831 musical compositions were included, and on August 18, 1856, authors of dramatic works were given — in addition to the sole right to print and publish — the sole right to perform such works.

2. For a further discussion of the topic of public domain, see pages 8 – 11.

3. There are some exceptions to this rule. In the area of music, the copyright law provides for a compulsory mechanical license for songs which have been previously recorded. A person wishing to record a previously recorded song may do so upon providing the copyright owner with written notice of his intention to obtain such a license and thereafter paying the statutory license fee.

There is another exception called "fair use," the purpose and intent of which is not relevant to the subject of this book.

4. The play licensing companies usually control only the stock and amateur rights. If the producer intends to present a "first-class performance," he would, in most instances, have to get those rights from the author or owner of the work. For a definition of "first-class performance," see Chapter 2, footnote 1.

5. Normally, when a musical play is written independently (not for a movie or publishing company), the composer and lyricist will assign their publishing rights to a music publisher for purposes of further exploitation; however, the composer and lyricist will retain ownership of the remainder of the copyright, including the grand performing rights.

6. Merger of rights will be discussed later in this book.

7. This common law copyright (which is eliminated by the new copyright law for works created after January 1, 1978) is sometimes referred to as the "right of first publication," since it exists until the work is first published, at which time the provisions of the copyright law become effective.

8. The word "publication" is a legal term of art and has no precise definition. The courts decide what is needed to constitute publication on a case-by-case basis.

9.   Registration of the work by sending in a copyright form to Washington did not grant copyright protection. Registration was merely a method of recording the work in a public place and a prerequisite to the maintenance of a lawsuit for infringement. Publication with the copyright notice was the key to copyright protection under the old law.

10.   January 1, 1978, is the effective date of the new copyright law.

11.   In certain instances the copyright term will be longer than fifty-six years as a result of the new 1978 copyright law.

12.   A complete explanation of these agreements can be found in the following chapters.

13.   The same title cannot be used if it has established a secondary meaning whereby the mention of the title brings to mind the producer's particular adaption of the play. This protection is derived from the law of unfair competition and not the copyright law. If, however, the title of the adaptation is the same as that of the public domain work being adapted, no secondary meaning can be established and that title is free to be used by all.

14.   In any translation there is, of course, an element of adaptation of the underlying work. For the purpose of clarity, however, we will call such translation/adaptation simply a translation.

15.   See Chapter 4 for a complete discussion on the reasons for a producer entering into a Dramatists Guild contract.

16.   As a point of interest, an area where this occurs more frequently than admitted is in the television industry. Writers often mail scripts to producers of a television series hoping to get a writing job or to sell their script. Since the success of a television series is sometimes based on not much more than an original idea with unusual characters, the script could be an easy target for copying. If an allegation of copying arises, it then becomes a question of fact to be decided by a court as to whether just the idea was copied or enough to cause a copyright infringement. Because of this potential problem, and because there have been numerous lawsuits in this area, many television producers refuse even to look at unsolicited scripts or scripts not submitted by agents or attorneys. Others insist that the writer sign a release stating that if they happen to produce a series with the same idea, the writer will acknowledge that such idea was developed independently of his script and that any similarities are purely coincidental and not a basis for a lawsuit by the writer.

17.   If an author conveys an interest in the subsidiary rights together with the license to an insignificant production, and if the chance for a first-class production later occurs, the needed interest in the subsidiary rights to give to the first-class production will already have been conveyed.

18.   See Chapter 4 for a complete discussion of the contracts required to adapt a basic work.

19.   For a discussion of the purchase of the adaptation rights for the basic work see Chapter 2 — Payments to the Author.

CHAPTER 2

1.   A first-class performance is usually thought of as a Broadway or pre-Broadway performance; the term, however, is much broader. A first-class performance is usually defined as one with a first-class cast (professional actors — that is, members of Actors' Equity), a first-class director (a director who is a member of Actors' Equity or the Society of Stage Directors and Choreographers), and a first-class theatre. Actors' Equity has a

different contract for a first class theatre than for other houses. If there is a question whether a particular theatre is a first-class house, the League of New York Theatre Owners and Producers or Actors' Equity could tell you. The first-class theatres are usually not used for one-night stands but for extended or open runs of plays on tour.

2.   The author or owner may own the copyright in the play, but the copyright is, in a sense, divisible. The copyright owner may, for example, grant someone the exclusive rights to present the play for a stage production, someone else the exclusive right to present the play on television, and someone else the exclusive right to record the play, etc, etc, etc. It is important for the optionee to know that the owner owns the rights being granted. It is also important to know what other grants, if any, have been made, because — as will later be seen — the optionee may be coming into other production rights in the play and other monetary interests in other uses of the play in other media.

3.   Some authors' representatives try to limit the extent of the author's liability to the producer to only those amounts which the author receives from the production of the play. This limitation is good for the author and bad for the producer, both for obvious reasons. If the play gets enjoined prior to opening, the producer's recovery is limited to only the advance he paid the author, whereas his exposure to liability could be extensive. This all but destroys the purpose of the clause and is usually avoided by all producers. The outcome, of course, depends on the relative bargaining power of the author and producer. The author should really be able to say, "I wrote that and I didn't steal it and I will pay you your damages if I did."

4.   Although payments for options are usually advances against royalties, sometimes the author's representative will insist that part of the payment be a fee and not such an advance. This is a favorite point for compromise. A shrewd producer might be able to convince the author or his representative to take a much smaller initial payment, which is an advance, if the larger second payment is considered a fee. For example, one might go with a total of $1500 as payment for a one-year option, with a $250 (which is low) advance against the royalties for six months and $1250 (which is high) as a fee for the second six months. The producer gets a cheap start and parts with the bigger money when he knows it is being well spent.

5.   There is marked difference of opinion on this subject. Some producers feel strongly that the production of the play in other media increases interest in the play and extends the play's run. Others feel that any other production detracts from the play. It is my feeling that the more productions and the more publicity there is, the better it is for the original production. The timing of the other productions is the critically important element.

6.   What constitutes unreasonably withholding approval? It may not be reasonable to withhold approval of a New Zealand production of the play during the Broadway run. A production in New Haven, on the other hand, could be directly competitive. Even if a movie release could compete, if the producer has earned a 40 percent interest in the subsidiary rights it might be reasonable to permit a movie, especially if the box office of the play is waning. The movie could rekindle interest in the play.

7.   Movies are different. There may be so much money involved in a movie sale that everyone's best interests will be served in making one. If the producer has earned his 40 percent, it may more than compensate for any lost ticket sales.

8.   It may simplify matters to think of the option payment as a fee for the rights to produce the play within a fixed period of time, and the royalty payments as a fee for the continuing rights to produce the play during its run.

9.   The usual compromise is 5 percent going to 6½ percent after recoupment of the production budget, or 6 percent going to 7½ percent after recoupment.

Most important during the early weeks of a show are the waivers (or deferrals) of royalties to help keep the show alive. The usual provision will provide for a waiver if all persons entitled to royalties similarly waive.

10.   The person of persons acquiring rights to adapt the basic work may, in the first instance, be the bookwriter, the composer, the lyricist, or any combination of these.

11.   The share of subsidiary income referred to is the total author's share. As will be seen later, a producer of the play may end up with some of this subsidiary income for his production company — as much as 40 percent. So the question is, how is the 60 percent (or whatever amount goes to the authors) divided up.

12.   The question boils down to this: who is making an important enough contribution to the new work that they can claim an interest in the play and all subsidiary uses of the play? We all know some directors who have this kind of bargaining power. The person to be avoided is the producer who includes himself or his girlfriend as a creator under some label so as to unfairly dilute the others' interest in subsidiary income.

13.   Any waivers are *pari passu* — that is, each party waives proportionately as to their royalty. For example, the author receives 6 percent, the director 3 percent, and the producer 1 percent (for a total of 10 percent). If the total royalties for the week in question are $10,000 (computed at 10 percent of a gross box office of $100,000), and if paying those royalties would cause the play to lose $4,000 for that week, the author would waive six-tenths, the director three-tenths, and the producer one-tenth of the $4,000 of royalties due them from the $10,000. This would make each participant's waiver $2,400 (6/10 × $4,000), $1,200 (3/10 × $4,000), and $400 (1/10 × $4,000) respectively for a total waiver of $4,000. This would also reduce each participant's royalty share for that week from $6,000 to $3,600 for the author; $3,000 to $1,800 for the director; and $1,000 to $600 for the producer.

14.   The next chapter will discuss the topic of subsidiary rights for a Broadway production as provided for in the Dramatists Guild Minimum Basic Production Contract.

15.   Although the agreement refers to the producer sharing in these receipts, as will be seen later, the producer assigns all his rights under the option agreement to the production company formed to finance and produce the play. The investors (and the producer to the extent he shares in profits) are the ultimate beneficiaries of the receipts from subsidiary rights.

16.   For a first-class production, the producer will share in subsidiaries after twenty-one performances on Broadway or under the other circumstances outlined in the later chapter on the Dramatists Guild Minimum Basic Production Contract. Other non-first-class contracts may vary to graduate the 10 percent to 40 percent between twenty-one performances and ninety-nine performances. The figures above set forth in the text are not only very usual, but also very fair.

17.   There are, of course, exceptions. Short runs usually mean, however, that the play's subsidiary uses are less valuable. Long runs usually mean that the subsidiaries are of greater value — but there are even exceptions to this. For example, "The Magic Show" could hardly be a big stock and amateur candidate because a trained magician is required and not every group has one.

18.   There are even exceptions to this. There are some few authors and composers who are so very famous and commercial that they could be financed for a Broadway production with little or no subsidiaries thrown in. The producer who argues that he needs the subsidiary income to interest investors knows, of course, that he, too, will share in subsidiaries only if the investor does.

19.   Authors will sometimes ask for and sometimes (but rarely) get 10 percent for twenty-one performances, 20 percent for fifty-six performances, 30 percent for seventy-five performances, and 40 percent for ninety-nine performances. They will also sometimes succeed in counting the performances from the official opening without counting any of the preview performances.

20.   An ABC ad is an ad in the alphabetical listings which appear in the *New York Times* and the *New York Post*. A teaser ad is one in which only the name of the play (and sometimes the star) is mentioned together with the name of the theatre.

21.   The classic billing dilemma was occasioned by Mary Martin and Ethel Merman when they did a benefit performance on the same program. The problem was neatly solved by having the program identical on both sides, except that on one side Mary Martin's name was first, and on the other side Ethel Merman's name was first.

22.   It may be provided that a determination will be made by one arbitrator rather than by three arbitrators. This will save some money, as the more arbitrators there are, the more it costs. Since an arbitrator's decision is, in fact, "arbitrary," I am not sure that a disputant will get more justice from the arbitrary decision of three arbitrators, rather than the arbitrary decision of one arbitrator.

23.   There is a big difference between the author's script control on a play and the author's script control on a film script. The play author has absolute script control and the screen play author, most usually, has none. I have speculated that the difference developed historically because plays were optioned with relatively little money being paid for the option. During the early Hollywood days in the 1920s and 30s, it was not unusual for studios to hire writers, pay them huge sums of money, and put them in a room with a typewriter. Under such circumstances the film company would expect to own everything that came out of the typewriter. Film options traditionally give the producers the right to alter, change, add to, subtract from, and amend the screenplay in any way they see fit. Of course, as was mentioned, this is not so with plays, where not one single word can be changed without the author's prior approval.

CHAPTER 4

1.   Very few Broadway plays have been produced without a Guild contract, since there are good reasons for using it. Most playwrights are members of the Guild or will insist on joining it and using the contract. But, most important, the contract — although a mess to read and comprehend — is, in fact, a very fair arrangement. It makes good business sense for both the author and the producer. In fact, in many instances of a foreign author (where a Guild contract is certainly not required, since foreign writers are not Guild members), the Guild contract is used anyway because of its fair terms. The Dramatists Guild Minimum Basic Production Contract is in the process of being renegotiated between the League of New York Theatre Owners and Producers and the Dramatists Guild. If past negotiations are any indication, there is no reason to believe that the present discussions will end in a new contract at a very early date.

2.   There is the lingering question of whether playwrights are, in fact, independent contractors as distinguished from employees — and, as such, not capable of banning together in concert to negotiate with the League for a standard contract without violating certain federal laws. The federal antitrust laws are intended to prevent the banning together of businesses in restraint of trade. Authors, not being employees, could be considered in restraint of trade if they collectively bargained with the producers for such contract terms.

3.   This should tell us a lot about when the royalty terms were first negotiated. Theatres now easily gross between $150,000 and $200,000 per week. If the shift from 5 percent is after a $5,000 weekly gross and from 7½ percent after a $7,000 weekly gross, it must have been established when the potential weekly grossess were on either side of $20,000. It may very well be a good bargaining tactic to give the author a straight 10 percent of the weekly gross. It only costs $300 per week and might subtlely be negotiated for other terms worth many times more than $300.

4.   There is an unanswered question at to whether the limitation would apply to a road company during the New York run. It may be argued that the contract limitations specifically state ''after'' the New York run and not during. The argument may be answered that if the limitation does not apply to a road company during the New York run, then the royalty payments fixed in the contract also do not apply, since they, too, specifically refer to ''after'' the New York run. What generally happens is that the parties accept, as applicable to a road company during a New York run, both the royalty payment and the limitation as set forth in the agreement applicable to a road company after the New York run.

5.   Although there were long and serious negotiations for this amendment to the contract, producers rarely — if ever — select this option. The reason is probably that the provision helps the producer, but not in the area where he really needs help at the time the option is negotiated and entered into. The producer's big job is raising the money to produce the show, and although this provision reduces running expenses, it does nothing to reduce the production budget — the amount of money which must be raised to produce the show. Also, if the producer elects this option (as will be seen in later discussion), he will lose a number of other benefits of the contract.

6.   The Dramatists Guild Minimum Basic Production Contract has much more limited warranties than were set forth in the previous chapter of options. It is for this reason that Paragraph TENTH will usually broaden the warranties and representations so that they are more inclusive.

7.   If a title becomes identified with a particular show, it is said to have a ''secondary meaning,'' which means that anyone else using this title, even though not protected by copyright law, would constitute an unfair business practice. If the title has acquired a secondary meaning and is identified with a particular show, anyone else's use would amount to a capitalizing on an asset which the original show's usage has made valuable. The law recognizes the fact that one ought not to be permitted to use such a title, or to confuse the title and capitalize on what someone else has made valuable.

8.   Anyone acquiring motion picture rights, on the other hand, traditionally acquires the right to alter, amend, or change the screenplay in any way. One can speculate that historically the development of the film industry was quite different from the stage and this could account for some of the differences. In the twenties and thirties, the Hollywood heyday, it was the vogue to hire very competent writers, pay them huge salaries, and put them in a room with a typewriter. Under such circumstances you would expect the studio — for its quarter of a million dollars, more or less — to want to own everything that came out of that typewriter and to do with it as they pleased.

9.   The contract refers to ''additional rights''; the term ''subsidiary rights'' appears only once, but is a colloquialism developed in the business to designate these additional rights.

10.   One must be careful to make the distinction between a monetary interest and control. Although, in a sense, a monetary interest and additional production rights could both be thought of as ''subsidiary rights,'' the usage here is only as a monetary interest. The distinction, however, is always important to bear in mind.

11. There is usually a provision in Paragraph TENTH to the effect that the terms of Paragraph EIGHT are effective only if the terms of Paragraph SEVENTH become effective; in other words, the right to the 25 percent is conditioned upon the producer's becoming entitled to the 40 percent by running the rights acquisition time.

12. Until recent years it was always believed to be disastrous to open a Broadway show during the summer months. This, undoubtedly, is the reason for this provision. During the last two years, for whatever reasons, this is no longer the case and shows do open during the summer months, stay alive, flourish, and become hits.

13. If the play runs the "rights acquisition time," as discussed, the percentage payable to the producer would normally be 40, 35, 30, 25, or 20 percent depending upon whether the rights are disposed of within ten, twelve, fourteen, sixteen, or eighteen years after the last performance of the first-class run; thus, under such circumstances, the original production's share of film rights would be reduced to 20, 17½, 15, 12½, and 10 percent depending upon when the rights were disposed of.

14. Again, one must be conscious of the difference between a monetary interest (40 percent of the author's share of subsidiary income which includes film money) and a producing right. The production which runs the rights acquisition time acquires (among other things) the monetary interest in film proceeds, and a preferred bargaining position to acquire the film rights in the play.

If the motion picture backer and the play producer are the same person or entity (motion picutre companies are sometimes financing and producing plays) the 40 percent monetary interest will be reflected in the price such backer– producer would have to pay, and it should, in fact, be 40 percent less since that is what the play producer would receive if someone else made the film.

This is all well and good if the motion picture backer producer is the sole investor. If he or it isn't, or if the motion picture backer and the producer are different entities, then something must be done to compensate the other investors and the producer who is not the motion picture backer. They would gain nothing from the motion picture backer's paying a reduced price for the film rights. So if the motion picture backer is not the sole investor and producer, the preference to the motion picture backer has nothing to do with price but, as will be seen, has to do with an inside track on the acquisition of the film rights. This should serve as the incentive to invest in the play.

15. The additional opening night house seats are usually not necessarily in the same preferred location as the regular run of the show house seats. The opening night seating plan requires both great wisdom and skill. It is necessary to accommodate (and hopefully also please) critics and investors, as well as the cast and crew's friends and relatives. This is not always an easy job — and sometimes it is not even possible.

16. For what it's worth, the producer's attorney may argue that the author's agent is trying to steal his job. It's always possible that the producer's attorney will be responsible for the film sale and may even handle a large part of the negotiations as well as the contract analysis. Under such circumstances it may be argued that the producer shouldn't have to pay both the agent and his attorney, that the author should pay the agent and the producer the attorney.

17. Of course, this reasoning — if the facts occur as in the text — would support a conslusion that the agent should pay part of the producer's attorneys fees as well.

18. In practice, the attorney for the producer is sometimes the attorney for the author, as the play often happens because the attorney gets his author– client together with his

producer – client. When this happens, the attorney acts as an arbitrator to get the producer and author together. After that, they have common interests and the attorney has no conflict. In what could be considered the conflict of interest stage, a good general manager can assist in the parties arriving at what are equitable terms.

19. Although some lawyers in the business disagree, I feel strongly that all theatre disputes should be arbitrated rather than litigated in the courts; for this reason I always include an arbitration clause in every contract I draw up that deals with the theatre. Besides the advantage of a quick decision, it is advantageous, I feel, to have any such dispute decided by persons with theatre experience, which the panel of arbitrators will have and which the judge may or may not have.

20. As a matter of good business, I believe that all agreements in the entertainment industry should include an arbitration clause. Special provision may be included requiring quick decisions. Sometimes the agreement will name the arbitrator, such as a director, to settle artistic disputes between co-producers, and the attorney or general manager to settle business disputes between co-producers. I know there are some attorneys in and out of the business who disagree with this philosophy and insist on their day in court. I will only appeal to your sense of reason by inquiring whether you would prefer to have a theatrical dispute settled by a judge — who may or may not have any special knowledge of the theatre business — at the court's usual slower pace, or by an arbitrator who is obligated to make a quick decision and who is selected especially because of his knowledge of theatre.

21. There are theatres in New York that do not fit into the category of either Broadway or Off-Broadway. Some of them are called middle theatres because they have over 299 seats but are smaller than the Broadway houses. Middle theatres usually have 499 seats, although some of these houses are expandable to more than a thousand seats. There are also some small theatres under 299 seats in the Broadway area. In any event each of these theatres must make its own special deal with Actors' Equity and the other applicable unions. The not-for-profit theatres are mostly referred to as off-Off-Broadway theatres and have problems similar to the not-for-profit regional theatres.

22. The author may enter into a contract with a producer with whom he has some rapport and may not want someone else to produce his play unless he knows them and agrees with their interpretation of the play. Hence the limitation on an assignment of a contract.

23. It is not unusual for the bookwriter, composer, and lyricist to share equally the proceeds from any advances, royalties and other income, that is, each receiving one-third. There are of course occasions when one of the parties is so important, so well known and has such bargaining power that his share will be more than one-third. An important composer, for example, could command and receive half of all receipts, while a less known bookwriter and a less known lyricist would share the other half.

24. There is recurring discussion as to what should be included as a "subsidiary right." The current dispute seems to center around whether television cassettes should be included in the definition or not. The predominant point of view at the present time would seem to include television cassettes in the definition.

25. Although the composer and lyricist control the publishing and recording rights (with the exception of the original cast album), the producer sometimes finds it necessary to solicit an investment from a publishing or recording company who would want the publishing or recording rights or at least an option of first refusal for such rights. A contract with the composer and lyricist will sometimes provide that the producer may make a deal with a publishing or recording company in exchange for an investment in the play if the composer and lyricist do not have previous commitments.

26. A stock producer who produces the play should have the first opportunity to move the play to Broadway or to tour it. Although the Dramatists' Guild frowns on changing the time, the contract will sometimes give the stock producer 60 or 90 days from the opening of the stock performance to decide whether he wants to transfer the production to Broadway, or to do a first-class tour.

CHAPTER 5

1. A limited partnership is a statutory entity, not a part of the common law. In order to organize a limited partnership, the statutory requirements must be complied with. In New York State this requires filing a Certificate of Limited Partnership with the county clerk in the county where the partnership will have its principal office and will conduct its business. The certificate contains facts about the partners — the amount of their investment and their relationship to each other. A digest of the certificate or the certificate must be published once a week in two newspapers in the county for six consecutive weeks. In New York County, one of the papers designated by the county clerk is always the *New York Law Journal*.

2. The Internal Revenue Service has arbitrarily determined that if the budget of the show is $2½ million or less, the assets of the corporation must be at least 15 percent of the budget or $250,000, whichever is less. If the budget of the show exceeds $2½ million (which is highly unlikely), the total assets of the production must be at least 10 percent of the budget. If the corporation has this kind of assets, it would defeat the purpose of limiting the liability of the party; this is the reason, in almost all instances on Broadway, that the producer is an individual or individuals.

3. This kind of arrangement, of course, has built-in dangers. The insolvent individual partner would have a general partners' liability, and also general partners' authority as far as creditors are concerned, and could obligate the limited partnership to commitments that might be unwise. If the corporation has little or no assets, and if the individual partner is insolvent, some of the creditors could end up unpaid and all of the principals in the limited partnership would have defiled their reputation in a very small business where one's credit and credibility is an essential asset.

4. One Broadway producer recently offered his investors 75 percent of the net profits. Instead of the usual 2 percent or 3 percent of the gross weekly box office receipts for a producer's fee, he was going to take 5 percent of the gross weekly box office receipts. The producer was offering a bigger percentage of the net, the pie in the sky, in exchange for a larger percentage of the gross, which is real money. Bear in mind that a percentage of gross is different from a percentage of net. The producer offering 75 percent of the net to investors was giving away ice in the wintertime in exchange for real dollars.

5. An investor can give permission to use his investment before the total budget is raised. It is most usual, however, that the total budget be raised before any of the funds are used. This is to insure the investors that the play will be produced and open if their money is used.

6. One of the newspapers will be the *New York Law Journal* if the partnership is in New York County. The county clerk of New York County always designates the *New York Law Journal* as one of the newspapers.

Until recently it was customary to file the Certificate of Limited Partnership only after the aggregate limited contributions had been paid into the partnership. Now it is better policy to form the partnership as soon as one limited partner signs the agreement. Publishing the name, address, and investment information about just one limited partner can save considerable money. Since the contents of an amendment to the Limited Partnership Agreement need not be published, putting the names, addresses, and investment information about all the other investors in the amendment avoids the necessity of publishing that information.

The other reason for filing a certificate of limited partnership as early as possible is that the attorney general of the state of New York issued an opinion that the partnership is not formed until the publishing is completed. To wait until the total budget is raised might delay use of the money when it is needed, for the limited liability promised would only become effective after completion of the publishing, and that means six weeks.

The Attorney General of the State of New York has recently taken the position that a Limited Partnership is not organized until the six weeks of legal advertising is completed. For this reason, the current thinking of most attorneys working in this area is to organize the Limited Partnership as soon as possible with a nominal dollar amount, and when the production is fully financed to file an amended Certificate including the additional limited partners and the amount of their investments which totals the complete budget. Since the law does not require the amended Certificate to be published, there is a considerable savings in the cost of the legal advertising as the name of only one limited partner is published rather than the many.

7. A well-known producer/director some years ago had to fire the director of a show he was producing and ended up directing the show himself. He could not be paid as the director because the partnership agreement made no provision for such a payment. Hence this blanket provision started appearing in agreements.

8. There is, of course, the more important tax consideration. As was discussed under "Characteristics of Corporation for Tax Purposes," it was noted that one of the corporate characteristics is free transferability of interests. For this reason it is wise to limit assignability to make sure our partnership does, in fact, end up being taxed as a partnership and not a corporation.

9. Some investors may object to the producer having the right to use the profits of the original production company to finance other productions. For this reason this provision may be eliminated from the agreement. Investors should realize whether or not this provision is in the agreement — and it usually is; if it is, it means that the investor is giving the producer the right to use profits from the original production to mount other productions.

CHAPTER 6

1. Who ends up with what depends on the bargaining power of the parties. A veteran producer would be reluctant to give bigger billing credit or more say so to his young new co-producer. If, on the other hand, the newcomer to producing brings in substantial money, he may make greater inroads. The bargaining power of each surfaces during the negotiations.

2. Do not underestimate the importance of the personnel who will be used on the show. A producer may have his own attorney or accountant that he insists on and his co-producer may want someone else. In all events it is vitally important to use specialized persons who know the theatre. I have wasted hundreds of man hours trying to work out agreements with some attorneys unfamiliar with theatre law and its special problems.

3. An associate producer is known to be one who is not a general partner, and thus not responsible for the obligations of a general partner. Some money raisers want to have billing as a co-producer instead of as an associate. What they must realize is when they get the co-production credit they may be exposing themselves to the liability of a general partner.

CHAPTER 7

1. The "blue sky laws" of each state in which money will be raised must be complied with. Blue sky laws are the securities laws.

2. One may not disperse any written information to investors unless it is filed with the SEC and accepted for filing by the SEC. The SEC wants to make sure that prospective investors have a full and fair disclosure. For this reason one may not pass out reviews of a previous production of a play unless one distributes all of the reviews. To permit an offerer to distribute only favorable reviews would not be the full and fair disclosure required by the SEC.

3. As was noted above, nothing may be given to prospective investors unless copies are filed with the SEC and accepted for filing. Until the prospectus is accepted it may not be used and the offering may not be made. It is possible to use a "red herring" prospectus on a full S1 filing, and a recent SEC rule also permits the use of a red herring on a Regulation A Exemption from Registration Offering Circular. This is discussed later in detail. It permits preliminary use of the prospectus with a warning in red ink that the prospectus is subject to change and the offering may not be made until the prospectus is in a form acceptable to the SEC for filing.

4. An investor may consent to his investment being used before the total budget is raised. He may waive refund if the budget is not raised or may opt to be reimbursed if the budget is not raised. The ticklish part of this is that an investor authorizing use of his investment before the limited partnership is organized may be exposing himself to general partner's liability until the limited partnership is formed. One of the risk factors in the offering circular calls attention to this fact.

5. The offering circular can refer only to cast members who have actually been contracted to act in the play. A star's interest or desires cannot be stated. Producers are tempted to state that a big star is interested or is considering the part. *This may not be noted* unless the star has, in fact, been signed and is committed to do the part.

6. As was noted in the chapter on the Dramatist's Guild Minimum Basic Contract, if the play runs for twenty-one performances on Broadway the producer will be entitled to 40 percent of the author's receipts from subsidiary rights for ten years, 35 percent for the next two years, 30 percent for the next two years, 25 percent for the next two years, 20 percent for the next two years, and thereafter nothing.

7. It is most usual that persons making loans to the partnership will be entitled to recover the amount of the loan before investors are repaid. The persons making loans will usually also be paid a percentage of the profits of the company, but such percentage is payable from the producer's share of such profits.

8. An investor may not realize that the profits of the original producing company may be used to finance other productions of the play instead of being returned to him. Such a provision is most usual. If the play is successful, such profits may represent a good investment in other productions. If not successful, there would be no profits for further investment. But investors should be conscious of the fact that the producer has such authority to use any profits for this purpose.

9. Note carefully that the offering can only be made to less than twenty-six

investors — not just that there are less then twenty-six investors. If there are, in fact, twenty-four or twenty-five investors, you can be assured that the attorney general of the state of New York will require evidence of the fact that the offering was not made to more than twenty-five persons. The producer will be invited to testify under oath concerning the number of persons to whom the offering was made.

CHAPTER 8

1. At the time of this edition the membership requirements are being reconsidered.
2. Owners of first-class theatres outside New York are not members of the League.

CHAPTER 9

1. Local No. 1, Agreement V.
2. Local No. 1, Agreement VI.7.
3. Local No. 1, Agreement VIII.
4. Local No. 1, Agreement XI.
5. Local No. 1, Agreement XII.
6. Local No. 1, Agreement XIV.20.
7. Local No. B – 183, Agreement 3.i.
8. Local No. B – 183, Agreement 3.i.
9. Local No. B – 183, Agreement 5.
10. Local No. 54, Agreement 13.
11. Local No. 54, Agreement 20.
12. Local No. 54, Agreement 6.

CHAPTER 10

1. The Actors' Equity Association's Agreement and Rules Governing Employment Under the Production Contract not only outlines rules governing the employment of actors but also details the actors' responsibilities to Equity.
2. Equity agreement rule no. 26.
3. Equity agreement rule no. 65.
4. Equity agreement rule no. 49.
5. Equity agreement rule no. 60C.
6. Equity agreement rule no. 72A.
7. Equity agreement rule no. 22.
8. Equity agreement rule no. 13.
9. Equity agreement rule no. 71.
10. Equity agreement rule no. 71B.
11. Equity agreement rule no. 10.
12. Equity agreement rule no. 51.
13. No more than two performances will be given in one day without the consent of Equity, whose consent will not be unreasonably withheld.
14. Equity agreement rule no. 52.
15. Equity agreement rule no. 60.
16. Equity agreement rule no. 60D (3) (a).
17. Equity agreement rule no. 60D (3) (b).
18. Equity agreement rule no. 63.
19. Equity agreement rule no. 60D (3) (c).

20. Stage managers are entitled to overtime payment whenever the actors receive overtime payment. Equity agreement rule no. 60D (4).
21. Equity agreement rule no. 73D (5).
22. Equity agreement rule no. 19H.
23. Equity agreement rule no. 19G.
24. Equity agreement rule no. 19H.
25. Equity agreement rule no. 13E.
26. *Ibid.*
27. Equity agreement rule no. 13F.
28. Equity agreement rule no. 48.
29. Equity agreement rule no. 5.
30. Equity agreement rule no. 55.
31. Equity agreement rule no. 72A.
32. Equity agreement rule no. 72B.
33. Equity agreement rule no. 16. The posting of a closing notice is often used by producers as a hedge against further loss. Often closing notices are posted weekly while the producer fully expects business to improve and the show to remain open. Should the producer give notice, however, an actor may consider this notice as final and take other commitments despite the intentions of the producer. It is not impossible to lose a star actor by posting a misunderstood closing notice, thus forcing the closing of the play despite the producer's intention to run.
34. Equity agreement rule no. 35.
35. Equity agreement rule no. 41.
36. Equity agreement rule no. 33.
37. Equity agreement rule no. 74.
38. Equity agreement rule no. 12.
39. Equity agreement rule no. 76D.
40. *Ibid.*
41. Equity agreement rule no. 71.
42. Equity agreement rule no. 42.
43. Equity agreement rule no. 63C.
44. Equity agreement rule no. 6.
45. Equity agreement rule no. 11.
46. Equity agreement rule no. 15.
47. Equity agreement rule no. 75E.
48. Equity agreement rule no. 54.
49. Equity agreement rule no. 3.
50. Local 764 article I.
51. Local 764 article IIIw.
52. Local 764 article IIIc.
53. Local 764 article IIIe.
54. The number of dresses employed is determined by the wardrobe supervisor and the stage manager, depending upon the particular production requirements and physical surroundings of the show.
55. Local 764 article V.
56. Local 764 article VI.
57. *Ibid.*

58.　SSC and D article 1.

59.　SSC and D article 5.

60.　SSC and D article 6e.

61.　SSC and D schedule A. 2c & d.

62.　SSC and D schedule A. 2e.

63.　SSC and D schedule A. 2f & g.

64.　SSC and D schedule A. 2j.

65.　SSC and D schedule A. 2k.

66.　SSC and D schedule A. 5.

67.　SSC and D schedule A. 9. Many knowledgeable theatre insiders feel that this clause is not used to its greatest advantage by producers of long-running shows, especially musicals.

68.　SSC and D schedule A. 6., 7., & 8.

69.　Local 829 agreement II.A.

70.　Although all designers are by contract obligated to obtain various estimates for the producer to make decisions on construction contracts, the designer will usually voice a strong preference for a particular construction house regardless of the various estimates. Designers will base this preference on previous experience at a particular house and the talent they know is available in that house to execute their designs.

71.　Local 829 agreement II.B.

72.　Local 829 agreement II.C.

73.　Local 829 agreement IV.

74.　Local 829 agreement VI.

75.　Local 829 agreement VI.F.

76.　Local 829 agreement VI.C.

77.　Local 829 agreement VI.D.

78.　Local 829 agreement VIII.

79.　Local 829 agreement XIV.D.

80.　Local 829 agreement IV.E.

81.　Local 829 agreement IV.C.

82.　Local 829 agreement X.

83.　Local 829 agreement XIV.G.

84.　Local 829 agreement IX.

85.　Local 829 agreement VII.

CHAPTER 11

1.　ATPAM Union #18032 agreement, article I, section 1.

2.　ATPAM agreement, article II, section 6.

3.　ATPAM agreement, article VI, section 2.

4.　*Ibid.*

5.　ATPAM agreement, article VII, section 3-A.

6.　ATPAM agreement, article VII, section 3-B.

7.　ATPAM agreement, article VII, section 2.

8.　ATPAM agreement, article VI, section 1.

9.　ATPAM agreement, article III, section 1-A.

10.　ATPAM agreement, article III, section 1.

11.　ATPAM agreement, article V.

12.　ATPAM agreement, article IV.

13.　ATPAM agreement, article IV, section 2.
14.　ATPAM agreement, article IV, section 5.
15.　Local 802 agreement, Fifth.
16.　Local 802 agreement, Sixth.
17.　Local 802 agreement, Third (2).
18.　Local 802 agreement, Third.
19.　Local 802 agreement, Fourth (II).
20.　Local 802 agreement, Eighth.

CHAPTER 12

1.　In some instances where the show has a superstar, it is currently fashionable and financially expedient to have an extended pre-Broadway tour, sometimes for as long as two years. In fact, sometimes the show makes a lot of money on tour and never gets around to opening on Broadway. Most big superstars are not anxious to commit themselves for such a long period of time, so the long tours usually have minor superstars — that is, those who have broad box office appeal but also can't command huge fees.

2.　A few Broadway and Off-Broadway shows find it expedient not to have an official opening. A show with wide box office appeal may not want to run the risk of the critics if it is the kind of show the producer knows the critics would not appreciate. One show with an overabundance of sex went this route.

3.　See the discussion of resident theatres as pre-Broadway tryouts, Chapter 2.

4.　The *Village Voice* is sometimes a source of advertising for a particular kind of play. Because of its readership, avant-garde works, gay life plays, and heavy serious dramas, to mention a few, would be particularly suited for the *Voice*.

5.　The last few years have produced just one exception to this rule of "never." A show was closed out-of-town before it ran out of money, but it was one of those plays with not even a remote possibility of success.

CHAPTER 13

1.　The theatre availability in Manhattan is a cyclical matter. There are times when a producer has his choice of theatres. Recently, however, it's been difficult to get one, and jam-ups have been causing waits of more than one or two months. The current situation Off-Broadway is particularly critical, with an extraordinary demand for good 299- and 499-seat theatres.

Another critical problem may be presented if the star's availability does not coincide with the availability of the theatre.

2.　There is a whole body of landlord–tenant law — both statutory and common law — which governs the landlord–tenant relationship. A license agreement relieves the landowner from the obligations imposed upon a landlord by these laws designed to protect tenants.

3.　The theatre owner and producer, as will be seen, are in reality partners in the play's success or failure. Consequently, the theatre owner will want to have some control over the elements which could make the show a success, such as the star. The theatre may be licensed to a particular producer because of the specific star, and for this reason the theatre owner will want to be assured of that star's continued presence in the show.

4.   Although the producer or the theatre owner may terminate the agreement if the stop clause amount is not raised for two weeks, the clause is really for the protection of the theatre owner. The producer has other means of terminating the agreement.

Index

Donald C. Farber, one of the country's leading lawyers specializing in entertainment law, is of counsel to the New York law firm of Conboy, Hewitt, O'Brien & Boardman. He has lectured throughout the country on the business of theatre, has conducted a theatre seminar for the Practising Law Institute, and has taught theatre law and business at York University in Toronto. He has also taught at Hofstra University Law School and Hunter College and currently teaches at New York's New School for Social Research where his course in the law and business of the entertainment industry is largely devoted to theatre. He is the author of *From Option to Opening: A Guide for the Off-Broadway Producer, Producing on Broadway, and Actors Guide: What You Should Know About the Contracts You Sign,* and he is the co-author, with Paul A. Baumgarten, Of *Producing, Financing and Distributing Film.* His wife, Ann, is a professor of mathematics, and they have two grown children, Seth and Pat.